The Petit Basset Griffon Vendéen

———

A Definitive Study

by

Valerie Link & Linda Skerrit

Doral Publishing, Inc.
Sun City, Arizona

Published by:
Doral Publishing, Inc.
10451 Palmeras Dr., Suite 225
Sun City, AZ 85373
1-800-633-5385
http://www.doralpub.com

Printed in the United States of America.

Edited by Nancy Hill
Interior layout by Mark Anderson
Cover design by Electric Loft Design Group

Link, Valerie.
    The petit basset griffon Vendéen : a definitive
  study / Valerie Link, Linda Skerritt ;
  edited by Nancy Young, Mark Anderson.
      p. cm.
    Includes bibliographical references and index.
    LCCN: 99-60290
    ISBN: 0-944875-58-0

    1. Petit basset griffon Vendeen.
I. Skerritt, Linda. II. Title.

SF429.P36L46 1999   636.753
                    QBI99-1412

DEDICATION

To my parents, Bill and Linda, who never understood what I did, but believed that I could do it.
VL

Remembering my husband, Bernie, a gentle man with a great love of our breed. My inspiration.
LS

ACKNOWLEDGMENTS

In our efforts to make this the definitive work on the Petit Basset Griffon Vendéen, we contacted those who played an important role in the development of the breed or whose dedication and devotion could not go unnoticed. This book would have been incomplete but for their enthusiastic interest and help.

It was not our intention to omit anyone or any influential kennel from these pages, but some did not respond to our requests, which in turn resulted in lack of detail. In researching every aspect of the breed, we received information from many countries. Some conflicted, even to the extent of major differences in old pedigrees. As years pass, records can be lost, memories fail, information is mislaid and old photographs that seem unimportant at the time are discarded. To our horror, precious glass plates of late 19th century British photographs had been used as hard-core for someone's driveway!

To quote canine chronicler "Stonehenge" from July 1, 1859:
These records have been carefully collected; and I believe it will be found, that though some individuals may hold different views, that in each case that which I have presented is the one which is maintained by a large majority of those who have made the subject their particular study. It is impossible to attain a certainty of this in every instance; but should I be wrong, it can, in all events be maintained that neither time, trouble, nor expense has been spared in arriving at it.

We also hope you will forgive where our best endeavors fall short of our aim for perfection.

It is impossible to mention everyone who supplied information on themselves, their hounds and their experiences. However, our gratitude goes especially to the following, including those whose contributions to the various chapters are self-evident: Ros Ackland, Helen Bamforth, Judith Barnett, William Barton, Kasmin Bittle DVM, Sir Rupert Buchanan-Jardine, Susan Buttifant, Holger Busk, Wendy Culbertson, Juliette Cunliffe, Nancy Dorsey, Dominique Fabre, Madeleine Hiemstra, René Huisman, Nickie Hunt, Wendy Jeffries, Betty Judge, Lauren Kovaleff, Per Knudsen, Suzanne Marlier (FCI), Gunnar Nymann, Geir Flyckt Pedersen, Inge Hansen Pettersson, Sue Polley, Sylvia Probert, Alton Ritchie, Dr. Jeff Sampson, Jim Scharnberg, Kitty Steidel, Nick Valentine, Marie José Van de Pol, Yolande Vlas, Martin Vuille, Major John Watson, and Pam Wright.

We thank Hubert Desamy, George Johnston, John Miller, Pierre Salaün and René Tixier for their kindness, help and immense interest; Renaud Buche for his support and for entrusting us with club records and original material dating back to the early 1930s; Carl White for his excellent services as an interpreter in France; and Darren O'Conor for translating letters.

We also thank two families: the Bannisters for their hospitality at Coniston Hall estate and for sharing their knowledge of the Tottie family; and the Millais, especially Jane Bowdler, for providing photos of Sir Everett Millais.

Our appreciation to Charlotte Allmann for wonderful artwork; to Pete Shea, Jenna Skerritt and Samantha Wheeler for contributing toward other illustrations; to Don McLeod for his input on genetics, technical writing and for translating old French documents; to long-time PBGV and Basset enthusiasts Michael McHugh, for his tenacity in aiding our research at the British Kennel Club, and Ron Green, for his invaluable help in designing and scanning; and to Quo'tass Photographic, Hillingdon, England for their careful and efficient handling of treasured photographs.

Although limited space precludes use of all the photographs we received, we are indeed indebted to so many who entrusted us with them. A note enclosed with one from 1987 simply said, "I am trusting you with my memories." Such confidence has allowed us to capture the history of the breed.

Last but not least, we thank our beloved hounds, who have suffered with dignity the shorter walks while we were writing this book. Thank you all!

Valerie Link & Linda Skerritt
March 1999

Valerie Link   *Linda Skerritt*

PREFACES

It is a great honor to be associated with a book that is surely destined to become the standard reference work on the Petit Basset Griffon Vendéen. Since childhood I have been interested in *vénerie française* and the *chiens courants*, which make up FCI Group VI, and therefore welcome a work that will increase knowledge of one of those breeds.

The first Basset Griffon Vendéen I ever saw "in the flesh" was in the very early 1950s when visiting the late Lionel Woolner to look over his West Lodge Harehounds. The little bitch was a descendant of the early imports made by Sir Rupert Buchanan-Jardine of Castle Milk. My next experience of the breed took place shortly afterwards when calling at the de Coeur Joie Kennels of Raymond Levoy in Normandy and then the packs of Messieurs Bassereau and Desamy in the Vendée. Subsequent journeys to France to purchase hounds, judge or research for books kindled an interest in all four varieties of Griffon Vendéen that has never subsided. In *The Basset Hound* 1968 when writing about the Basset Griffon Vendéen I stated, "I am convinced that, should the breed be reintroduced into Britain, it would stand every chance of becoming firmly established." Happily that has proven to be the case.

That a breed—so popular in its homeland and now a familiar feature in the showrings and hunting fields elsewhere in Europe, North America and the Antipodes—has not had many literary works devoted to it, has always struck me as being a pity. Dr. Jean Auger's *Les Chiens Courants de Vendée* published in 1942 is considered by many to be a classic, but is not a specialist work on the Petit Basset Griffon Vendéen. In more recent times several other authors have covered the breed—

notably Claire Dupuis, also Mlle. Berton's and Messieurs Leblanc and Miller's superb books dealing with the *basset* breeds. Their chapters on the Basset Griffon Vendéen are indicative of great research and knowledge of hounds and hunting. The admirable early works by Kitty Steidel and Jeffrey Pepper have played a significant role in introducing the PBGV to North American hound lovers—whetting the appetite for more knowledge. Like the reintroduction and acceptance of the breed to British shores 30 years ago, I feel that this book will also be welcomed and regarded as the source of information English-speaking readers have long required.

Linda and Valerie are well-known breeders, exhibitors and judges in Britain and the USA. They have also been closely involved with the breed societies in those countries. This gave them ample qualifications to co-author this book, but, not content with that, they have consulted with colleagues and also European and American huntsmen and field-trialers. This process provides a wide range of the experiences and views of contemporary PBGV breeders that will be appreciated by all devotees of the breed.

The co-authors have been especially fortunate in locating, and then being given access to, previously unexamined kennel records, albums and archives. A researcher's dream come true! The new information and especially the photographs published for the first time bring great freshness and unique appeal to a timely book.

Those who value the Petit Basset Griffon Vendéen for exhibition, hunting or companionship will welcome this book—so, too, will other hound-breed enthusiasts and lovers of the chase. Certainly all will derive great pleasure. Linda Skerritt and Valerie Link should be very proud of their achievement.

George Johnston
Wigton, Cumbria 1999

Préfacer un livre sur le Petit Basset Griffon Vendéen où vous avez mis toute votre volonté et votre passion pour recueillir sur cette race Vendéenne son histoire, sa sélection et son utilisation, est pour moi un honneur bien sûr, mais aussi un grand plaisir.

Vous avez su à force d'abnégation convaincre les éleveurs français d'abord, et ceux du reste du monde où notre Petit Passet Griffon Vendéen s'implante, doucement mais sûrement de vous confier leurs anecdotes, leurs connaissances et leur expérience pour permettre à vos futurs lecteurs de découvrir cette race fabuleuse au milieu de toutes les autres.

C'est donc une comble de joie que d'exprimer en cette préface la reconnaissance du Club du Griffon Vendéen de France, origine de la race qui petit à petit est découverte par la cynophile internationale.

Fidèle et joyeux à la maison, grouillant et passionné à la chasse, il rassemble à lui tout seul beaucoup de qualités, mais aussi quelque défauts, car je n'ai pas la prétention de dire qu'il est parfait, car la race parfaite existe-t-elle?

Non bien sûr, mais ce Petit Basset est un grand sur le terrain de chasse: pas trop vite, bien criant, pas trop têtu, courageux, passionné, il fait découvrir à ceux qui osent vérifier ses qualités le plaisir de la chasse bien sûr, mais de la chasse pour le chien.

Les récris d'une petite meute de Petit Basset Griffon Vendéen égayeront votre environnement, mais si vous n'êtes pas chasseur alors il vous convaincra par la fidélité de son caractère joyeux et son intelligence.

Merci à vous d'avoir voulu rassembler son 'histoire'; merci à vous de m'avoir permi en quelque lignes d'exprimer ma passion.

(It is both a privilege and a pleasure to provide this preface for your book on the Petit Basset Griffon Vendéen, especially since I am aware of the earnest dedication with which you have researched its history, selection and function.

Gently, firmly, and not without some sacrifice, you have managed to persuade breeders from France and around the world to entrust you with their anecdotes, their knowledge and experience. All of this will enable future readers to discover this marvelous breed for themselves.

It is therefore a sublime joy for me to acknowledge in this preface the Club du Griffon Vendéen of France—birthplace of a breed that is gradually coming to the attention of dog lovers all over the world.

Faithful and exuberant at home, lively and enthusiastic in the hunt, it is a breed distinguished by many qualities, as well as the odd flaw, after all, who could claim perfection in any breed?

Nonetheless, the Petit Basset is one of the great hunting dogs: not too quick, a good voice, not too stubborn, brave and full of passion. For those who have admired the breed close up, the Petit Basset reaffirms the great pleasure taken in hunting, by dog as well as man.

The cry of a small pack of Petit Basset Griffon Vendéen will brighten any environment. Even if you do not hunt, you cannot help but be won over by such cheerful fidelity, and such intelligence.

Thank you for taking the trouble to piece together the story of the breed, and thank you also for allowing me these few lines to express my own enthusiasm.)

Renaud Buche
Huest, Normandy 1999

TABLE OF CONTENTS

Dedication iii

Acknowledgments v

Prefaces ix

Chapter One: In the Beginning 15

Chapter Two: The Art of French Venery 25

Chapter Three: Evolution in France 49

Chapter Four: The Hunting Tradition 73

Chapter Five: The PBGV in Great Britain 95

Chapter Six: Crossing the Atlantic 143

Chapter Seven: Popularity in Other Countries .183

Chapter Eight: The PBGV Standard 207

Chapter Nine: Pet Petits—Personality Plus! . . .243

Chapter Ten: Your PBGV's Health 263

Chapter Eleven: Mating, Whelping
    and Puppy Care 281

Chapter Twelve Genetics 307

Chapter Thirteen A Versatile Happy Breed 321

Appendix 345

Glossary 363

Bibliography 373

Index 377

CHAPTER ONE

IN THE BEGINNING

By viewing nature, nature's handmade art
Makes mighty things from small beginnings grow.
—John Dryden 1631–1700

What are the origins of the Petit Basset Griffon Vendéen, whose unkempt appearance and extrovert character set him apart? Whether new to the breed or a long-time devotee, sometime you feel impelled to discover what distinguishes it. Inevitably, the beginnings of many breeds are lost in the realm of antiquity and so to explore the exciting world of these delightful hounds, one must rely on general historical information—and your imagination!

Think of Petits Bassets Griffons Vendéens and your mind turns to France, the acknowledged home of the hunting tradition. However, hunter-man with his canine companion predates the days when French nobility kept packs for sport, and glancing at the evolution of this man/dog association perhaps explains our attraction to the bustling little hounds known simply as

The Petit Basset Griffon Vendéen—small, low-set, rough-coated hound of the Vendée.

PBGVs, or Petits, and characterized by the nickname "the Happy Breed."

Early Hunter

Three million years ago primitive man existed on vegetation and small animals. His later, upright posture freed his hands to make tools and catch even larger animals. With wild carnivorous dogs scavenging nearby, *Homo Erectus* and *Canis* soon united for hunting food. Evidence of this abounds from prehistoric times, and illustrations worldwide indicate the existence of short-legged hunting dogs, from Bronze Age Germanic cave-drawings (6000–3000 B.C.) to Assyrian, Indian and notably Egyptian monumental inscriptions.

Pharaonic Egypt glorified hunting, from paintings in V Dynasty tombs (c2500 B.C.) to the Middle Kingdom necropolis of Beni-Hassan (2125–1795 B.C.) where tall, elegant dogs are accompanied by a small one. From the XII Dynasty on, a long-bodied, short-legged dog with erect ears and pointed muzzle appeared. However this later vanished from Egyptian iconography and it is for the dog with excellent eye, the sighthound, that the Egyptians became known.

To see how hunting by scent, or venery, evolved, we go to Europe of Greek and Roman times. The Greeks were probably the earliest breeders of hare-hunting scenthounds, which mirrored Celtic hounds. From the Rhine, in 5th century B.C., the Celts settled in Gaul (modern-day France), becoming renowned for their highly prized dogs. Hunting essayist Xenophon recommended: "Do not take the first dog that comes along for hunting wild boar; and for hunting hare, for Celtic dogs are preferable to all others."

Detail of Tutankhamun's ostrich-feather fan.

As the Greeks colonized Mediterranean areas, the Romans became equally fond of hunting. They had various breeds of dogs, calling those that hunted by scent "sagaces," and the Greek Artemis soon became their Diana, Goddess of the Hunt.

In 1st century B.C., Julius Caesar conquered Celtic Gaul. When the Gauls finally accepted life under Roman rule, they kept packs for sport, and they, too, became masters of hunting.

Although the French passion for hunting never became as popular elsewhere in Europe, centuries later it did have some influence, especially in England. Following 1066, hunting became a fanatical pastime among Norman conqueror kings of England. By 1200, a third of England was royal forest devoted purely to hunting. By contrast, throughout the Middle Ages, hunting was frowned on in Cromwellian England and banned by the Puritans, though revived under the 17th century reign of Charles II. In France, however, hunting developed to an even grander scale, becoming the renowned "Sport of Kings."

So what *are* the origins of the PBGV? We can only speculate on how and when the PBGV's predecessors evolved. We do

Movement of hounds throughout Europe, France and the Vendée.

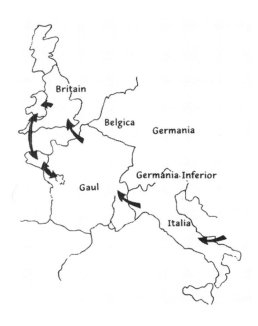

know that the Romans bred rough-coated hounds. On moving north, one Gallic breed especially attracted them, rough-haired Segusian Hounds.

Arrian, the 2nd century authority on hunting, compared them to swifter but less reliable dogs, finding them shaggy and ugly. They gave plenty of tongue when hunting even a cold line, but their voices were lugubrious. He wrote that the Gauls compared their tone to beggars imploring charity. Their name, Segusii, originated from the Segusians, or Celtic people, who settled in western Gaul by the River Rhone.

The Vendée

West of the Rhone, the rugged terrain of the Vendée presented a challenge to huntsmen. Dense, thorny vegetation made pursuit on horseback difficult, requiring a hardy dog with physical and mental stamina, and a coat resistant to brambles and thorns.

Possibly selective breeding of descendants of the Segusii and inter-breeding with hounds from nearby Brittany produced the powerful, rough-coated (Griffon) hound for which the Vendée became noted and, eventually, the shorter-legged Basset Griffon Vendéen, which could be followed on foot.

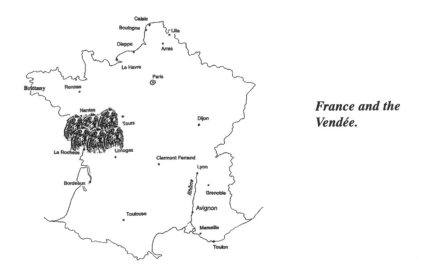

France and the Vendée.

However, the Vendée suffered greatly during the political and social upheaval of the 1789–1799 French Revolution, halting all thoughts of hunting for pleasure.

In 1793 Louis XVI was executed and France declared war on the rest of Europe. Impending enforced conscription incited the Vendéens to riot. Local royalist Chouans revolted. Their rallying cry imitating the screech-owl (*chat-huant*) terrorised Republican armies in the remote Vendéen marshes and forests. Initially successful, by that winter the Chouans were defeated. In 1794 most Vendéens were exterminated and the 1795 peace treaty was broken. Not until 1799 did law and order come. Thirty-three years later the Vendée was at peace and thoughts again turned to hunting.

The Royal Races

In happier times, when hunting was at its peak, Charles IX (1550–1574) wrote in his 1570 book, *La Chasse Royale* (published 1625), that all hounds descended from four "Royal Races":

- Chien Fauve de Bretagne,
- Chien de St. Hubert,
- Chien Gris de St. Louis, and
- Chien Blanc du Roi

His interesting theories give possible alternative and varied origins of the Griffon Vendéen, which we can take forward beyond the years of turmoil in the Vendée.

Chien Fauve de Bretagne

In the latter 5th century, Welsh people and their hounds emigrated to the area of Gaul, subsequently called Brittany. Since these ancient Britons originated from Celtic Gaul, their animals were almost certainly of Gallic origin; and Arrian wrote that the native hounds there were rough-coated. Thus the hounds taken from Gaul by ancient Britons were probably reintroduced into

Brittany by the Welsh colonists. Their Fawn Breton had a rough, reddish-fawn coat. It possessed qualities in the field similar to the Griffon Vendéen, being a big powerful animal of 25 inches (63.5 cm) admirably suited for boar or wolf hunting.

Chien de St. Hubert

The vision of St. Hubert.

Legend has it that, while out hunting in A.D. 708, the Duke of Guienne's son was miraculously converted when he saw a stag with a cross between its horns. Hubert (A.D. 656–727) devoted the rest of his life to God but continued his avid interest in hunting!

Bred at Hubert's Ardennes monastery, the St. Hubert was possibly the earliest hound selected for nose and other hunting qualities. Each year the monks sent several hounds to the Royal Kennels. In turn, the French king offered them to his noblemen, thus helping to proliferate this breed. Some hounds reached 24 inches (61 cm), making them powerful and fast; others had short legs, which slowed them down, as testified by Jacques Du Fouilloux in his 1585 book, *La Vénerie*.

Chien Gris de St. Louis

From 1250–1470, royal French packs consisted exclusively of these hounds. The devout King (Saint) Louis IX had returned from the Crusade in 1248 with several rough-haired, reddish-gray specimens whose scenting ability ensured pack domination for the next 200 years.

Possibly they descended from the old scenthounds known to Xenophon. Hounds from the Holy Land would have resembled Greyhounds or Salukis with no rough, reddish coat, which Du Fouilloux attributed to the best hunters. This description also fits the Fawn Breton.

It follows that the Breton hound descended from the St. Louis strain or, more probably, both the Breton and St. Louis came from the native breed of France descended from the Segusii known to Arrian.

Chien Blanc du Roi

About 1470, a squire from Poitou presented Louis XI with a white St. Hubert-type dog named Souillard, who sired several litters. About 1500, Louis XII's secretary, the Greffier du Roi, acquired a fine Italian Pointer bitch. A mating with Souillard produced an outstanding, predominantly white puppy, and, in *La Chasse Royale*, Charles IX testified that few stags escaped him. In subsequent years, further out-crosses helped strengthen the breed.

Souillard's birthplace of Poitou was the home of French venery. Before the French Revolution, the squires of Low Poitou (the Vendée) belonged to a hunting club, the Société de la Morelle. They bred some outstanding hounds, up to 33 inches (84 cm) high. These suffered in the French Revolution and Vendéen War but, fortunately, a few survived. When crossed, they produced the modern Vendéen hounds.

Form for Function

The widely distributed "Royal Races" helped in the development of French hound breeds. By crossing them with their own hounds, the aristocracy established *chiens courants* (hunting dogs) of distinct breeds such as: *d'Artois* (Artesiéns), *de Bretagne* (Bretons), *de Gascogne* (Gascons), *de Normandie* (Normands), *de Poitou*, *de Saintonge* (Saintongeois) and *de Vendée* (Vendéens).

As these evolved, geographical isolation, climate, local conditions and desired use dictated differing type, size and even color. Hounds, such as St. Huberts, could carry genes of the low-set type, and throwbacks to the shorter leg resulted. Thus three types of each breed emerged.

Chiens d'Ordre Invariably full-sized hounds, standing 23 inches (58.5 cm) or more. Used for stag, boar and wolf hunting, without the aid of a gun. Their method was *chasse-à-courre*, pursuing to death. Also used for hunting smaller game.

Chiens Briquets Between 15–23 inches (38–58.5 cm), with origin often uncertain. Poor pack animals, so often used singly or as a couple, to flush game out of bushes towards the gun-carrying huntsman (*chasse-à-tir*). Intelligent and quick but inclined to cut corners or run wide of the line. Used on smaller game such as hare and roe deer. Formerly, interbred with *chiens d'ordre* to achieve the best strains for hare hunting.

Chiens Bassets Low hounds, under 15 inches (38 cm), for hunting hare, rabbit and occasionally fox. Deer and boar hunting had long been the preserve of kings and nobles, who could afford to ride on horseback following swift, large hounds. Smaller game required a slower hound, so the poorer huntsman could follow on foot, and the best way to restrict speed was to shorten length of leg. The shortest-legged hounds at the time were interbred and, gradually, a useful and practical low-to-the-ground hound evolved.

This low-set hound became known as the *"basset"* (pronounced "bah-say," from Latin *bassus*, meaning 'low') and Du Fouilloux was apparently the first to specifically use the term.

The earliest known illustration of bassets—the **Charrette de Chasse,** *Sigmund Feyeraband's woodcut in Du Fouilloux's 16th century La Vénerie.*

In *La Vénerie* he recognized two types of basset, the crooked front (*à jambes torses*) and the straight front (*à jambes droites*).

In general, the crooked-legged bassets were short-coated (*à poil ras*) and went to ground better, whereas the straight-legged (or, at most, slightly crooked—*demi-torses*), hunted above ground as well as working terrier-like. These were mostly rough-coated (*à poil dur*), the early Bassets Griffons.

Thus we see how a French hound breed could be either full size, *briquet* or *basset*, for example:

- Grand Griffon Vendéen,
- Briquet Griffon Vendéen, and
- Basset Griffon Vendéen.

The Basset Griffon Vendéen could be further subdivided into:

- Grand Basset Griffon Vendéen (*basset de grande taille*) and
- Petit Basset Griffon Vendéen (*basset de petite taille*).

Smaller in stature but by no means a lesser animal; with intelligence, an independent mind and stamina, the PBGV soon proved his worth as a hunter and became greatly valued by French huntsmen.

CHAPTER TWO

THE ART OF FRENCH VENERY

*There is a passion for hunting something deeply
implanted in the human breast.*
—Oliver Twist, *Charles Dickens (1812–1870)*

From early days all huntsmen have sought to breed sound hounds possessing strong working abilities. In France, the science of venery has always played a large part in the successful hunt and, in his 1882 work *Les Chiens Courants Français pour la Chasse du Liévre dans le Midi de la France*, Comte Élie de Vezins expounded that general characteristics fell naturally into two qualities:

physical – those emanating from good conformation and physical qualities; and

mental – those linked with instincts, intelligence and how the hound works.

Hounds, like humans, have individual skills and not all in a pack work equally expertly in every aspect of the hunt. Skillful breeding over many years is necessary to produce the ideal hound.

The diagram on the following page, from Joseph P. Thomas' *Hounds and Hunting through the Ages*, 1937, illustrates the importance of heredity to breeding good hounds. Heredity at the hub carries qualities, such as Cry, straight to the rim, whereas others such as Shape (proportion/balance/soundness),

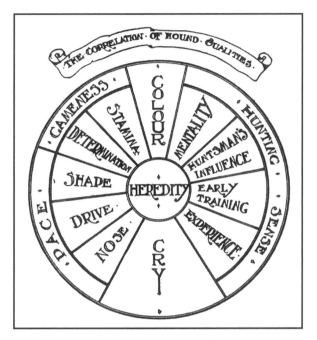

Drive and Nose, in turn, support Pace, the outer segment of the rim.

A brief look at some of these qualities, so important to breeding hounds that work well together, gives an insight into the strength of character within the PBGV.

Shape, or physical soundness in conformation, is essential. Muscle tone and the storage of energy in muscles and tendons are important to the hound's staying power, its ability to maintain stamina. However, in keeping with the principles of good architectural design, bone structure is perhaps more vital. It takes into account the function of the hound—and a good design helps the structure to serve its purpose. Straight shoulders or poor hind angulation create stress on joints in movement. The dog will either pound its front feet heavily on the ground or use its rear legs inefficiently. When the dog is standing everything must fit together and be pleasing to the eye—a balanced dog is one that is structurally sound and will perform effectively the job for which it was originally bred.

Voice not only gives the huntsman much pleasure, it is also important for telling him exactly where the hound is and what he is doing, especially when hunting in woodland or in country prone to fog and winds. A hound that babbles excitedly when not following a scent will distract others, but one who howls magnificently, with long drawn-out notes, will dominate the rest of the pack. His cry tells the other hounds when to rally quickly and points hounds and huntsman in the right direction. The voice, though, should be proportionate to the size of the dog. Too much voice in a little body saps stamina and energy.

Drive derives from an acute mind coupled with scenting ability. Any hound that casts about because he does not possess the patience and calmness to keep the line, that runs up and down and hunts only in fits and starts, or that lacks drive will be a poor hunter. A hound with a good nose hunts with perseverance and without hesitation. Without these qualities he will not be able to sustain a quick and unhesitating style of hunting.

Scenting Ability

For over 2,000 years man has been trying to understand the mysteries of scent. In the 5th century B.C., Xenophon observed of hunting hare in Greece:

> In the spring, on account of the mild temperature of the air, the trail would be very strong, if the earth, being full of flowers, did not puzzle the dogs by mixing with it [scent] the odor of the blossoms. In the summer it is slight and imperfect; for the earth being hot, it destroys the warm particles it contains, and the scent itself is not only slight, but the dogs also smell less, on account of the relaxation of their bodies. ...The scent is also stronger in woody places than in open ones, for there, sometimes running and sometimes sitting, she [the hare] is touched by many things...

To understand what hounds do, we must try to understand how they do it. The mind of a dog is his sense of smell and a scenthound especially is a unique creature with extraordinary abilities. Bound up with that part of the nervous system that forms the link between the brain and nasal cavities, his marvelous sense of smell is much more highly developed, possibly over one million times keener, than that of man. This aspect alone makes it a quality worthy of greater detail than the other qualities described in this chapter.

The complex nose of a dog includes a bulky nasal bone and short ventral turbinate (scroll-shaped) bone, with diverticula (small sacs), and a pitted surface. The latter occupies roughly three-quarters of the cavity, which opens partly into the nose and partly into the throat. The ventral turbinate bone is covered with mucous membranes rich in nerve endings. They receive the slightest olfactory impression and transmit it to the brain.

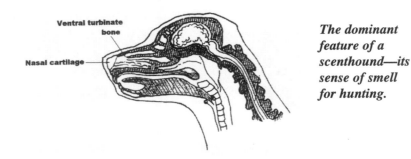

Ventral turbinate bone

Nasal cartilage

The dominant feature of a scenthound—its sense of smell for hunting.

The external architecture of the muzzle also plays an important part. A healthy dog's nose is always moist. It is this wet surface that retains and absorbs the emanations floating in the air and which probably communicates them to the taste papillae to reinforce this outstanding sense.

Scent depends on trampled earth and crushed plants on which the pursued's residual odor lingers; on varying degrees of humidity and moisture in the ground, brush and foliage; and on atmospheric conditions. Melting, cool conditions usually give the strongest scent; freezing conditions or dry ground combined with hot, humid air the least. Scent must also be "lying" and not "rising." This is an added confusion. Although all conditions may appear to be the ideal combination of moisture and calm, if the scent is rising, it will be at human level and hounds at ground level will have difficulty identifying it. Imagine a light fog rising and rapidly disappearing—scent acts similarly.

There are two ways in which a scenthound follows its quarry—that of body scent floating in the air and of pad scent on the ground. Peter Beckford (1740–1811) stated that "particles of scent, which are constantly perspiring from the game as it runs, are the strongest and most favorable to the hound when kept, by the gravity of the air, to the height of his breast; for then it is neither above his reach, nor is it necessary that he should stoop for it."

The hunted also plays a large part in the way scent behaves. A fox or a rabbit may mislead the hounds by lying still, since there is often little or no scent if it remains quiet. Once on the run, however, the body scent becomes stronger and the full imprint of the pad on the ground immediately makes conditions better for the hounds.

Methods of Hunting

At the height of venery, during the 17th century, there were close to 40 hound breeds of varying sizes that had been developed to hunt different types of game.

Grande vénerie, or hunting of large game with a pack of full-sized Chien d'Ordre scenthounds, was, and still remains, a very formal occasion with huntsmen and staff all wearing livery. They pursued the quarry to its death (*chasse-à-courre*). Although not as large as ideal hounds such as the Poitevin and Billy, the Grand Bleu de Gascogne, Griffon-Nivernais, Grand Fauve de Bretagne and Grand Griffon Vendéen were often used.

For *petite vénerie,* hounds were used to drive game toward waiting guns (*chasse-à-tir*). This was far less formal, with medium or small hounds used to hunt smaller game. The Petit Bleu de Gascogne, Artois-Normand and the Basset Griffon Vendéen were ideal for this type of venery, which saw a great rise in popularity after the World War II.

The Great Hunting Packs of France

The French Revolution abruptly ended hunting. The monarchy collapsed and most of the nobility fled the country or were sent to the guillotine. Large hunting establishments were disbanded and the carefully bred hounds were dispersed to avoid destruction. Although some breeds disappeared, the intervention of devoted older huntsmen, coupled with an understanding between the peasantry and their lords of the manor, helped to save representatives of most of the noble races.

Restoration of the monarchy (Louis XVIII) in 1815 heralded re-establishment of the aristocracy and resumption of hound breeding and hunting. However, by then everyone wanted to experience the thrill of the chase. Restrictions followed. Aspiring huntsman needed a license to carry a gun and, to conserve game, "open" and "closed" hunting seasons were introduced. Landowners raised no objections since this provided the opportunity to repopulate game and rebuild their packs. With hunting rights given to everyone, smaller hunts became more popular. This badly affected packs of full-sized hounds but, in contrast, saw the number of *basset* breeds rise as they suited these new supporters particularly well.

Nevertheless, not until Louis Philippe ascended the throne in 1830 did hunting increase substantially. In granting the right to hunt in some state forests, his reign became noted for *chasse-à-tir*. The number of hound packs grew as the passion for hunting spread and, though often initially quite modest, the packs gradually became worthy of their predecessors.

At the beginning of the 19th century, there were just about enough good specimens of Artois, Normand, Saintongeois, Bleu de Gascogne, Fauve de Bretagne and Vendée hounds to reestablish the breeds. The smaller *briquet* and *basset* varieties could also be found in greater numbers. The hunter of small game soon realized the benefits of short-legged dogs, which additionally were more suitable for use with "Le Faucheux," a new type of gun that appeared between 1840–1850. This gun replaced the flintlock, which was prone to misfire in the rain. Before long, *petite vénerie* surpassed in popularity the *grande vénerie*. In time, a few hunts with full-sized hounds formed, some disbanded; but not only were bassets seen at the smaller hunts, they were often found beside the larger hounds. For relaxation during *grande vénerie*, a dozen or more bassets were uncoupled to pursue hare or rabbit.

In subsequent years references to *bassets à jambes torses* were made, such as in *Le Journal des Chasseurs* (1836), *Le Chasseur* (1850) and *Les Chiens de Chasse* (1875), most acknowledging the bassets to be eminently suitable for hunting small game. In the latter, de la Blanchère considered the Griffons de Vendée to be the finest dogs in the world, capable of hunting in the most difficult terrain.

Comte le Couteulx de Canteleu

As the great hunting packs were being encouraged to enter the innovative canine exhibitions in Paris, Comte le Couteulx de Canteleu's reputation grew from his series of publications on all aspects of hunting. These appeared between 1854 and 1901. His authoritative work, *Les Races de Chiens Courants Français au XIXᵉ Siècle,* was completed in 1870.

His book *Le Manuel de Vénerie Française* was published in 1858 and covered all *basset* breeds. Acknowledged as the first of its type, and later serialized in *Le Journal des Chasseurs,* this work by the young nobleman from Étrepagny described each breed of French hunting dog in detail and traced its origins. He cited the Gascogne, Saintonge, Chien de Vendée (*poil ras* and *poil dur*), Haut-Poitou and d'Artois breeds as still in existence and having been regenerated for hunting. Like his predecessors,

Comte le Couteulx de Canteleu considered the *basset courant* to be a "breed" or "strain" of dog, like the large hound breeds, and he recognized both coat types and leg structures.

As the son of an officer in Napoleon I's army and himself a former cavalry officer, Le Couteulx's interest in hunting with hounds was passionate and, with his cousin the Vicomte d'Onsenbray, he saved several hound breeds from extinction. In 1852, he left the army and established a pack of Griffons Vendéens-Nivernais to hunt wolf.

However, after the death of his only brother in 1862, family obligations prevented him from continuing with his favorite sport. He sold the pack in 1870 but soon obtained four Saint Huberts from Scotland. Subsequent attempts to revive packs of *chiens d'ordre,* at a time when popularity for the larger hounds was on the wane, proved costly. He was always the only supporter. So, from about 1872, he also took up breeding bassets and hunting with them. As a result of his prominence in official canine activities and forthright ideas on quality breeding, he became influential to the history of the smooth-coated basset, notably with those in England.

Le Comte d'Elva

A female Basset Vendéen and a *fauve*-colored, male Basset de Bretagne formed the basis of Comte Christian d'Alincy d'Elva's premier breeding kennels of Bassets Griffons Vendéens. From 1875, it took ten years to perfect his pack of hounds, a passion he successfully combined with a military and political career. Born in 1850 at Changé, near Laval in la Mayenne, he taught military law at the École de Saint-Cyr before becoming an aide-de-camp at Rennes. After leaving the army, his political career soared from becoming mayor of nearby Changé in 1884 to appointment as a senator by 1906.

By 1885 he considered his Kennel Ricoudet hounds good enough to enter at the canine exhibition in Paris and his pack of twelve won top honors. They had a typical Griffon Vendéen coat—mainly white, marked lightly with orange or tri-color, with straight front or feet turned out slightly. They measured 13.5–17 inches (34–43 cm), with an average height of 15.5 inches (39 cm).

Royal Combattant attracted the most attention, a straight-limbed, tri-color male of 17 inches (43 cm) who became the Count's favorite stud dog. He was only the second *basset courant* to be registered in the Société Centrale's *Livre d'Origines Français* (studbook), as Number 93. Coincidentally, Number 92 was also a rough-coated basset, Tambour, born in 1883 like Combattant. He belonged to M. Tribert, who lived in Paris but hunted elsewhere. In subsequent years this resulted in confusion over portrayal of these hounds and another, Tambourin (one of several similarly named), owned by Vicomte de Villebois-Mareuil.

Although d'Elva's hounds achieved a certain amount of success at exhibitions towards the end of the 1880s, they did not dominate the *bassets à poil dur*. Being used for *chasse-à-courre* and *chasse-à-tir*, they looked something between a *basset* and *briquet*. Because of this, they were penalized when exhibited. The Count therefore decided to form two separate packs, one of bassets for *chasse-à-tir*, the other of briquets for *chasse-à-courre*. In doing this, his bassets retained features such as straight front or only slightly turned out feet, and ranged from

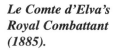

Le Comte d'Elva's Royal Combattant (1885).

13.75–17.75 inches (35–45 cm).

Despite a conflict between his parliamentary duties and passion for hunting—and constant rumors that his pack was being disbanded due to regular sales of dogs—he attended the Paris show every year. With his hounds improving all the time, from 1885 to 1905 he made a great contribution to establishing type. A small fortune secured a Grand Vendéen stud dog from M. Baudry d'Asson, one of the most prestigious French breeders. When no longer needed, the Count generously gave this stud to the hunt kennels of the zoological gardens (Jardin d'Acclimitation) in Paris for the public to use.

D'Elva's reputation grew from his immense influence at exhibitions and his capabilities as a judge of all types of bassets, and he eventually took over from Le Couteulx de Canteleu on his retirement from official canine activities. Without doubt, he was the first person to seriously care for breeding method, which he did for more than 40years, earning him the sobriquet "father of the Basset Griffon Vendéen."

E. Ambaud

At the end of the 1870s, M. Ambaud, who lived in Le Havre, started a breeding program at Grandcamp in La Seine Maritime. It was based on *bassets à poil dur*, which were not purely bred but, following lengthy endeavors to eliminate any traces of smooth or silky coat, he perfected a small basset (*petit basset*) with harsh coat and fairly straight legs. Success at exhibitions followed, his dogs often being placed above the original Comte d'Elva type. Like others of a color other than *fauve*, these hounds could be called Griffons Vendéens.

The extent to which he influenced development of Bassets Griffons is difficult to say but, for his time, M. Ambaud was one of the most important breeders. His favorite stud dog, Castilleau, measured 15.25 inches (39 cm) at the withers but weighed only 26.5 pounds (12 kg). He claimed that his line had a tendency to reduce in height and, for this reason, he liked to keep stud dogs whose height was greater than the average in the pack, which he calculated was 14 inches (36 cm) for about 25 pounds (11.5 kg).

In the 1890s M. Ambaud often judged the *bassets français* breeds at shows organized by the Société Centrale. L'Eleveur of 1890 associated his bassets with *chasse-à-tir*, hunting hare and roe deer. They wrote that these suited the amateur well, being easy to handle. All worked well together and followed a straight line confidently, making it easy to follow on foot, regardless of the terrain—through woods, brambles, gorse. Nothing would stop them and they would hunt eight hours a day for three consecutive days.

Vicomte de Villebois-Mareuil

Experience as a cavalry officer gave the Vicomte Roger de Villebois-Mareuil the skill to win horse races. His many other sporting accomplishments also included outdoor activities, especially a weakness for hunting hare on foot with his *briquets griffons*. As a friend and one-time neighbor of Comte d'Elva, the Viscount based his breeding on Ricoudet stock but, preferring a shorter basset, he worked hard to standardize this type.

Despite having some excellent bassets, Villebois-Mareuil was known primarily for his *briquets* at the Bois-Corbeau à Montaigu meet in the Vendée. These hounds were some 19.75 inches (50 cm), used for hunting on foot and regularly took 40 to 60 hares in a season.

In tandem with his passion for hunting, the Viscount also became involved in exhibitions and, as an organizer of the canine exhibition at Nantes, he was the first to have an interest in exhibiting dogs in cages instead of being tethered.

Louis Lesèble

At the end of the 19th century no one was more knowledgeable about all aspects of the canine world than Louis Lesèble, the Jardin d'Acclimitation's first manager. His kennels provided a good grounding for pure-bred stock and he showed particular interest in the *basset courant*. Although his duties did not permit him to favor any particular breed from the kennels, he nevertheless expressed a preference for the *fauve*-colored Bassets Griffons.

In 1894 his draft book on bassets was serialized in articles on the *basset courant* in *La Chasse Illustrée*. Unfortunately, World War I disrupted full publication of his work, illustrated by P. Mahler, but it did eventually get to author's final correction stage and binding.

At the 1884 Paris Dog Show, a stud dog belonging to M. Béjot was offered for sale. He became the first of several to be acquired by the Jardin Kennels. In 1886 they bought Santanas, a 16-inch (41 cm) tri-color *basset griffon* from Comte d'Elva. At the same time they bought Clairon, a 12-inch (30 cm) Basset Fauve from the Monti de Rezé stock in Brittany. In 1887 the Jardin acquired another *basset fauve*—Victor, who was 12.25 inches (31 cm)—from the same kennels and Piston a white and orange 12-inch (30 cm) *basset griffon* from Vicomte de Villebois-Mareuil. At the end of that year they reduced the number of bassets to one *basset griffon* stud dog, Piston.

However, Louis Lesèble admired another of the Viscount's bassets, the white and orange Tambourin, a *basset griffon*, born in 1887. Despite being only 12 inches (30 cm) at the withers, he displayed all the qualities of a larger hound. After seeing him at the Paris dog show in 1889, Lesèble acquired Tambourin, who replaced Piston.

Vicomte de Villebois-Mareuil's Basset Griffon Tambourin; and Jules Machart's basset d'Artois Chicaneau II (Le Chenil 1892).

For a long time the Jardin relied on the Comte d'Elva, Monti de Rezé Kennels and Vicomte de Villebois-Mareuil. From this, it is evident that they tried to obtain rough-coated bassets from breeding establishments that were winning at shows and had a good reputation for working ability. Then the beginning of the 1890s saw a change in public opinion about *bassets courants*. For the first time the price of Bassets Griffons puppies exceeded that of the smooth-coats.

As a huntsman, it was Lesèble's responsibility to make the kennel hounds work. With his own Bassets Fauves, he hunted rabbit in Sologne, in Normandy and the Ile de France. Considering the basset as essentially a rabbit dog, he was an ardent follower of the *basset de petite taille*.

He praised Bassets Griffons Vendéens for their hunting ability.

> Their great love of hunting makes them a little ambi-tious and zealous, but their daring to enter into thick woodland and the most impenetrable brambles makes them a valuable asset for the modest hunter and the country landowner who is forced to destroy rabbits. Formerly, in the Vendée, many of these dogs were under 30 cm at the withers. The locals and landowners became addicted to hunting hare more than rabbit and increased the size of their dogs. Their crooked legs became straight and their height increased up to 36 cm or even 40 cm.

> I admit to not understanding the objective of the Vendée stock-breeders. If the bassets lack speed for hunting hares, they should take up briquets, in strong numbers in this region; as the dogs actually called Bassets Griffons Vendéens are actually, for the most part, small briquets.

> An unfortunate apathy in the laws of reproduction, and absence of selection, have resulted in the degeneration of this breed and the lack of type. In the same litter, you

see some with long, woolly coats, some smooth-coats and even rough-coats. It's principally with the latter that the stock-breeders need to pay attention for, in winter in snow, the dogs with woolly coats are more prone to cold and, in summer, more susceptible to heat than the animals with harsh coats.

Consequently preference should be given to breeding from the rough, wiry-coated animals. The ear of the Bassets Griffons often leaves a lot to be desired. In most it is set too high, flat and too short. Let us select stud dogs and brood bitches with correct tail set, carried candle fashion; with long ears, extending down well and curled inwards, with short legs, strong with slight crook. We will soon have good stock that will be in public demand.

An Enduring Tradition

Two world wars in the first half of the 20th century badly affected hunting in France, but by the end of World War II the French could take stock of, and resume, their sport and, today, hunting to hounds is as popular as ever.

This is not, however, necessarily a pursuit for the thrill of the sport, the kill, the excitement. In many instances it is as simple as putting food on the table. This informal, spontaneous event may be merely a few men and their hounds out in the early hours of the morning, walking the fields. They can be seen in countless

A good day's hunt. Neptune, owned by Hervé Tenailleau, Belleville Sur Vie, Vendée.

small villages, crossing country lanes at dawn. These huntsmen are *amateurs*—fanciers, enthusiasts, or, more accurately, lovers of the hunt. And this is a passion, a way of life, a history.

The *amateur* is not alone in his passion, the hounds, too, are ardent in their desire to hunt. In the PBGV, however, such zeal often replaces method and discipline, which can be a challenge. The French describe this impetuosity in the breed as "*bouillant.*"

Hervé Tenailleau is experienced at harnessing this natural hunting instinct. Breeding under the prefix Du Parc des Chaumes, Hervé lives in the Vendée and is the area representative to the Club du Griffon Vendéen. He has owned PBGVs since the late 1980s, had success in the conformation showring at the Nationale d'Élevage but his consuming interest is hunting. During the season, which runs from late September until mid-January for rabbit and through March for hare, he is out with six to eight of his eleven homebred hounds twice a week, more often if training.

Puppies begin tuition as young as three months and are typically taught by the adult, mentally sound dogs. This careful training at an impressionable age, the *débourrage*, is what forms the hound. For Hervé, the human side of training has two vital aspects—the use of the horn and teaching recognition of the word "*Écoutez.*" This is not a signal to listen to him but a command to listen to the hound on the scent. As the hounds set out into the thick hedgerow, "*Écoutez!*" rings out repeatedly.

Hunting in the Vendée takes place over the *bocage*—varied terrain of small cultivated plots put down to maize, other cereals and vegetables, interspersed with ditches and dunes of undergrowth, thick with brambles, bushes and shrubs. It is the ideal habitat for rabbits that burrow into the banks and come out to feast on the crops. The farmers therefore welcome the huntsmen, sometimes armed with guns, out with their packs of PBGVs, Beagles, bassets, and other hounds of the *petite vénerie.*

A small pack may be only four hounds, larger packs numbering upwards of 20. The skilled huntsman trains his hounds from a few months of age to be absolutely obedient to his calls and commands (vocal and on the horn). Hounds work the undergrowth—under brambles, in the shadows of bushes, at the mouths of burrows, until their quarry is sprung. They worry their prey into a place where it cannot escape, to be killed by the huntsman (and not devoured by the hounds) usually by breaking its neck, occasionally by shooting. The PBGV is truly a hunter for all game, if he is allowed. His tenacity and fiery personality will see him off in the woods after roe deer or boar if he is not controlled. It is only by small numbers in the pack (and discipline) that they can be managed.

For René Tixier also, this pursuit is the core of French tradition. He hunts with a confidence in his de Fin Renard hounds that comes as second nature. A desire to control with constant commands to keep the hounds in line is not M. Tixier's way. With slightly different style, he is patient and understands. Despite an ardent hunting ability, his hounds exude a similar confidence, while M. Tixier walks behind reacting only if needed.

Hunting with PBGVs is not new for M. Tixier, a retired rail-

René Tixier with Minos, Minerve, Leda and Hipie de Fin Renard.

road engineer. For over 35 years he has participated in trials and hunted for his own pleasure. As one of the earliest breeders specifically of the PBGV, M. Tixier acquired his first in 1963, a dog named Tito. A true *petit* in type yet of *origine inconnue* (unknown origin). Next came Miss Foxy; then Bel Oscar de la Lipaudière and a bitch, O'Croa de la Lipaudière (breeder M. Désdouets). These were the foundation of his de Fin Renard line. Great success has come in the showring but for M. Tixier the reason for his hounds, and indeed for their integrity, is hunting.

He keeps around 20 hounds at his home in Allassac in the far southwest of France, near the Spanish border. The acreage is divided into large pens where the hounds are separated by sex and age. Young puppies are put in pens with tall grass near a cement house containing several rabbits. Thus, scenting ability is instilled from an early age. They are turned loose for evaluation of hunting instincts at ten weeks before any decisions are made as to which will be retained in his breeding program. M. Tixier, who has become noted for his black and tans, said, "Having a PBGV for other than hunting is a formula against natural selection, and detrimental in the long term."

In France the *Brevet de Chasse* is approached with similar passion. This organized hunting trial run by breed clubs offers points towards the working title, or BC (*Brevet Chasse*). With an estimated 150 packs registered, the governing body of this sport is the Société de Vénerie. Working trials are run with each small pack (*meute*), consisting of between two to four hounds for rabbit, six for hare and eight for roe deer. Being steadier mentally, bitches are more commonly worked together.

Each variety is used according to the game:
    Grand Griffon – Roe deer, boar
    Briquet – Roe deer, boar, fox
    Grand Basset – Rabbit, hare, fox
    Petit Basset – Rabbit
Noise, barking and bustling greet the day of the hunting

*A **meute** arriving at the hunt.*

trials. Drivers, helpers and hunters busy themselves unloading hounds. Judges, huntsmen and followers congregate to drink coffee, discuss the conditions, terrain, tactics of the prey. Paradoxically there is calm excitement, expectation, eagerness, anticipation. A judge throws several discs onto the table. One by one the huntsmen select a disc, turn it and call out the number, thus giving the order and location for hunting. They consult the map. Each is allotted an area, usually scrubland or woodland inhabited by rabbit, and has one hour to work his dogs with the judges following.

Before setting off, the dogs are fitted with colored collars for identification and inspected by the judges. This examination is important, as each must conform to the written standard. It is a routine matter, not only for general conformation but also to identify the hound by a tattoo number in its ear. A comparison with the number in the judge's book (taken from the entry) confirms that the dog hunting is the one that was entered.

The dogs are then released to set off steadily in search of the local wildlife. Once a hound has sprung, or roused, a rabbit, the chase begins. He will bay, give tongue or, more aptly defined, make music. In this way he makes verbal contact with his master and the other hounds. The *meute* rallies and routs the rabbit from the brush, then continues on the trail.

Judges grade the dogs on scenting ability, how they work together and, if they loose the scent, how they search to retrace it. The pack is not judged as a whole; hounds are judged individually on hunting ability. This includes how well a hound harks to the line, or picks up a scent, and in turn how well he communicates this to other hounds. Some dogs are vocal whether they have found a scent or not, they babble. Others learn when to take heed and when to ignore. Huntsmen naturally prefer to hunt with a pack with a strong lead-hound, hounds that work well together and achieve great uniformity.

Rabbits forage close to their burrows, then typically circle around to return to them. Therefore, unlike the long drawn-out chase in fox-hunting where hounds cover great distances, only a small area is needed for this pursuit. Any huntsman will acknowledge the importance of understanding how his dogs work, but he places equal importance on knowing how the rabbit works and how it thinks.

At the November 1998 Club du Griffon Vendéen hunting trial in Huest, Normandy, 27 *meutes* were entered—primarily PBGVs but also GBGVs, Basset Hounds, Beagles and Fauves de Bretagne. Huntsmen travelled from France, Holland and Belgium to compete. And compete they did—but not with each other. One pack is not judged against another, rather each huntsman and his hounds are out alone in the *bocage*, understanding the environment, the wildlife and

Jannie Dekker setting off at the hunting trial in Huest.

working well together as a unit.

There is not necessarily a Best Meute award at the end of the day, or even at the end of the event, since conditions and areas always differ. To the huntsmen, the most important thing is not winning; it is how their hounds hunt, both individually and as a pack. In his address at Huest, Judge Gilles Rhul said there was no doubt that, from watching the dogs working, PBGVs were the best, most passionate hunters.

Scoring is based on every aspect of the hound's working abilities and how he uses them. A typical judge's card is given on the opposite page.

Once a dog has gained 100 points at a *Brevet de Chasse*, the letters BC can be added after his name, indicating hunting aptitude. To become a working champion a dog must receive two Excellents—that is, 150+ points at each of two separate events under two different sets of judges (*juries*)—and, at minimum, a Very Good rating at a conformation show. A working champion is recognized by the letter T (or Ch. T). Once a dog is a working champion, it may no longer participate in working trials.

Some European huntsmen believe that the *Brevet de Chasse* parallels the dog show—a competition for selecting the best, and that the undedicated will hunt once to achieve a minimum score, thus gaining the right for their hound to use the title BC. The real passion comes from hunting in solitude with hounds for personal pleasure. Whatever the motive, it is clear that the PBGV excels in and enjoys his natural environment.

The *Brevet de Chasse* is an essential part of what the French call *"la sélection,"* identifying those hounds that are good hunters and those that do not meet the standard. In stark contrast to a more pet-oriented way of keeping hounds, most French breeders manage theirs like livestock. Although personal contact is essential for bonding of hound and huntsman, few keep hounds as pets. Therefore, the PBGV's function in a working capacity is paramount. Dogs that excel in hunting at the *Brevet de Chasse* will further lines used in breeding since

SUGGESTED SCALE OF POINTS

	Deer hunt	Hare hunt	Hare shoot	Rabbit shoot class D	Deer shoot	Fox shoot	Boar shoot
Origin, species, conformation				10 x 3			
Scenting ability				10 x 3			
Quality of cry, voice				10 x 2			
Aptitude for working together and for picking up the trail				10 x 3			
Activity, demanding nature, persistence in work				10 x 3			
General style, attitude *							
Temperament for rallying to-gether and hunting in a pack				10 x 2			
Confidence on the track, obedience, flexibility				10 x 1			
Tenacity, strength				10 x 1			
Tenacity in undergrowth **				10 x 2			
Esteem							
Total points				**200**			

* Deer hunt	Soundness and steadiness when the trail changes and breaking through on difficult trail changes.
Hare hunt	Aptitude for hunting on the trails and for working together.
Fox shoot	FAULT LEADING TO ELIMINATION: Dogs not closing on the fox
Boar shoot	Aptitude in water and standing ground in undergrowth. FAULTS LEADING TO ELIMINATION: Refusal in the boar's lair, going away from the group, refusal to stand ground; dogs not closing on the boar.
** Deer shoot	Soundness and steadiness on the trail of the deer.

SCORING:

100–124	**Good**
125–149	**Very Good**
150+	**Excellent**

they prove good hunting traits that can be passed on. One huntsman, who has had PBGVs since 1942 as a young boy, explained, "You can achieve beauty in two or three generations, but for working it is very difficult. Once instinct has gone, the breed is diverted from its function—it is unwilling to hunt. This is very hard to regain. A hound with its origins in hunting will always be balanced because, if he is not, the huntsman does not keep him."

Not to be confused with this seemingly casual event is the

tradition that comes with the more formal hunt. It includes the flourish of horns (fanfare). Although not seen at most *Brevets de Chasse*, or indeed at many independent hunts, this age-old tradition holds a place that is unparalleled. Each different, identifying piece of music (*trompe appelle*) heralds a particular pack, and the prey. Each pack's individual fanfare is played at various, significant times during the hunt itself. The repertoire of calls is immense and usually composed in honor of the Master of Hounds or to recall a particular location connected with a hunt. As each type of prey also has its own fanfare, this is also played at the kill.

Fanfare for La Rallye Bocage.

The hunting horn, or *trompe de chasse,* is large, circular and worn around the chest and over the shoulder. The most common used has two-and-a-half turns and, if unrolled, would be about 13 feet (four meters) long. It is the function of the Fédération Internationale des Trompes de France to encourage the teaching and playing of horn music throughout the country. Old recordings exist of traditional hunt fanfares and calls; and two

Tradition at its best, Hubert Desamy listening to the fanfare.

museums, the Musée de la Vénerie in Senlis and Museé Internationale de la Chasse in Gien, are dedicated to hunting with hounds. These cover all aspects of venery and are a reminder that the tradition of the "Sport of Kings" lives on in France.

CHAPTER THREE

EVOLUTION IN FRANCE

Aimer la Chasse pour les Chiens avant d'aimer les
Chiens pour la Chasse.[1]
—*Henry de Falandre*

With masters of French hunting packs also exhibiting their dogs in the late 19th century, the canine exhibitions brought about a change in attitude towards the hunting basset breeds.

The first dog shows stemmed from the founding of the Société Zoologique (Impériale) d'Acclimation in Paris in 1854. Its members, both amateur and scholastic from the Muséum d'Histoire Naturelle, were keen to introduce foreign species of animals and plants into France. They negotiated with the city of Paris to find a suitable location and, with Napoléon III's influence, secured 20 hectares north of the Bois de Boulogne. In 1858 the Société du Jardin d'Acclimation was born and by 1860 visitors were able to see all sorts of aquatic and zoological specimens. Eager to find other attractions, they commissioned Pierre Amédée Pichot, son of the director of *La Revue Britannique*, to study the existing British canine exhibitions, with the idea of mounting something similar in France.

As a result, at the end of 1862 the society formulated plans for the first dog show in France and encouraged owners of all types of dogs to attend. They contacted masters of wolf-hunting packs and urged them to spread the news to other quality packs.

---

[1] Love the hunt for the dogs before loving the dogs for the hunt.

They also invited foreign dogs, but an admissions panel eliminated any considered unworthy of competing. This process took three days, with a mêlée of families and dogs, having arrived mostly by train or carriage, all crowding around the judges' table hoping to take part. From the 900 or so undertaking this initial assessment, about 700 dogs were eventually admitted.

The exhibition opened in May 1863 with 27 in the basset class. There was no distinction between smooth-coat and rough-coat, only between the Bassets Français and Bassets Allemands (German). Quality was poor, with dogs of all coat types and sizes. Purity of breeding was lacking to such an extent that it was thought unlikely that any progeny would resemble their forebears and the rough-coated bassets that had arrived from areas far from Paris were unmemorable.

One name of interest in "other breeds entered," who was subsequently to have some influence with the *bassets courants*, was Charles Bocquet. In 1863 his Paris shop dealt in animals and game for restocking. His face was soon familiar at the canine exhibitions and, for over 30 years, he visited all the European shows. Often the only exhibitor of both smooth and rough variety, he frequently entered 30 or 40, most of which were for sale. Two dogs bred by him and sold at Crufts became the foundation of rough-coated Bassets in late 19th century England.

In 1865 the exhibition moved to Cours-la-Reine, in central Paris. Reduced to eight days and better prepared, it attracted more exhibitors. The *bassets* headed the *chiens courants*, and three times more entered than previously. With division according to height and no clear distinction between Bassets Français and Allemands, the *petits bassets* class was apparently all Bassets Allemands.

In the *grands bassets,* Comte d'Incourt de Metz had a *meute* of nine. Although at that time there was great irregularity of type, they were probably all Grande Taille; and his rough-coat Reveillo won first prize.

A small irregular pack from Sologne before 1870, illustrating the enormous strides breeders made since then in seeking uniformity of type.

Poor organization blighted the 1867 exhibition, held as part of the Exposition Universelle on the Ile de Billancourt. The lack of definitive description of the French breeds and doubtful suitability of the judges, especially for the *chiens courants* (hounds), resulted in much discussion. A main problem was that all hunt people wanted to take part and, up to this show, top stockbreeders and huntsmen were exhibiting as well as judging, and Le Couteulx was even sitting on the admissions panel as well! There was no immediate solution since the owners of *chiens courants* preferred to be judged by their hunting colleagues, and the problem caused great discord for years to come.

The society's last exhibition took place in 1873 at the Jardin d'Acclimitation, its 10th anniversary show. However, the Jardin suffered financial difficulties stemming from rebuilding and restocking. Therefore, to guard against financial ruin, Le Couteulx and Pierre Pichot laid down a guarantee, which they expected to be covered principally by entrance fees. This was a wise precaution since torrential rain during the exhibition rendered access to the Jardin almost impossible. Despite this disaster, Albert Geoffroy Saint-Hilaire, Jardin manager since 1870, was satisfied that the show had made great strides in recognizing the growing widespread popularity of the dog and in ensuring that those suitable for breeding would be chosen wisely and future shows would see the fruits of improved breeding.

Again at this show the Bassets Français and Allemands were simply divided into two height categories, with smooth and long-coat in each. Although not gaining first prize, the bassets belonging to the Marquis de l'Angle from Rennes and M. Poulet were placed above other French packs.

Not everyone agreed with the judges' decision. Reporter M. de la Rue was astonished that dogs belonging to de l'Angle, Poulet and Bocquet were classified as *chiens courants* or as *meutes*. In an article for *La Chasse Illustrée*, he wrote that he had only seen wretched, small dogs, mostly black and tan or red, of poor color, shown by foolhardy huntsmen. He recognized German Dachshund in many of them but said they had lost all desirable qualities. Some were good rough-coats, notably Tambourin, although he did not take an award, and in general although numerous bassets were shown, de la Rue criticized them for lacking breed characteristics.

The Influence of the Jardin d'Acclimitation

The year 1873 also saw the birth of the great hunt kennels of the Jardin d'Acclimitation, a unique establishment that was to have remarkable influence on breeding and knowledge of French hunting bassets. In recognition of the developing public infatuation, the operation of the kennels was both an educational and financial venture. It was hoped that an increase in visitors would follow from their practice of selecting good stud dogs and brood bitches, thus giving the public benchmarks for desirable type in each breed. Dog fanciers and huntsmen alike also benefited from the great service the kennels provided by making quality dogs available at affordable prices.

Built not far from the present-day Musée d'Arts et Traditions Populaire, the first wing was finished by autumn 1873. The aim was to have three sections, one for Greyhounds and utility breeds, one for setters and pointers, one for hounds (*chiens courants*); also a special building for "boarders." Less than 24 different breeds were housed there on completion, amongst which were eight Bassets Allemands and one Basset de Vendée.

The kennels sold weaned puppies, but adult dogs only left when they needed more room for better specimens. However, it was far from being a puppy mill. In not restricting themselves to establishing their own lines, seeking good stock from outside sources was of paramount importance. In this way they could offer to dog fanciers the widest possible choice of breeding stock.

In an effort to improve the quality of French livestock, full-time kennel manager Louis Lesèble, who was an ardent lover of Bassets Français, bought the better studs and bitches available on the market. With public favor, the number of dogs gradually increased from 67 in 1873 (24 breeds) to 113 a year later (37 breeds) and, by 1877, 168 adult dogs representing 32 breeds. It averaged 250 adults and 150 young dogs at its peak the following decade.

Bassets Français soon rose in popularity and, from four Bassets Griffons in 1874, the kennel had 12 (four dogs and eight bitches) by 1877. At that time the smooth-coated bassets were more sought after. The stud fee was 15 francs for either type of coat but a smooth-coated basset puppy cost 50 francs, 10 francs more than a *basset griffon* puppy.

Thanks to establishment of smooth-coated bassets in England during this era, where they kept good records, much is known about the breed in the kennel. However, documentation to show how the *bassets griffons* were bred in the 1870s is limited. According to a description given in the kennel catalog, color was rather mixed. In 1877, there were four white dogs lightly marked with brown or orange, two tri-colors, two blackened fawn, two ash-gray, one wolf-haired and one light fawn. They were, however, rather similar in height, being between 11–13.5 inches (28–34 cm). Essentially they were *petits bassets* for rabbit hunting.

Louis Lesèble probably selected the Bassets Griffons from the province of Sologne. Following usual practice, the kennels often crossbred them with smooth-coated bassets. There was, therefore, very little chance of finding at the Jardin *bassets griffons* corresponding to the known large Vendéen breeds. It would be some years before the first *bassets griffons* appeared bearing the Griffon Vendéen type.

By comparison with the first exhibition in 1863, it was obvious that in little more than a decade the breed progressed from unsettled and poorly defined type to being in demand as an established type. This was all thanks to exposure to the public at the dog shows and to breeders who gradually developed the *basset griffon* type, bringing it closer to that which we know today.

The Twentieth Century PBGV in France

The existence of the Basset Griffon Vendéen and the development of Griffon Vendéen hounds since the late 1800s is linked to the Dézamy family from La Chaize-le-Vicomte in every way. Without this family it is unlikely the breed would exist as it does today. The development of the BGV and subsequent division to a Grand and Petit variety over this time period is a complex issue. Because of this genetic complexity, two world wars and difficulty obtaining records from a somewhat closed community, making an accurate, complete portrait of the breed in France is difficult. It is simpler to look chronologically at the PBGV in his country of origin.

1896—Club du Basset Français (CBF) is Founded

In the late 19th century an attempt was made to separate the French bassets as definitive in their own right and to encourage their breeding, so in 1896 the Club du Basset Français was founded. Count d'Elva became president of the long-haired bassets section of the club and devoted himself to writing a standard for the breed known as the Basset Griffon Français. This was provisionally approved in 1898 and, with some minor alterations, fully approved and published in 1904.

During this time there were two important breeders who dominated the smooth and rough-coated bassets until the outbreak of World War I: Léon Verrier for his *bassets à poil dur* and Paul Dézamy for the *bassets à poil ras.* Despite the Griffon Vendéen name, most rough-coated bassets, which mainly belonged to Comte d'Elva and Vicomte Villebois-Mareuil, showed limited type. Even so, at the time, the count was the only Société Centrale judge who hunted with BGV and concentrated on a proper breeding program.

However, in the late 1890s Paul Dézamy's BGVs became the breed role model. In 1901, he formed the Rallye Bocage, his own hunting pack of between 15 and 20 BGVs that hunted hare.

The Club du Basset Français stemmed from the Société Centrale, located just outside Paris where the general assembly was held each year. Over the next few years it became apparent that it was somewhat insular, convenient only for Parisians. The club, which was attempting to include all basset breeds, found it was isolating members who lived far from Paris, such as the Vendée.

1907—Club du Griffon Vendéen (CGV) Founded, Livre d'Enregistrement du Basset Griffon Vendéen is Opened
By 1907, Paul Dézamy had won many awards at Paris dog

Bassets Griffons Vendéens belonging to Comte d'Elva.

Paul Dézamy's Farino.

shows and had established himself as an important breeder of true BGVs with straight legs. His dog Farino was crowned a champion at the 1903 Paris show, his first champion BGV.

He and his hunting companions in the Vendée felt that a locally run club would better serve the Griffon Vendéen interests, and, with its headquarters at La Chaise-le-Vicomte, they founded the Club du Basset Griffon Vendéen on May 30, 1907. The members of this first of the individual scenthound clubs in France adopted the motto *"Amélioration en Vue de l'Utilisation"* (Improvement with an Eye to Use), which is still used to this day. Being almost exclusively friends who hunted together, very few of the original members lived outside the Vendée. At the first general assembly of the club, Comte d'Elva was elected as "President of Honor" and Paul Dézamy as president. In 1909, club members accepted Paul Dézamy's revision of the Club du Basset Français breed standard. This contained a reference to two sizes, but with classification based primarily on crook of leg.

M. Dézamy continued to devote himself to the improvement of the taller Basset Griffon Vendéen with straight legs, where he tried to combine type and the best hunting traits. However it was evident that, at the beginning of the century, all BGVs were not of a uniform standard, including Paul Dézamy's. There was a definite variation in type, primarily between the taller straight-legged hound and the smaller, crooked and shorter-legged hound.

At this time members also affiliated themselves to the Société Centrale and the Société de Vénerie. They opened their own studbook called the *Livre d'Enregistrement du Basset Griffon Vendéen* (LBGV – the registry of all BGVs, later to become known as the RCGV). Farino was registered as Number 1. The guidelines were initially simple. To be included, a dog's parents had to be recorded in a recognized book, either in the LBGV or *Livre d'Origines Français* (LOF – the Société Centrale stud-book in existence since 1885), and the dog must have obtained a first or second place prize in a show organized under the aus-pices of the Société Centrale.

It was clear that the primary interest was the working ability of the hound as the LBGV also catered for notation of working performance of each dog listed. Even though each entry was countersigned by the club president, the accuracy of some early registrations is difficult to define since recordings were hand-written until mid-century, frequently by the breeders who wrote in the pedigrees themselves. Indeed we only have to look back at more recent pedigrees to understand how human error can lead to discrepancies from one generation to the next.

"At Rest" by John Emms, c1900, illustrating the early 20th century PBGV.

1912—The CBF Delegate Organization of Working Trials to
the CBGV, Which in Turn Draws up First Regulations in
France for Working Trials

In 1912 the committee of the Club du Basset Français
decided to turn over organization of working trials to specialist
clubs such as the Club du Basset Griffon Vendéen. This became
a great asset to the CBGV since it extended their club to additional members, giving them greater importance and recognition. On July 8 that same year, their committee adopted what
was certainly the first regulation in France, governing the organization of *chasse à tir* working trials.

Paul Dézamy devised a certificate of *Brevet d'Aptitude à
Chasser* (BAC). This later became the *Brevet de Chasse*, as it is
known today. The event was to be judged by two competent
huntsmen chosen from the club's list of approved judges. The
dogs were judged on ability to seek, how well they worked
together, on scenting ability and tenacity. Baying or babbling
when not on a scent or chasing a trail in the wrong direction
would be severely penalised. In addition, the dogs would be
examined to ensure that they had no serious physical faults in
conformation.

The nature of the trials would be to work the dogs in small
groups, though they would be judged independently for demon-
stration of individual qualities. From birth of the *Brevet de
Chasse,* the Scale of Points remains accurate to this day. It
includes willingness to rally to the pack, tenacity and strength,
scenting ability, voice, and "*mépris du lapin*" (contempt for the
rabbit).

The first hunting trial took place shortly after. Following a
disorganized start at La Roche-Sur-Yon, where there was little
control over the hounds, they decided to move the hunt to the
nearby Château de Resteau, which belonged to Comte Henry
d'Andigné, president of the Société de Vénerie. Here the trials
were a great success, with hounds in a containable area and the
public able to watch from the terrace. However, it was almost

12 years before their popularity grew since trials were either infrequent or remote and the huntsmen sceptical. As interest increased, trials were held primarily in the park of the Château de Resteau. Six judges officiated, with each of four judges watching their designated sector and the remaining two following the hounds. Paul Dézamy and Comte d'Andigné were both great promoters of these trials and strove to make them an enduring tradition.

In the 1951 *La Chasseur Français*, Paul Daubigné, an influential judge and writer during the early and mid 1900s, wrote, "And what delightful days those were at Resteau, where we found ourselves among enthusiasts, where we escaped from reality, where from sunrise to sunset we lived hunting, where during meals we spoke of hunting, where during the evening, after discussing and writing notes of the day, we spoke of hunting again."

1922—CBGV Recognizes Smaller Variety of Hunting Hound

The breed flourished in the hands of the new Club du Basset Griffon Vendéen and under the direction of Paul Dézamy. Most importantly, due to the Vendée's somewhat isolated geographic position, the BGV suffered less from World War I than other breeds. The original club members continued to hunt with the larger *"type Dézamy,"* as they had become known. These swift, taller bassets were ideal for hunting hare in large, open areas. However, in July 1922 the Club recognized the need to nurture the smaller, rabbit-hunting variety. They did this for several reasons. With smaller hounds, less land was needed as they worked in a tighter group in less space, not hesitating to go into the thick underbrush to seek out rabbit, something the larger variety was not as apt to do. And, quite simply, they were easier and indeed cheaper to keep.

Many of these hounds existed, distinguished only by type of leg. With classification still based on crooked and straight leg, greater emphasis was now put on height: 13.5–15 inches and

15–16.5 inches (34–38 cm and 38–42 cm). Straight legs were always stipulated for the larger variety of BGV. However, despite many hounds of the smaller variety being of mixed type, evidence shows that there were dogs exhibiting true *petit* type from as early as 1927.

A catalog album of the May 1927 meeting of rabbit-hunting packs at the Château de Chambord shows that both varieties co-existed in the same kennel. Of the 14 hounds photographed at Hubert Devaulx de Chambord's hunt, five are *demi-torses* and, of those, three have heads that are not typically *grand* in type. Also, the album shows two hounds, Gambade and Mirliton, both of whom show all the appearance of the modern PBGV.

Above: Equipage H. Devaulx de Chambord.
Below, left: Gambade.
Below, right: Mirliton, 1927, courtesy of Dominique Fabre.

In 1927 the Société Centrale evolved into the Société Centrale Canine, thus strengthening its link with the canine world. Three years before, on July 15, 1924, the Club du Basset Griffon Vendéen had also changed its name after accepting the

Briquet and, shortly after, the Grand, into its register. It became the Club du Griffon Vendéen, and Comte d'Andigné started work on a set of standards for all French scenthound breeds. With Paul Dézamy's contribution on the Briquet and BGV, already drafted a few years previously, these were published in 1930.

One way of establishing the quality of a hound of unknown origin, or origin not demonstrated (*d'origine non démontrée*) was through the *Feuille de Déclaration pour l'Enregistrement au Registre Initial* (the RI or Initial Register). This formed part of the LOF. Owners could ask a qualified judge or approved SCC official to examine a hound when it was eight months and old enough to enter a show. A 'Good' qualification delivered by this person at a show organized by the SCC or an affiliated group qualified the hound for entry into the RI. The club president countersigned the completed form.

There was also provision in the register for dogs of parents already admitted to the RI. This allowed the owner to take advantage of generations previously recorded as pure. These had to be declared in the month of their birth. Any successfully examined fourth generation dog, from hounds registered in the RI, could be directly registered into the LOF.

1932—Paul Dézamy Resigns as CGV President; 1933—Abel Desamy Takes over CGV Presidency

In July 1932, Paul Dézamy, already ill for some time, resigned as club president. He continued to look after the register and club events until January 1 the following year. Then Abel Desamy, his son-in-law and successor designate, officially took over. Following Paul's death later in 1933, the committee elected Abel as president.

Over the years there has been much confusion over the spelling of the Dézamy family name. It is in fact a very common name in the Vendée, spelled either with a *z* or an *s*. Therefore when Paul's Dézamy's daughter married Abel

Desamy, the name changed. It was not simply a change in spelling over the years as some have believed.

On March 19, 1935, at the Exposition Canine Internationale d'Orléans classes of BGVs were separated into "*à jambes demi-torses de 0ᵐ 34 à 0ᵐ 38*" and "*à jambes droites 0ᵐ 38 à 0ᵐ 42*" for the first time. However, with another world war looming, hound showing and hunting had another setback. Fortunately, again favored by the location of the region and their concentration, BGVs suffered less than other hunting breeds. Some stock was depleted, though mainly due to less breeding and hunting throughout this time. During the war, it was the Briquet that suffered most, becoming virtually extinct.

The war also affected the existence of the Grand Griffon Vendéen. Having survived a previous decline, with wolf and stag now almost disappearing, the Grand began disappearing as well. By 1946, it was practically extinct outside the Vendée and even there the type had deteriorated seriously. (It wasn't until 1969, under the direction of Abel Desamy, that a new standard was approved by the committee of the SCC.)

Only four BGVs were registered in the RI during the war years, but shortly after World War II the

A young Grand Griffon Vendéen in France.

PBGV began to come into its own as its popularity grew. Hares became almost extinct. Rabbits, however, were abundant and so it was from a practical viewpoint that the dedication to the smaller hound began. The huntsmen needed a smaller, more capable hound to hunt this game, sometimes for as basic a reason as providing food. Although this kind of informal hunting was prospering, the organized *Brevet de Chasse* had suffered due to the war and it wasn't until 1964 that Abel Desamy actively began reorganizing them in the heart of the Vendée.

1952—New Standard for PBGV Agreed on, RCGV
Registration Rules Changed

The role of the PBGV was reviewed during the late 1940s through the early 1950s. Paul Daubigné convinced the committee that the breed needed an independent standard, as it had become clear that they had separated themselves from the Grand Basset. From 1947 the club put this question to the test and Abel Desamy set out to write a standard specifically for the Petit. This was not only based on the method of hunting and size, but it recognized that evolution had led to two very different breeds. The Petit was more square in construction with less dramatic features than those of the Grand Basset, and in character and type it seemed to model the Briquet. Separating the two also aided in the rebirth of the true Paul Dézamy type of Grand Basset.

In 1952, a new standard was agreed upon, giving the breed its own distinct identity. In November that year, with the agreement of the full committee, the PBGV could be registered as an independent, separate breed within the pages of the RCGV. This was not done, however, without some reluctance on the part of the SCC.

Paul Daubigné's early 20th century definition of the breed

A gathering of Briquets.

captured the harmonious, proportionate reduction in size and assumed natural hunting instinct. Applied to the '50s revision and now in the current standard, it endures as a perceptive cameo—*"Ce n'est plus un Petit Vendéen par simple réduction de la hauteur, mais un Petit Basset réduit harmonieusement dans ses proportions et son volume, et naturellement pourvu de toutes les qualités morales que présuppose la passion de la chasse."*[2]

Crossbreeding was done on a regular basis to import new qualities and traits. In this manner, it is thought Basset Fauve de Bretagne was introduced into the PBGV some decades ago to create new blood. Due to the depletion of Briquet stock during this era it was necessary to introduce Grand Basset blood into the remaining hounds to try to save the breed. From the resulting litters, it was impossible to tell at birth whether they would be of Briquet or Grand Basset type, or something between the two. Also, as the club rules stood, a puppy registered as one breed could be changed to the other when adult. For this reason, the club decided in 1952 to give non-specific registrations in the RCGV until after examination at one year of age.

Seeing the merits that such an examination could bring to charting reproduction, the club decided to extend it to the PBGV. After much evaluation and discussion, approximately ten years later the SCC also saw the benefits. It adopted this examination or confirmation process before definitive registration in the LOF, which also took place at one year of age.

1967—Abel Desamy Resigns

With the backing of committee vote, in 1967 Abel Desamy asked his son Hubert to take the position of president elect.

---

2 It is not a Petit Vendéen by simple reduction of height, but a Petit Basset reduced harmoniously in size and volume; and naturally provided that all qualities presuppose the passion for hunting.

From the beginning of 1970 Hubert assumed charge of the club and eventually took over presidency in June 1975 after his father's death. Hubert had obviously been involved with hounds, hunting and the Griffon Vendéen all his life, and he had taken over the famous Rallye Bocage from his father and grandfather (although the pack was given to a friend of M. Desamy in 1993).

The Rallye Bocage.

In February 1972 the French Ministry of Agriculture recognized the CGV as an approved Breed Association. It was the first hound club (and one of the first clubs of any breed) to hold this honor. The CGV was also the first hound association to hold club shows, now known as the Nationale d'Élevage.

The first Cup of France hunting trial took place in 1975, organized by the SCC for hounds of the *petit vénerie*. Held in the grounds of M. Mangin, president of the Hunting Federation of Seine-et-Marne, all hound breeds of the *petit vénerie* took part except the Basset Bleu de Gascogne. Four of René Tixier's PBGVs represented the Griffons Vendéens.

In 1972 president-elect Hubert Desamy asked breeders to cease inter-breeding between the Grand and Petit. However, the practice continued for some years until 1977 when, as president, he banned it. So, from January 1, 1977, the Grand and Petit became officially separate in breeding terms. Although from then on they were two distinct breeds bearing different standards, with numerous inter-breedings having taken place beforehand, no one could tell with any certainty what would appear in a litter.

Consequently, from that date puppies born out of a PBGV litter could still be registered as Grands, or out of a Grand litter as Petits. This complicated matter was handled through the club RCGV by Secretary Pierre Bourguet. Initially each puppy in the litter was simply registered as a Basset Griffon Vendéen. So, continuing the process adopted in 1952, at one year of age the dog went to a *confirmateur* for assessment as to whether it was a PBGV or a GBGV and, following the appropriate paperwork, the dog was fully registered as one breed or the other. The *confirmateur*, a judge or knowledgeable person acting on behalf of the club, examined the dog to establish quality and type, allowing full registration to take place.

During this era, Hubert Desamy accepted the black and tan (although at that time this was never officially recorded as such in the written standard). He did so on the grounds that one of the classic colors was "badger hair" and, in some respects, this is black and tan. He also said it was an original color, since it appeared in the 1909 standard written by his grandfather. Therefore, until publication of the 1999 PBGV standard, black and tan had been an unofficial, yet acceptable, color in France only. Ninety years later, it is now in the French, and also appears in the FCI standard.

1985—Renaud Buche Takes over the Presidency of the CGV; the RCGV is Closed

In 1985, the committee (16 voting members) met to review new statutes and Renaud Buche, then club treasurer, was voted to succeed Hubert Desamy as president from September of that year. It was a difficult transition, as the Desamy family had controlled the Club du Griffon Vendéen since inception almost 80 years before. Also, although it was felt the time had come to bring the club into a more modern era, M. Desamy believed that affairs of the club should be a traditional, family matter. Committee records and the RCGV were handed over to the new

Above: Examination/ confirmation certificate of Lucrèce du Grangeot de Callou, March 12, 1975.

Right: Corresponding RCGV entry countersigned by Hubert Desamy.

Excellent example of a working/show champion PBGV in France.

president. Unfortunately, many historical records, including photographs and writings, were not passed on. These would have included the club approval for any possible crossbreeding of PBGVs dating back to the 1950s, requiring the president's signature.

At the time of the new presidency, the decision was made to close the RCGV, which gave the origins of the club, to turn the studbook and all registrations over to the SCC and to adopt the Société's LOF system of registration. (At the time the CGV was the only club in France to keep a personal register and it showed that about 80 percent of the dogs registered were Petits.)

Transfer to the SCC system of registration was relatively straightforward since the CGV had used a similar one with their own RCGV. (Every year the SCC issues a letter of the alphabet to be used for registration. This means that all dogs of whatever breed born in that year must have a name beginning with the given letter). It was also decided to discontinue the practice of allowing the two varieties to be registered out of the same litter. If a Grand should appear in a litter of Petits (or vice versa), it would simply be unregistrable; and a hound lacking the quality to pass the examination at one year of age would not be given an LOF number.

The standards were changed slightly to greater reflect the difference between the Petit and Grand. Until then the height of the two breeds had overlapped with the Petit maximum and Grand minimum both 15 inches (38 cm). Renaud Buche felt the division should be more defined. A tolerance of 0.5 inches (1 cm) was added at the higher end of both Grand and Petit scales, and the minimum height for the Grand raised to 15.5 inches (39 cm). (In 1999 it changed again to reflect a height increase for males).

The system of registration and evaluation remained. Even today puppies are registered, but not fully until one year of age. The full registration is issued by the SCC following examination by the *confirmateur*. General points leading to non-confirmation include size exceeding the limits of the standard and lack of type. Specific points regarding type might include: insufficient construction and bone, resulting in inability to hunt; cottony or silky coat; defective tail; flat or overly long ears; severely crooked front; or excessive lack of pigmentation. Furthermore, abnormalities are accessed, such as being monorchid or cryptorchid; having a severely undershot or overshot bite; and aggressive or timid temperament.

In assessing suitability for an LOF number, the *confirmateur* will also indicate whether the dog is:

apte – able to be shown and passed for breeding;

inapte – unable to be shown and not passed for breeding (although, in reality, such hounds are used for breeding, but their progeny will never be registrable); or

ajourné – put on hold. At assessment a dog from registered parents may be lacking in some way, for example out of condition or underweight. The decision is therefore deferred and the hound brought back six months later for reassessment.

Thus, if the French-bred or French-registered hound has been passed by the *confirmateur*, it is technically impossible for it to be disqualified at the National d'Élevage. As the standards states, there are two sets of faults, "*défauts*" (flaws or undesirable traits) and *"défauts éliminatoires"* (faults considered significant enough for disqualification, therefore not passing the test at one year of age).

The club asks breeders to sign *"une charte"* (a pledge) concerning their breeding activities and, in particular, promising to replace or refund the monetary difference for loss in value if a dog is refused at confirmation. These breeders must have a registered prefix and must have been a member of the club for more than three years. Some of the longest standing members are René Tixier (de Fin Renard), 1963; Pierre Salaün (des Ajoncs de l'Aulne), 1967; Maurice Perraudeau (de la Jaranne), 1970; and Gilbert Pène (des Rives de la Garonne), 1975.

A breeder has always needed formal, written permission from the club, with the president's signature, to introduce new bloodlines and improve hunting abilities by crossbreeding. Any resulting hound, once having shown hunting aptitude in a working trial and awarded a prize at a show, could then be registered with the SCC. It would be recorded as *"origine inconnue"* or, as it states on the SCC registration certificate, *"Titre Initial"* (First Generation). On the next and subsequent generation, when bred to a dog of known origin, the pedigree develops and, after four generations, it is thought that the blood is pure. Since taking over as president, Renaud Buche has given no such formal permission for the Petit.

The year 1998 saw the CGV celebrate its 25th anniversary Nationale d'Élevage. There was an entry of 380 Griffon Vendéen hounds, 162 of which were Petits. As usual, classes were divided by sex and as *Jeune* (Youth), Debutant, *Ouverte* (Open), Champion and *Travail* (Working). Awards were given as Excellent, Very Good and Good.

At such shows, at the judge's discretion, all the dogs awarded Excellent usually compete further for Best of Breed. There may be an SCC official or possibly a trainee accompanying the judge. There is also a secretary to document the oral critiques that are given in the ring. It is not unusual for a discussion between exhibitor and judge to begin during judging. This may involve additional judges present as well as spectators. However, the breed judge's decision on placement is final. At the 1998 show, one such debate about an injury to a dog's tail stopped judging for 30 minutes!

Judging the
Open Class.

Following in the footsteps of the Dézamy dynasty founded a century ago, Renaud Buche's presidency has ensured that not only has the PBGV become a strong contender in the showring, it is also firmly established in France as one of the most popular hunting hounds of outstanding quality. There are approximately 600 entries annually in the LOF and, together with the Beagle and Basset Fauve de Bretagne, they form the basis of hound breeding in France today. The BGV has now come full circle. The Grand Basset suffers from small litters, lack of uniformity of size and type variation resulting in a decline in the breed, whereas PBGVs are thriving. With an extensive gene pool, there is no need to introduce new blood by out-crossing to another breed.

CHAPTER FOUR

THE HUNTING TRADITION

The next best thing to a good day's hunting is a bad day's hunting—but the reading of a book on hounds must, in my humble opinion, be a very close third.
—*Sir John Buchanan-Jardine,* Hounds of the World 1937

The Hunting Scene in Great Britain

In late 19th and early 20th century England the use of Griffons Vendéens as a pack animal was a completely new experience for many huntsmen. William Mure of Caldwell House near Glasgow in Scotland, who hunted a pack of rough-coated hounds, gave testimony to their tenacity by saying that, once on a scent, not even a stone wall would stop them, so it was quite understandable that they would account for more hares.

These hounds hunted more like a terrier, being neither as steady nor as pleasurable for the huntsmen to handle. They also did not have the quality of voice other of hound breeds. However, their longer legs (indicating they were Grande Taille) gave them the advantage of being able to cover the ground faster. Soon huntsmen saw the benefits of using Griffon Vendéen blood. This played a considerable part in the making of a new breed of English Basset or Harehound.

In the years spanning World War I the Bassets were crossbred with Griffons Vendéens, Beagles and Harriers, with the intention of reproducing the earlier *basset à jambes droites*. This "new" basset retained many pure characteristics, such as tone of voice, scenting ability, substance, length of body and depth of chest, but the type of leg conformation lost favor and gradually disappeared from every basset breed except the Griffon Vendéen—today's Grand Basset Griffon Vendéens.

In *Hounds of Britain* (1973), Jack Ivester Lloyd wrote that genuine hunting folk had displayed elasticity of mind by introducing out-crosses when these would benefit the breeds that interested them. This was why all hunting hounds in Britain possessed stamina, health and intelligence. By contrast, the closed gene pool of Kennel Club registered dogs recognized the unthinking pursuit of high breeding—leading to low breeding!

This had concerned Captain Godfrey Heseltine who, early in the 20th century, resigned from the Basset Hound Club in protest against the bad effect he thought showing was having on soundness of the breed. His concern was maintaining genuine type and capability for hunting. With his brother Christopher, he had started hunting badger in the New Forest in the early 1890s with a few couple, which soon increased to form their Walhampton pack. Hare later took preference, and their fixture card humorously specified "No riding is allowed unless the rider is under seven or over 70 years old."

Following the rift between the showing and hunting fraternity, in 1912 the Heseltines were instrumental in forming a Master of Basset Hounds Association. Their aim was to promote the breeding of correct type. Their first show specifically for working bassets took place at Rugby in May that year. Queen Alexandra, who with King Edward VII supported the basset during this low ebb, was the only Basset Hound Club "show-minded" person permitted to exhibit at MBHA events. At Banbury in 1914, the last show before the outbreak of World War I, she exhibited a couple of rough-coated bassets in a class not restricted to working hounds, gaining second prize with

Sandringham Valens who "lost in head but was as sound as a bell, with irreproachable front and quarters."

The renowned Walhampton pack was maintained by various people at several localities before and after the war years and while Godfrey served abroad. It was finally disbanded after Godfrey killed himself at his home in 1932. The brothers had briefly kept a few rough-coats, which Christopher Heseltine said "were excellent in their work, but they had a different style of hunting. If they had not been drafted they would have spoilt the pack."

The Westerby

Lieutenant-Colonel Eric Morrison was one who admitted to "the dreadful crime of crossing the basset with other hound breeds." Having been whipper-in for Godfrey Heseltine for many years, he reformed the depleted pack after 1932 and changed its name to Westerby to differentiate it from the Walhampton show-prefix.

In a 1959 letter to French hound expert George Johnston, Morrison wrote, "I would like you to know that I did this solely to keep the breed alive, as in the middle thirties it was in danger of becoming extinct." Morrison achieved this by crossing the pure Bassets with Harriers for greater activity, and introducing Petit Bleu de Gascogne blood and some Griffon Vendéen lines from Sir Rupert Buchanan-Jardine's Castle Milk pack.

Castle Milk

It was largely thanks to the efforts of Sir Rupert Buchanan-Jardine that the Basset Griffon Vendéen became established as a pack-hound in Britain. Sir Rupert's father, Sir John, owned the Dumfries Foxhounds in Scotland.

Sir Rupert followed on in the hunting tradition and, in 1938, he imported six straight-legged Griffons Vendéens—five dogs and a bitch—from M. Sellier in France. These hounds formed the foundations for his Castle Milk pack.

Griffons Vendéens imported from France 1938, in Castle Milk kennels.

Castle Milk Blazer 1948 (Beagle Caldbeck Fell Bloater ex half Beagle/half Griffon Vendéen Saucebox).

By out-crossing with the Westerby hounds that were shorter coupled, more active and leggier, he bred several litters and hunted hare fairly successfully for quite a few years. He also reared an average of at least one litter every year of pure Griffon Vendéen and described them in general as:

Very useful little hounds, possibly more numerous in France than the Artésiens-Normands, although not so popular in this country. This breed is divided into two groups, one with straight, the other with slightly bent legs. The straight-legged strain is shorter coupled and more active. In color these hounds are usually lemon and white or badger-pied; they are rough coated and very hardy. The straight-legged variety reminds one very much of a small Welsh Hound both in appearance and in working qualities. Each is full of activity, has a good nose, is inclined to be riotous, but does not possess quite the stamina of some other breeds.

Of his own hounds he remarked:

The pure Griffons Vendéens had good noses, plenty of cry, though not the wonderful voices of the smooth coated Artésiens-Normands, but were faster than the latter. They were also hardier and had more drive; their main drawback, however, was that they were very riotous and headstrong. They used to start off the day with a terrific dash but after two hours or so used to tire and get tailed off. This factor, I think, is in the breed of them, as a great deal of trouble was taken to get them really fit.

Nick Valentine, Master of the Bradley Vale (subsequently Ryeford Chase) pack, took up the story.

He found the Vendéens suited the Dumfriesshire country of rough heather and stone walls better than other bassets, being longer on the leg and more athletic. However, they had two failings. Firstly, they proved too wild and headstrong to make good pack hounds and secondly they were lacking stamina. So, by 1945, he came to the conclusion that the only way to progress with the breed was to use an out-cross to rectify these faults. Sir Rupert was fortunate in obtaining the great Beagle sire Caldbeck Fell Bloater from C. N. de Courcy-Parry. Bloater's pedigree does not appear in any stud book; on his sire's side he had a line to Border Stormer, a Foxhound; and his dam, a blue mottled bitch, went back to Romney Marsh and Clifton Foot Harrier blood. Bloater was a great hare hound, many packs of Beagles owe much of their excellence to his blood. He ended his days with the West Lodge.

The Bloater/Griffon Vendéen cross proved a huge success. From them Sir Rupert bred his hounds on these lines and quite a few of them found their way to the West Lodge. From this source the West Lodge have always had a number of rough-coated hounds in the pack clearly showing their Griffon Vendéen ancestry.

The West Lodge

The West Lodge was originally a Beagle pack but resurrected as English Bassets by Lionel Woolner in 1950. However, he admitted he had always been addicted to shaggy dogs.

In his 1988 article "Speeding up the Basset," Major John Watson wrote, "In the late 1940s, he began to take a close interest in the broken-coated French breeds. In 1949, as an experiment, he mated a Beagle dog-hound with a pure Griffon Vendéen Basset bitch from Sir John Buchanan-Jardine's Castle Milk."

Lionel Woolner told him, "At that time the possibility of starting a pack was not even in mind and the resulting litter of broken-coated hounds, ranging in size from 15–19 inches, was disposed of in the Barnet area. The following winter these pups were, on several occasions, collected together and, with my single couple of old hounds, gave the local hares a little light exercise. It was towards the end of that season, and as a result of the considerable interest which these activities had aroused, that the possibility of reviving the West Lodge was first mooted."

Major Watson continued, "He then acquired some unentered hounds from Colonel Eric Morrison's Westerby Kennels—Artésien-Normand Bassets crossed with small Harriers." The pack gradually expanded and, in the late '50s, Mr. Woolner took most of the Castle Milk Basset-Harrier pack (following their disbandment), thereby greatly increasing the element in the

West Lodge. However, despite the undoubted attraction to the Griffon Vendéen, Lionel Woolner did not want pure griffon in the pack. His country bordered London, sometimes hunting within ten miles of Hyde Park, and he had to be sure of keeping them together!

In later years, Lionel's passion for hunting led him to translate Comte Élie de Vezins' *"Les Chiens Courants Français pour la Chasse du Lièvre dans le Midi de la France,"* which was published in 1974 under the title "Hounds for a Pack."

As well as the West Lodge, Sir Rupert Buchanan-Jardine knew of one other pack of crossbred bassets: the Casewick, which hunted in Lincolnshire and, he believed, had a good deal of Griffon Vendéen and Beagle blood. The Casewick later became the Crowcombe Harehounds. They eventually changed to using Beagles and most of the bassets were exported to America, where they became the Tewkesbury Foot.

Isle of Wight Foot Beagles
In August 1970 Basset Griffon Vendéen bitch Sanda de la Réote, born on July 9, 1969, (Quibiche de la Brèche des Charmes ex Qualine de la Réote), arrived on the Isle of Wight. Bred by Claude Guy, a ladies' hairdresser from Essay, near Cherbourg, she went through quarantine to join Colonel Francis Mew's Beagles. Sanda was mated to Parson and produced eight puppies with markedly rough coats. Known as the "Fluffies," they caused considerable interest both in the kennels and hunting field. Sanda was always kept at the Master of Hounds' home as a pet and never hunted but, in the 1972–73 season, when the puppies were old enough, they were entered.

Current master (Mrs. Mary Chapman) records show that the "Fluffies" were bred to improve voice and nose in their notoriously cold-scenting country. It was a success. They hunted with a deep and lovely cry, which was easily recognizable, and they were usually well to the fore. On the debit side, they were terrible fighters in the kennels and had to be lodged separately.

Sanda was never mated again and Nina, the last of the litter, spent her old age with the master as his pet.

The Ryeford Chase

Formerly known as the Bradley Vale, this pack, which is the best known to British PBGV owners, has moved several times with Master Nick Valentine's employment. They have hunted in several different areas in England, Ireland

Feeding time at Bradley Vale.

and Wales, always assuming their name from current location. In May 1995 permanent kennels were acquired at Ryeford, near Ross-on-Wye, in the countryside bordering Wales. Nick appropriately added the name Chase in recognition of the nearby Chase Woods and acknowledging that his hounds will follow anything!

Nick was first introduced to hunting at the age of ten when his father took him and his sister out hunting with the West Lodge Harehounds. His sister was unimpressed as she failed to see any point in running around after a load of screeching dogs, but Nick was enthralled. He wrote,

> From the first moment a hare popped up, as if by magic from nowhere, and the clamoring music of the hounds rose as they tore off in hot pursuit, I was caught by an impulse that gave wings to my legs and sped me along in their wake. The excitement of that day has never been lost; since then hunting has been the one passion of my life. I played truant from school on hunting days and between times relieved the boredom of a dull academic career by dreaming of the pack of hounds that I would one day possess myself.

In 1974 Nick spotted Joan Wells-Meacham's and Mildred

Seiffert's imported dog Rigolo de la Vrignaie at the Hertfordshire County Show and he saw the chance for his dream to become a reality. His first dog, Jomil Fanfare, started hunting at the early age of four-and-a-half months and possessed the best voice Nick had ever heard.

Encouraged by this, Nick contacted Jack Powell-Williams, West Lodge Master, to beg for any rough-coats available. He acquired Mischief, a white and lemon six-year-old direct descendant of Castle Milk Songster, with some Beagle blood and a line of West Country Harrier from Sinclair's Venus. Thisbee, a young, nervous, rough-coated Beagle of unknown breeding from Wales, was the next brick in the foundation of his pack. By using Fanfare on these two bitches of such different type, the resulting progeny were beyond all expectations; they seemed to inherit the virtues of their parents while leaving the faults behind.

By 1984 Nick realized further progress was impossible without introducing fresh blood. He achieved this by obtaining hounds from different sources. He first acquired two rough-coats from West Lodge, Clansman and Cobweb, by Westerby Crofter out of Winsome, one of their rough-coated bitches. Cobweb, who proved to be too wild for the West Lodge, was a great-granddaughter of Jomil Angelo, owned by Basset Hound Club Chairman and Albany Basset hunt master John Evans. She hunted brilliantly and, in carrying the best of the old West Lodge lines through her grand-dam, West Lodge Majestic '78, featured strongly in all future lines.

Two pure Griffons Vendéens also arrived; Arthur, a Wakelyns dog bred by Anne and Sandy Mackenzie, and Future Amnesty (Gambol) bred by Jan Baker. Born on July 23, 1982, Gambol's sire was Jomil Flambard, litter brother to Fanfare. Reared in a domestic environment and with a successful show career, the somewhat bad-tempered Gambol adapted easily to pack life and proved to be a deep scenting hound, hunting well into old age. Her progeny displayed similar characteristics. Nick's hounds rapidly became very popular amongst farmers and landowners who waged war against a plague of rabbits that constantly ravaged their crops and caused other damage.

Nick bred from another Jan Baker PBGV in subsequent years. Jaby Arrow Bright Crocus, born on June 18, 1984, (Alabeth Avide ex Folly Acre Buttercup) possessed good conformation and, like Gambol, had strong lines to Jomil Flambard and the imported Pacha des Barbus d'Entre Lac. However, she was excitable and sadly passed epilepsy on to her offspring. This line was therefore bred out and continued careful selection produced a fast, hard hunting, straight-legged 15-inch hound. Spree of Sweetdean arrived from Pam Aldous and Graham Telfer in 1989. Unfortunately, her soundness and sensible nature were not matched by hunting ability, although her descendants number in the pack. After hunting with the pack, Linda Colbert's Ch. Rillaton Solace was used at stud in 1990. Bred by Mrs. D. Hounslow (Dan. Lux. Ch. Salto de Crislaure of Morebess ex Maquisard Bonjour of Tollydane), Solace later joined the pack for a year. Although Nick found him too noisy, his line is well represented through offspring of his one daughter, Softley. From 1992, several Teckels (working wire-haired Dachshunds) have been kept and run with the pack in place of terriers.

The pack's Silver Jubilee year was 1999, and Nick remi-

The Ryeford Chase, Nick Valentine, center, in front of the Stable Yard at Althorp (now the Diana, Princess of Wales Memorial Museum), Falconry Fair 1996.

nisced about the great progress made. Initially he been unable to breed enough puppies and had only one litter every other year. He also had a high failure rate with whelps being born with bent sterns, bad mouths and, worse still, bad shoulders. He also had puppies not making the grade in their work. Now, Nick now has up to six litters a year of more fixed type. Structural faults disappeared long ago and the required level of performance in the young hounds is more easily achieved. By out-crossing, he has also introduced a fresh line (de Fin Renard) into 12 generations of his own breeding.

The hunting season generally extends from the end of August to April, with about 40 to 50 hunts a season and the annual tally being over 100 brace; mainly rabbit, but also fox and hare. Invitation meets are numerous and, during the summer, Nick is often asked to parade the hounds at country fairs, where they are always well received, especially by children. These hounds now represent 12 generations of his own breeding and have evolved into a characteristic type that Nick freely admits would find little favor in the showring. However, in the field and working in unison, they leave most others standing, as René Tixier will vouch. After well over 30 years of showing and working his hounds, he will long remember the sight of Nick's pack at the August 1998 Houndshow, where he was agog at the sight of so many Bassets Griffons all under control.

Nick's enthusiasm for hunting has spread to many, some of whom have started up small packs with stock provided by him. Starting with eight couple of 11–12.5 inches (28–32 cm) Pocket Beagles, Dai Large has had PBGVs since the early '70s and his Mid-Glamorgan pack hunts regularly. David Vaughn's Morfe Vale started in the early '90s with English Bassets. Hunting near Bridgnorth in Shropshire, David took on a pure-bred PBGV from Nick, also a Basset Fauve de Bretagne. With a limited gene pool, he has since crossed Fauves with Griffons and English Bassets with Griffons. In addition to hunting over the winter months, like the Ryeford Chase, the hounds are paraded regularly at shows. And, in 1997, Bedlington Terrier expert John Williams started the Black Mountain Bassets, a primarily Griffon Vendéen pack, with a couple of Bleu de Gascogne crosses and four couple from Ryeford Chase. This all serves as evidence that Bassets Griffons Vendéens have played, and will continue to play, a valuable part in the English hunting scene.

Hunting in North America

The hunt, if it evokes for many a number of colorful images, is much more than certain clichéd stereotypes: the horses, the horns, the red clothes...And if we are more particularly concerned with this mode of hunting, it is that the element which is most important in this "art," is the dogs.
—*G. P. Larcher, 1973*

Traditionally, the working pack has been primarily Beagle or Foxhound throughout the United States and Canada. The opportunity to see a pack of little tri-colored hounds charging through the fields with their hunt master and whipper-in dressed in traditional clothing, is rare in most parts of North America. More usual is the sight of ordinary people out with their few Beagles, enjoying what comes naturally in the form of a weekend hobby.

But for those studying the art of venery, the pleasure is derived from the hound, achieving what it is bred to do, working out in the fields and forests. Thanks to some breeders and owners, intent on preserving an age-old tradition and protecting the well-rounded hound, hunting has been reborn and rekindled.

The Chaparral

For Susan Buttifant from Ontario, whose prefix Chaparral is also the name of her pack, this is a deep commitment. She grew up with an assortment of dogs, spending summers at the family cottage of accompanying neighbors who ran a pack of Beagles. They were out in the fields daily and Susan would follow them. Although it may have started with the boredom of a ten-year-old girl, the fascination began. In 1985 Susan spotted an advertisement in the newspaper for PBGVs. They had just been recognized by the Canadian Kennel Club. Being a fancier of different scenthounds, she knew what they were but had never seen one before.

She replied to the advertisement. Noreen Beasley (Belray) was leaving the country and wanted to place a litter of pups (Jomil Pascal – Wakelyns Angelique) and an adult dog. Susan took them all and spent the next six months sorting out which ones to keep and which to re-home.

At that time Borzoi was Susan's main breed and she would take them lure coursing as well as hunting rabbit. Naturally, the PBGVs accompanied them into the fields. The breeds worked well together and the combination of hunting dogs and styles created "a deadly team." Soon the breeds were separated and Susan began to concentrate her efforts on the PBGVs.

However, Susan found that their hunting style differed so much from the Borzoi that she needed a greater understanding of how scenthounds really worked. Jim Wellheiser, a long-time friend who raised hunting bassets, became her mentor. They spent hours in the field with his bassets to compare the breeds. Jim had never heard of the PBGV, so he was also unfamiliar with their style of work. With perseverance, they were able to determine how the breed ran, what training methods worked, and how to work through problems, such as the dogs running deer and poor working habits. Most important of all, they concentrated on how the dogs' minds worked.

The terrain where they hunt compares with that of the Vendée—thick brush, forest and stony land full of thorns and bramble thickets. With the dogs more than eight feet in front of her, Susan can rarely see them, although she found that this helps them begin to develop confidence in their own abilities.

Training method came by trial and error. The youngsters start going out from the age of six months. They are trained in brief sessions, about 30 minutes once a week.

As stamina and muscles develop, each pup is taken out with an older "training hound," who works slowly so that the youngster can keep up. This is done for a short time so the pup can get the right basics instilled in his mind before going out alone. Vocal commands and horn sounds are then introduced and the dogs begin to learn discipline.

At around one year old, the PBGV in training accompanies the other hounds out hunting. Outings become longer and the youngster continues to work with very reliable, experienced hounds. As Susan says, "Learning never ends. This is part of what keeps my interest."

Vocal commands vary from words to a particular sound. When out exercising, the hounds will respond to "Heel up," which means they must walk beside or behind her, not in front. The young hounds are always trying to take an inch so they can have a mile so "Back" is used if they start to forge. A hound under a year or two old will have a rope dragging from it and, if it goes too far ahead, a quick stamp on the rope helps reinforce this critical command.

When hunting, the hounds are trained to respond to "Over here," which indicates the direction Susan wants them to turn. They also take this command from a distance with a wave of her arm. Continued hunting in a particular area is encouraged with "Yut-yut-yut." If Susan spots the rabbit first, the hounds respond immediately to Susan's "Hi-yi-yi-yi-yi" from wherever they are going and take the direction she points out.

The horn offers several different sounds. One indicates a change in direction. The hounds may look up to follow their master or continue working, simply following the sound of the horn. There is another sound for "no" if they have found the scent of a deer. Yet another sound indicates the hunt is done and it is time to head home.

Over the years the pack has learned much and progressed well, and correspondence between Susan and Nick Valentine forged a mutual appreciation of the problems and blessings of running a *basset griffon* pack. In 1988 Nick wrote to her, "It is so nice to hear from someone interested in using the PBGV for the purpose which centuries of careful breeding created and molded into the hound we now have."

He saw all characteristics so important to the hunting hound as "virtues invisible to the eye that can only be possessed in their entirety by well-bred individuals from parents who proved their ability in the field" and advised Susan not to keep hounds that were a disruptive influence as they would surely spoil the rest. This meant having the courage to weed out any hound persistently hunting on its own, that babbled, was too slow or too fast, not true on the scent or plain lazy. "Seventy-five percent of a pack's success in the field is due to its breeding, you can't make a hound hunt, the love of it must be born within him. Similarly, the desire to cooperate as a team member must emanate from the hound itself. The other 25 percent ingredient needed to bring a pack to perfection is correct handling in field and kennel; and discipline—this, however, is an art in itself." Both have shared a common goal of preserving and improving what they cherish as their heritage.

Usually only three or four Chaparral hounds go out together.

Susan Buttifant with her Chaparral Hounds.

While hare hunting is more successful in larger packs, hunting rabbit is best with two or three, a manageable number. Being a passionate breed, they feed off each other's excitement, but they are also independent hunters. If one hound gets on the scent of a rabbit, the others will rally to his call; however, they like to find the trail first, on their own, then rejoin the hunt. Contrary to others' belief, Susan thinks that PBGVs do not lack stamina. Rather the dogs tire, become messy and lazy in the way they work; although they do not stop working altogether.

Susan's writing encapsulates perfectly her passion for her hounds.

I have had Deucy for a few weeks now, getting to know her and vice versa. She is a year old and I have a lot resting on her so it was with a little trepidation that I took her out for the first time into the fields.

We set out along the leaf-covered paths into the bush. The sky was overcast and the air heavy with an impending storm. I unclipped Deucy and off she went at full gallop, free at last. I eventually turned a corner and could see her silhouette 500 feet in the distance looking back on us. When I saw her, I gave a quick blow of the horn and turned off the path into the brush.

I released Nick at that point and he went about his usual work. Within a minute or so Deucy was right there behind us and, from then on, she realized the party was with me and not off in the distance. The rest of my time was spent watching her work, her style, her drive, her desire. It was all there, sometimes misplaced, but with practice I would expect her to improve.

The rain started. This never deters the hounds from the job but it does affect their scenting abilities and they weren't able to follow very well. My boots began to fill with water, so I started heading in the direction of home. Near the edge of the field I blew the two wet hounds in and they obediently came over to be hooked up.

We'll continue this kind of routine throughout the season. Whatever problems we run into will soon be forgotten when the hounds are running together on a great line with their melodious voices echoing through the hills and dales.

Currently Susan is the only person in Canada to hunt a pack of PBGVs. Although she continues to show her dogs successfully in the conformation showring, the skill, the dedication and the intensity comes in the field. Her Can. Ch. Fredwell Calabash not only won at the Canadian Specialty, his excellent hunting qualities earned him Best in Field in 1993. This Working class win was her proudest moment.

The Skycastle

In 1948 John and Elizabeth Streeter established a private working pack with some hounds from England. They had moved to Chester Springs, Pennsylvania, buying a 320-acre farm, which they named Skycastle. There they brought up their children, established an equestrian center, raised horses, chickens, a rare breed of cattle—called Belted Galloways—and Basset Hounds. Their Bassets were a reflection of the less polished, natural lifestyle that Elizabeth loved. She did not want the typical, heavy, slower hound but preferred the English Hunting Bassets—longer legged, swifter dogs. They worked the pack for enjoyment but were very competitive in Working trials.

In the years that followed, they acquired more Bassets, AKC registered, from local field trial enthusiasts and packs such as the Timber Ridge (Maryland) and Coldstream (Newtown Square, Pennsylvania). During this time Elizabeth's passion for hunting grew and eventually turned to a different type of basset. As early as 1967 a hunting publication made reference to the Skycastle being a "private pack of partially rough-coated hounds..." There is evidence that, at that time, other packs contained rugged bassets, rougher in coat and physique, whose coarse hair on the underside of the tail was six inches or more long. They possibly originated from the Dalby Hall pack in England. Although not of the *griffon* type, these long-haired bassets were extremely good hunters and Elizabeth was often asked whether she would like them, as they did not meet the show standard. Possibly she was tempted.

By the mid '70s, Elizabeth's fascination for rough-coated hounds had turned to the PBGV and inspired a trip to England. She met breeders, saw many dogs and gleaned what she could from the limited information available there at that time. With her sights set on developing a hunting pack of purely rough-coated hounds, in August 1975 she imported a dog, Jomil Gallant, and litter sister, Gabrielle (Rigolo de la Vrignaie ex T'Annetta). Shortly after, still keen to learn more about the breed and their working style, Elizabeth visited France to spend time with huntsmen, including French Club President Hubert Desamy. Two bitch puppies accompanied her on her return to Pennsylvania.

Elizabeth Streeter MBH showing her five-couple pack at the Bryn Mawr Hound Show in 1982.

The PBGVs worked well, but Elizabeth soon realized that performance together as a pack was poor. Learning from European huntsmen, she embarked on improving their working abilities by introducing missing elements.

Incredibly, quite independently and with the Atlantic separating them, that year she set about this in exactly the same way as Nick Valentine had in the U.K. She went to the Tewkesbury Foot, descendants of Castle Milk. Elizabeth acquired Tewkesbury Foot Artful '72, an English Hunting/AKC cross-breed from New Jersey. By crossbreeding her PBGVs and the traditional English Hunting Basset, the first generation saw obvious improvements in cooperation and uniformity of working. Artful produced several litters, one having great influence on American Basset packs. Quince, Quicksilver and Questling came from the 1979 "Q" litter, which was sired by Skycastle Napoleon '77, whose sire and dam were Pelloquin's Ciro and Pelloquin's Propriétaire, bred by Vendée inhabitant M. Pelloquin (du Pays de Retz). Quince was drafted back to Tewkesbury and produced several outstanding working hounds for them and other packs. Elizabeth eventually let the old Basset line die out and never went back to her English Hunting Basset cross. Over the years she took great care to keep the pure-bred Griffon Vendéen line separate from the crossbred hounds (who were at least three generations away from pure-bred PBGV).

Curiously, she had only one stud dog at a time. While she kept other young males at Skycastle for a year or two, the stud had the run of the property with many of the bitches—a hound with his harem. This one dog would be used regularly, being replaced every few years. He would hunt, though rarely in trials. When in competition, Elizabeth hunted with an all-bitch pack.

In 1983 she traveled back to France and to the Ajoncs de l'Aulne kennel of Pierre Salaün, Vice President of the Club du Griffon Vendéen. There she bought the young Turenne, born on July 16, 1982. He hunted so well that any door left open meant an absence of up to three days on the trail of rabbit and deer. He would return exhausted but happy. He also excelled as a stud dog, and when Elizabeth eventually had a pure-bred son to keep, she felt able to part with Turenne.

As one of the early enthusiasts in North America, undoubtedly Elizabeth helped development of the breed. Her devotion came from a deep understanding of the hound and a desire to continue to let it flourish by using its natural instinct. Her not unfounded fear, in those early days, was what would happen when the PBGV was transformed into a show dog and a pet?

Elizabeth died in 1987 as she would have wished, while returning from hunting. Her son, Nick, decided to keep the pack going. As a private one supported by subscription and renamed the Skycastle French Hounds, he asked James Scharnberg, MBH, to take over as huntsman. Jim, an art director for an advertising firm, native New Yorker and experienced foothunter, did so in June 1987 and within a year the committee appointed him as the new master.

As a conservationist, Jim fought several battles over the land on which they hunt and about preservation of local habitat and wildlife. The Streeter family sold much of their property but gave permission for the pack to occupy the barn kennels and use the house until it were sold for development. This allowed fundraising time for building new kennels, completed in 1994. Two years later the original house and acreage was sold. Happily, with permission from the various owners, Skycastle still hunts on most of the land.

When Jim took over, the better hounds had been taken by a couple that had worked for Elizabeth. The remaining pack consisted of 19 hounds, five of which were puppies and only three pure-bred. Much to his surprise, some were shy, some aggressive—and there were no males! After two wasted breeding seasons and drafting out the fighters, Jim obtained good workers from Ripshin Bassets, which were rough-coated descendants of Quince '79.

In the summer of 1992 Skycastle turned once again to Pierre Salaün and Jim imported Estèle des Ajoncs de l'Aulne (Bissol des Ajoncs de l'Aulne ex Savane des Ajoncs de l'Aulne), in whelp to Fr. Ch. Baldo de la Côte d'Olhette. She delivered nine

1994 Bryn Mawr Hound Show. Jim Scharnberg with Skycastle Duchess, Grand Champion Basset and Skycastle Estèle des Ajoncs de l'Aulne, Reserve Grand Champion. (photo James Carr)

puppies in 1993. Three remained with Skycastle—Dalesman, Dervish and Doubtful. Being too big and fast for Skycastle, Duchess became lead hound with the Ripshin, winning many titles at Bryn Mawr Hound Show.

With the new infusion of French blood, Skycastle hounds showed their prowess in hunting and conformation. Dalesman was Bryn Mawr Champion Dog and won many other firsts, the start, after a long hiatus, of pure-bred hounds winning once more on the flags at National Pack Basset Trials. Others have been regular winners at trials in Aldie, Virginia, and Bryn Mawr. Hounds from, or sired by, Skycastle have also become AKC and Canadian champions in the showring.

Strong workers came from a Dalesman – Reba '92 mating (Ripshin granddaughter of Quince). Dervish also produced a litter, sired by an excellent Ripshin hound, Rebel '98, for whom Jim has high hopes.

There have been other imports. In 1994 Hecto (El Diavolo de Fin Renard ex Fanny) arrived from France, a strong little hound, though aggressive in the kennel and either outstandingly good or bad in the field. A Hecto – Estèle mating produced nine, one of which (Guilty) went to Nick Frost, while the two Jim kept have proved to be outstanding in the field. Luron des

Mounaidières, from Christian and Pierre Isern, is turning out to be a superb hunter and, with Pierre Salaün's assistance, anther import was Oscar des Bords de l'Anse, bred by André Domelain.

Jim maintains a pure-bred and crossbred line in the kennel. He finds the PBGVs to be bold, driving hunters. "Their intelligence is eerie and they have excellent noses and cry is either very high and shrill or a good deep bay. Their agility is awesome and they will tackle the worst undergrowth and bramble, which most smooth-coated bassets would quit."

Jim summed up his passion by saying, "Hunting with PBGVs is super. They live up to their reputation of being '*trop requérant*' or '*trop chasseur*'—trying too hard to find their quarry and not listening to the huntsman or fellow packmates— they do not settle down in their work until maybe their third season. The crossbreeds, which are 50/50 or 75/25 French/English, are much steadier in their first and second season and are the glue which holds the pack together. This is why the pack consists of 40 percent pure-bred hounds and 60 percent crossbred. What a grand madness it is!"

Jim Scharnberg with the Skycastle.

CHAPTER FIVE

THE PBGV

IN GREAT BRITAIN

Your Roman-Saxon-Danish-Norman English.
—Daniel Defoe 1660?–1731

The present-day PBGV arrived in England in 1969, when Joan Wells-Meacham and Mildred Seiffert imported Rigolo de la Vrignaie from France. We cannot, however, ignore the exciting era of Victorian/Edwardian England when the rough-coated basset existed alongside its cousin, the smooth-coat.

This rough-haired basset, often a product of crossbreeding practiced in France between smooth basset and Griffon Vendéen, was distinctly different from our present-day PBGV. Few publications of the era used the name "Griffon Vendéen," favoring the title "rough-coat," thereby leading to present-day differences of opinion on the rough-coats' historical significance. However, looking at its appearance and the part which smooth-coated basset fanciers played in this, illustrates how Griffon Vendéen blood was first introduced into England.

Arrival of the Basset in England

In common with other French breeds, smooth-coated bassets had doubtless been imported centuries ago, but probably the bloodlines became mixed within other varieties of dog so gradually they lost their true identity. Thus, the first true smooth-coated bassets to arrive in England in recent history were two which Comte de Tournon presented to Lord Galway in 1866. In 1872, he passed his small, established pack to Lord Onslow, who also owned "straight-legged, half rough-coated bassets, with remarkably short ears."

Then, in 1874, Everett Millais, son of prominent artist Sir John Everett Millais, saw two smooth-coats at the Jardin d'Acclimitation in Paris. Both were Le Couteulx stock. Millais was impressed and bought one, the famous Model. Over the next seven years his hard work helped to establish Basset Hounds firmly in England.

The Millais Legacy

Millais gained an over-whelming interest in hounds from his father, whose passion for hunting led him to spend several months every year shooting and fishing in the Highlands of Scotland. Everett's own claim to renown was as an animal geneticist, having studied at London's St. Thomas' Hospital to increase his knowledge and relate it to the basset world.

Sir Everett Millais.

With no suitable bassets to breed Model to, Millais suc-cessfully out-crossed with a Beagle to keep his bloodline going. In 1892 he out-crossed with the Bloodhound to restore certain features which the *basset* breed had gradually lost. This experiment proved all the more remarkable since he achieved it by artificial insemination.

Many considered out-crossing harmful. However Millais' prolific essays on the subject demonstrate his advanced theories, and it is thanks to his many enthusiastic writings on the basset that we gain a marvelous insight into the origins of the rough-coat in England.

In Vero Shaw's 1881 *Book of the Dog*, Millais quoted from a December 1875 letter sent by eminent French author, Monsieur A. Pierre Pichot. As editor for *La Revue Britannique* and a Jardin d'Acclimitation manager, Pichot had written to the editor of the *Live Stock Journal*: "The Basset Hounds, which differ in almost every point from the Dachshund, are, on the contrary, of every color and both rough and smooth, and of these there are still more numerous varieties than of the Dachshund, the Bassets having in my own opinion, sprung from the different local breeds of large hounds, and therefore connected with the Vendée, Saintonge, Artois, and Normandy types."

Millais continued "I may mention here that the only Bassets yet exhibited in England have been of the Normandy type, *à poil ras*, and one of the Vendée type, a Basset Griffon. I have only lately received a letter from a gentleman in Wales who informs me that he has imported a leash of the latter hounds for rabbiting, and so I now hope to see an increase of them, as the only one I mention above is a dog belonging to Mr. de Landre Macdona—a very fine specimen, but deficient in leather."

Enter the Rough-Coat

Macdona's Romano appeared at the June 1880 Kennel Club show at London's Crystal Palace in the Basset Français class. Apart from Romano and one nondescript tri-color, the class was wholly of imported bassets or those bred from imported parents. All belonged to Lord Onslow and Millais. With the Earl of Onslow's and Millais' bassets taking top places, Romano's debut in a breed class was inauspicious.

Previously, Dr. Seton of Potters Bar, Hertfordshire, owned Romano. Records show that he exhibited a dog listed variously as "Ramoneau," "Ramonneau," "Ramonneur" or "Ramoneur." The latter spelling seems likely; French for "chimney-sweeper." In December 1875 in the Foreign Class at Birmingham he placed 3rd to Millais' Model and at Alexandra Palace, London, he shared top spot with Millais' Model and the Prince of Wales' Molodetz, a Russian Wolfhound. Dr. Seton continued to show Ramoneur with some success and in the turn-of-the-century book *British Dogs*, A. Croxton Smith quoted from Millais' early reference to him.

Millais was aware that, at that stage, the recently imported French Bassets could scarcely be called British dogs, and he explained that they could be subdivided into:

1. Couteulx Hounds
2. Lane Hounds
3. Griffons

"Of the first two varieties we have many examples at present; of the third, only one, to my knowledge, has been exhibited in England, namely Ramoneau, though the type is common enough at Continental shows." Millais described the Griffon type as:

Color:	Tri-color, blue-gray, hare-pied, lemon and white
Coat:	Thick, hard, wire-haired, and like that of the Otterhound
Head:	Such as that of the Otterhound, and well flewed
Eye:	Dark and hawed
Ears:	Long and pendulous, low hung
Bone:	Good
Legs:	Torses
General appearance:	A strong, active hound, powerful, and well knit together
Example:	Ramoneau.

By May 1880, in the Dublin show Any Variety class, the name "Romano" appeared, owned by de Landre Macdona of

West Kirby, Cheshire. Later that year, at Birmingham's 21st Exhibition, he came equal 1st in the Foreign Class, Sporting with Mr. Krehl's basset, Fino de Paris. With no further records of Ramoneau, this tends to confirm that the gray, brindled pepper dog Dr. Seton imported from France was the dog subsequently owned and registered at the Kennel Club by member de Landre Macdona as "Romano, French Basset."

Other French Bassets did exist about this time. Mr. Humphries of London exhibited his imported Romance at Dundee, Scotland, in November 1879, where one of the judges was Rev. J. Cumming Macdona from Cheshire, doubtless a relative of de Landre. Dr. Seton showed St. Bernards bred by the Reverend, a friend of the Prince of Wales and Charles Cruft, the man who subsequently instigated the annual great dog show in London, later dubbed "Crufts."

Although traditionally accepted that the Basset Français was the smooth-coat and Basset Griffon the rough-coat, French Bassets were sometimes listed as either smooth or rough-coated, and both types were often shown in the one class. Pedigrees too were frequently listed as "unknown," making definition of type difficult.

Thanks to Millais' records, we know that Romano was a *griffon* type and he has been traditionally accredited with being the first rough-coated (Vendéen) hound in England. By 1881 records became clearer, the white, tan and grizzle Rallie being registered as a Griffon Vendéen. He belonged to exhibitor Mr. Ramsay of Bray, Berkshire.

From France to England

The early 1890s saw interest in the rough-coat growing. Despite traveling difficulties before the advent of the automobile, it was quite usual for breeders and exhibitors from both England and abroad to send dogs to Crufts for sale or auction.

Basset breeder Mrs. Challoner Ellis, then of Maidenhead, Berkshire, was another of the first to buy a rough-coat. In 1891 she registered the white and lemon Rocket, bred June 9, 1888, by Monsieur St. Hilaire. The Prince and Princess of Wales were also early fanciers showing at late 1880s Crufts. At Crufts 1893 Captain Ronald Cannon exhibited four from the same litter they had bred; Princess, Sandringham, Royalist and Prince, born January 1, 1892 (Babil ex Bijou).

Monsieur Puissant of Merbes le Château, Belgium, was a regular contributor at Crufts. In 1893 he sent rough-coats, bred by Monsieur Bocquet, for exhibition and sale. He asked £80 for Babonneau, born April 1890 (Ramoneau ex Mirabelle), and £40 for Bamboche, born June 1890 (Barbouillon I ex Ravande). For the two which were to become a great influence on the breed, he asked £80 for Tambour, born May 1, 1889, (Caporal ex Musette) and £100 for Pervenche, born February 1891 (Tonnerre ex Pimpante). Both were white and tan.

Ch. Pervenche.

Tambour went to basset breeder J. Roberts of Garforth, Leeds, who immediately used him at stud, siring the Prince of Wales' litter out of Bonnet, which produced Beauty II and Bonnie II. That year saw 1sts at Crufts, Bath, Crystal Palace, Birmingham and Brussels but, by Crufts 1894, he was again for sale, this time for £50. Unsold, in April Tambour won at Crystal Palace and Mr. Roberts registered him with the Kennel Club,

Mabel Tottie, at rear, with two of her daughters, Helen and Mabel.

while M. Puissant registered Pervenche.

Crufts 1895 saw Tambour again owned by M. Puissant and being auctioned with Pervenche and her daughter Merbes Fanfarde, born March 23, 1893, sired by Babonneau; and litter-mates Merbes Fantome, Sans Peur and Talisman, born April 14, 1894, sired by Tambour.

Major Tottie's wife, Mabel, was tempted. Soon her successful show kennels of Bassets and other breeds at the 1,448 acre Coniston Hall Estate, near Skipton, West Yorkshire, became noted for its rough-coats—all thanks to her foundation stock, Tambour and Pervenche. She soon became recognized as the main breeder of rough-coats.

Tambour was used regularly at stud both before and after his move to England, siring many winning show dogs such as Mr. Lowe's Barman of Kippen and M. Puissant's Merbes

Ch. Tambour.

CRUFTS 1897

AT STUD, the ROUGH BASSET-HOUND
CHAMPION TAMBOUR
(37,743)

Winner of fourteen 1sts, four championships, and many specials, including cup; gold medal for best dog in show, Bristol 1895; stud dog medal; Crufts 1896. Acknowledged the best Rough Basset living. A sure stock-getter. Sire of numerous winners, including Merbes Aventurière, Norman o' the Border, Pierrot, and Truelove (2nd novice, Birkenhead). **Fee £5 5s**

Photos and stud cards on application to
JOHN GIBBS, Head Kennelman, Coniston Hall, Bell Busk, Leeds.

All bitches to be addressed to Bell Busk Station, M.R., carriage paid

---

Aventurière, born March 20, 1893, out of Bamboche; and, born October 26, 1895, out of Rametta, Mr. Krehl's Trompette d'Erpent who was "very hard and carried the Otterhound head." Tambour – Pervenche breedings produced Mr. Lowe's Trueman of Kippen and Mr. Robinson's Fifine, born April 1894; Mr. Gerrish's Pierrot, born March 1, 1895, and Mrs. Tottie's Peerless and Perpetua, born March 19, 1900.

By Crufts 1897 Tambour was a champion and Pervenche, absent due to whelping, gained her crown shortly after. This litter born February 6, 1897, proved most successful, producing Puritan (originally known as Peppermint) and Priscilla. Both were tri-color. Puritan was of such quality that, a year later, he

Ch. Puritan.

became a champion. He was described as "a splendid hound with immense bone, perfectly sound, full of quality, with grand coat." Priscilla was also soon a champion.

In common with the practice of crossbreeding, Ch. Tambour was also used on smooth-coats or bitches with unknown pedigrees producing Rev. Shields' white and hare-pied Norman o' the Border, born January 1893 out of Dynamite; Captain Swaffield's tri-color Treasure '96 and Mr. Gerrish's Gay Boy, born April 2, 1896, out of Spinster; and Dr. Isacke's tri-color Ragimunde, born September 1, 1896, out of Bluebell.

Mrs. Tottie's head kennel-man John Gibbs, with whom she had a close association, was sometimes shown as the breeder. On November 28, 1895, his mating between Ch. Tambour and smooth-coat Leyswood Venus produced Miss McDonald's Truelass, Dr. Isacke's Truelove and Mr. White's Snyed Princess, who Mrs. Ellis said excelled in all points as a rough hound but was "unfortunately for breeders, a crossbred, and consequently unreliable from a stud point of view." Conversely, Mrs. Tottie's Periwinkle '96, born on February 28, 1896, (smooth-coat Solomon ex Pervenche) and shown as a smooth basset, gave 'too much evidence of the rough cross.' "

During this era Ch. Tambour was seen as "a pillar of the stud." With his progeny, Ch. Puritan and Ch. Priscilla, he represented the very best of rough-coat blood in England. Aged nine and despite having whelped countless litters, Pervenche

Mrs. Tottie's Ch. Tambour – Bagatelle litter of one smooth and three rough-coats, including Mary Smith, born January 6, 1898.

still managed a 2nd at the 1901 Crufts. By 1903 Puritan and Priscilla belonged to Mr.Taylor who, at Crufts that year and the following, sought £1,000 for each.

Other veteran supporters who exhibited rough-coats "of the Puritan blood" were Mr. Stone—whose home-bred tri-color bitch Sturdy, born July 19, 1900, (Ch. Puritan ex smooth-coated Syren) was a regular winner at 1901 shows—and Mr. Lawrence of Cambridge. He had some success with Mary Smith, bred by Mrs. Tottie, although by Crufts 1901 he had reduced her sale price from £100 to £20.

Soon after, distemper wiped out his kennel. The same tragedy befell others, including Mr. Gerrish. Some thought that dubious breeding methods, while trying to maintain type, made dogs more susceptible. Others attributed the disaster to general weakness in the breed, and evidently many rough-coat breeders had not bred with such dedication as they had with smooth-coats.

In a letter to the *Stock-Keeper* journal, Mabel Tottie later admitted, "I made a mistake in crossing rough and smooth Basset Hounds; but one learns from experience, and what I did has done the breed no harm, as it was not carried on." At that time she felt the breed was robust. "As to the rough hounds, I also wonder they are not more taken up; they are hardy, easier to breed than smooths, very plucky and sensible."

Millais remained convinced that English fanciers who bought foreign imports obtained inferior specimens. As their ancestry is impossible to trace, we will never know how pure the strains were that arrived from Belgium and France. We can only draw our own conclusions from knowing that the rough-coats were from basset breeders.

The Umbrella of the Basset Hound Club

In the intervening years, Millais (by now knighted), with other devotees, founded the Basset Hound Club. Comte le Couteulx de Canteleu was its first president. This united enthusiasts of both smooth and rough-coated bassets. The club prospered and had its first show in 1886 at Westminster Aquarium. The judge? Everett Millais.

Following registration with the Kennel Club, at a meeting held on May 6, 1891, the Kennel Club committee decided to define the Basset Hound into two classes, rough and smooth. In 1905 the BHC revised its rules: "The objects of the Club are to promote the breeding of smooth and rough-coated Basset Hounds...any respectable person favorable to the object of the Club shall be eligible for membership, except professional dealers. Ladies shall also be eligible for membership."

Unfortunately, Millais did not live to see these changes. In 1897, shortly before his death, he reminisced:

> Some twenty years ago, when I was at school in Paris, I used to frequently adjourn to a dog dealer's, whose shop still exists close to the Arc de Triomphe. I was there not long since, and on asking Mons. Ravry if he could find me a couple of Bassets Griffons, such as he used to keep years ago, he informed me that he could not, unless I put my hand very deeply into my pocket.

Millais mentioned noticing a similar rough-coat about 1874–75, adding, "Since then I have never seen a hound like Romano in type and size except Mrs. Ellis' Rocket, which though not of exactly quite the same character, comes nearer to that mentioned than the smaller varieties, which might pass better as rough-coated Dachshunds than do duty at our shows as Bassets Griffons."

Royal Patronage

The Prince and Princess of Wales, later King Edward VII and Queen Alexandra, kept a veritable menagerie at their Sandringham, Norfolk, estate. Among innumerable hounds, the Prince of Wales was especially attracted to the rough-coats. He hunted with them and exhibited at leading shows.

Alexandra devoted her affections to many breeds during

Queen Alexandra with her rough and smooth bassets at Sandringham.

Edward's frequent absences. Bassets were one of her favorites and their prominent kennels boasted beautiful specimens of both rough and smooth. Mrs. Ellis presented the king and queen with most of their original stock. Shortly beforehand, they had acquired the white and gray rough-coat Babil (registered in 1891) from the Comtesse de Paris. They also sent their rough-coats to exhibition regularly and the breed would undoubtedly have disappeared from the English show scene earlier if it had not been for this royal patronage.

Like others, the royal family used favorite names more than once in their breeding programs. On January 1, 1896, the successful Sandringham Babil '96 was born, the result of cross-breeding between the smooth-coated basset Zero (Ch. Forester ex Ch. Zena) and Beauty II (Ch. Tambour ex Bonnet). Their first Babil, exhibited at Crufts 1891 with progeny Bran, Bustler and Bendigo III, born July 8, 1888, was listed as breeder and pedigree unknown.

Having had some success with Babil '96's litter brother, Snyed Prince, Mr. White obtained other rough-coats from the queen's kennels—Prince Zero, born February 15, 1904, from a mating between his smooth-coat Loo Loo Loo (soon after a champion) and Sandringham Flo; and Young Prince, born

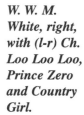

*W. W. M.
White, right,
with (l-r) Ch.
Loo Loo Loo,
Prince Zero
and Country
Girl.*

February 24, 1906, from a repeat breeding. From this litter, the queen kept the tri-color Sandringham Vanity.

Among other consistent prize-winners was Sandringham Bobs, born June 18, 1899, (Sandringham Babil ex Sandringham Vivian), a "deep, long-bodied hound, with dense coat and excellent in head properties." A later mating between Ch. Sandringham Bobs and Ch. Sandringham Vanity produced Ch. Sandringham Valens, born on March 5, 1909. By 1912 Ch. Sandringham Valour and Sandringham Vero were also regular winners.

Decline of the Rough-Coat

Despite enthusiastic breeders' efforts and the interest of the king and queen, who continued to exhibit mainly roughs "with a steadfastness that should give some encouragement," the breed failed to attract great attention. Mrs. Ellis felt that previous large entries spoke wonders for the persistent energy of the breeders who had produced so many excellent types "with such infinitesimal matter to work on." However, like Millais, she considered the Griffon Vendéen to be less hardy than the smooth-coat. This, coupled with deaths from distemper, may be why it failed to achieve popularity and attract more breeders. Undoubtedly, introduction of quarantine regulations in 1901 also contributed towards the decline.

In the late 19th century, heated words appeared in the *Stock-*

Keeper over the ethics of crossbreeding. In those days corre-
spondents sometimes used noms-de-plume. This angered many
who felt unable to judge whether the writer spoke with any
authority. "Old Tyke" was adamant that in olden days "breeders
never thought of crossing the rough and smooth (two distinct
varieties)," prompting the editor to comment that this regret-
table crossing was proof of ignorance. "If the breeders knew the
origin of these varieties they would realize that their course was
no less absurd than if they crossed Setters and Pointers under
the impression that because both are shooting dogs therefore
they must be one breed, and one variety."

In Robert Leighton's *New Book of the Dog*, published 1907,
Mrs. Tottie changed her opinion on the breed's constitution,
saying it had failed for some reason to receive great attention.

> In type it resembles the shaggy Otterhound, and as at
> present favored it is larger and higher on the leg than the
> smooth variety. I have myself imported several from
> France, but have found them less hardy than their vel-
> vety relatives, and not so staunch or painstaking in their
> work, and for packs they do not appear to be generally
> liked.

> Their coloring is less distinct, and they seem generally
> to be lemon and white, gray and sandy red. Their note is
> not so rich as that of the smooth variety. In France the
> rough and the smooth bassets are not regarded as of the
> same race, but here some breeders have crossed the two
> varieties, with indifferent consequences.

> Some beautiful specimens of the rough basset have
> from time to time been sent to exhibition from the
> Sandringham Kennels. King Edward always gave affec-
> tionate attention to this breed, and took several first
> prizes at the leading shows, latterly with Sandringham
> Bobs, bred in the home kennels.

From 1903 Kennel Club registrations were minimal, with
none for several years running. Show entries gradually

declined, so much so that at Crufts 1904 smooth and rough-coat classes were combined. By 1907 only two entered at the Crystal Palace Kennel Club Show. Judge Christopher Heseltine of the Walhampton (later Westerby) Bassets wrote that he was disappointed with the rough bassets, finding them untypical.

> Their coats were thin and not rough, which is not surprising considering they were by the Smooth hound who won the Open Smooth Championship. Where are the rough Bassets of years ago? Are there none left? Surely someone must have kept some of the old breed and type. Surely there must be in existence some descendants of those typical hounds Tambour and Pervenche. Let me beseech breeders of Rough Hounds not to forget the type of the two hounds I have named, they were models which breeders should look to for type.

> The two I judged are altogether removed from that type, and are not Rough Bassets, their coats being broken and not rough. They may be good for sport, but so were the typical ones which Mrs. Tottie used to breed. I do hope and trust that the Rough Bassets of olden days will not be allowed to die out, but that someone will make an earnest endeavor to breed to the type of Tambour and Pervenche, so that once again we may have the pleasure of seeing the true type of Rough Hound.

His words were to no avail. From 1906, Mrs. Tottie's kennels suffered from the flu. She had moved to Ashbourne, Derbyshire, and, by April 1908, given up her duties as secretary of the BHC and gone abroad, creating a further void in the breed.

Only 14 rough-coats were registered with the Kennel Club in 1909, two in 1910, none in 1911 and one in 1912. In 1910 the King died and, with no Sandringham contingent, A. Croxton Smith had only two to judge at the Kennel Club show, the

Marquis of Bowerham and Chantress, both owned by Mrs. Olive. In 1911, judge Harding Cox bemoaned, "Not a single rough-coated hound entered! Alas and woe is me!" The following year the Queen's Valour, Vero and Vally, the only rough-coat representatives, were withdrawn from Crufts due to the death of the Duke of Fife. At the October Kennel Club show, judge A. Croxton Smith only had her "charming couple and a half of the old-fashioned type" to consider. In 1913 there were again only two registrations with Sandringham Valour, Vero and Vally taking 1st, 2nd and 3rd at Crufts. Later that year just the Queen Alexandra supported the Kennel Club show with her entry of three rough-coats, Sandringham Bobs and Vanity going 1st and 2nd. Five rough-coats appeared at the following year's Crufts, Valens, Vally and Vero taking 1st, 2nd and 3rd.

The onset of World War I in 1914 effectively put an end to showing and further registrations and, Valens, Vero and Valour, at age seven, were the last rough-coats to appear at Crufts in 1916. In all, less than 200 were registered in the BHC's Stud Book, which Everett Millais started in 1874. It was updated by a succession of subsequent BHC secretaries, including Mabel Tottie.

Despite the disappearance of the rough-coat from exhibition and Mrs. Ellis' views that they were a poor pack animal, they did maintain some presence in Great Britain over the following decades through the introduction of Griffon Vendéen blood to the hunting scene, notably amongst the Westerby, West Lodge and Castle Milk packs. However, it was to be over half a century before Bassets Griffons were to reappear in the showring.

The Renaissance

The year 1969 was memorable for it marked the revival of the Petit Basset Griffon Vendéen, or Basset Griffon Vendéen as it was then simply known, for British show people. Following earlier tradition, many of these were distinguished basset breeders and judges of long-standing.

In 1967 two such people, Mrs. Joan Wells-Meacham (Fredwell) from Ringshall, near Berkhamsted, Hertfordshire, and Mrs. Mildred Seiffert (Maycombe) of Oxted, Surrey, visited the Paris show. Joan had judged bassets in France and was again captivated by the happy-go-lucky PBGVs, who displayed the most wonderful, outgoing disposition. She and Mildred were enchanted, so much so that the following year they joined BHC members going to France, their hearts set on importing. After much persuasion, Hubert Desamy set the wheels in motion for these determined ladies.

In 1969 a six-month-old dog, Rigolo de la Vrignaie (Pillou ex Noisette de la Vrignaie), bred by Eugene Roquand and born October 6, 1968, arrived in quarantine. Orée, an older bitch from Henri Mounac, stayed in France to be mated to M. Desamy's best dog, Petit Prince de la Levraudière, then sent to whelp in U.K. quarantine. Unfortunately, a rabies scare in England foiled these plans and a cable to M. Desamy arrived too late to prevent the mating. On May 28, 1970, Orée, registered as born on September 26, 1965, though possibly older, duly whelped...in France! She arrived in England with two female puppies, T'Annetta and T'Arlette. After quarantine, they

Below: T'Annetta.
Right: T'Arlette. (photo Keith George)

joined Joan Wells-Meacham's Clipperdown Cottage Kennels set deep in Ashridge Forest.

The Jomil Influence

Importing three bitches rather than one became a blessing in disguise as Orée only produced one more litter. On July 4, 1971, five dogs and the Jomil (*Jo*an and *Mil*dred) kennel name was born!

Of this "A" litter, Aiglon went to the Bergishagens in Michigan, Ajax to Edith Hurling in Australia, Asputin to Betty Mitchell in Ireland, Aristotle to Joan Walker and, later, Angelo to John Evans.

T'Arlette, rather longer on the leg than T'Annetta, produced two litters when mated to Rigolo. Of the "B," two females and four males, born October 26, 1971, Bernadette went to Mrs. Mitchell, Bacchante to Mildred, Bolero to Mr. Warrington, Bartolo and Bolivar to Switzerland, and the other dog, Bourbon, to Mrs. S. E. (Nickie) Hunt's Huntersbrook kennels near Needham Market in Suffolk. From the "D," born November 30, 1972, Danielle was Nickie's foundation bitch, while Delice went to Carla Gerber-Niedenzu in the Netherlands. When mated to Angelo, on July 24, 1974, Bacchante produced one puppy, Elisette. She went to Martina Hoffman in Sweden who subsequently had more Jomils.

Despite return visits to France, Joan and Mildred were unable to buy another hound as nobody would sell. Puppies entered packs at five months and, at that stage, Joan lacked confidence to pick a good, younger one. In Britain there was great interest in the breed, but only for bitches and the early litters were mainly dogs, some of whom they gave away! Eventually T'Annetta, true *petit* in type, produced four litters; three to Rigolo ("C," "F" and "G") and her last, the "L," to Armand of Jomil, who was by Joan Walker's imported Windsor von Schloss Isabella and Jomil Farandole.

From the April 17, 1972 "C" litter, Claudette joined first

Australian import Ajax in 1973. He had arrived earlier that year. The new settlers created quite a stir, as did their first litter of eight males. Despite such setbacks, several of Edith Hurling's Majesty Kennels PBGVs excelled; Nicholas in the showring and Benjie as the first to hold an obedience title.

Jomil Fauvette. (photo Foyle)

In England, not until the July 22, 1974 "F" litter did Joan Wells-Meacham keep one of the scarce bitches herself (Jomil Fauvette). Fanchette went to Rita Rossi in Italy, Flambard and Farandole were Ruth Brucker's first PBGVs at Twinrivers; and Fanfare was Nick Valentine's eagerly sought pack foundation bitch. When mated back to her father, on November 15, 1976, Fauvette produced the "H" litter. This included Jomil Hotspur, Per Knudsen's foundation dog in Denmark.

The notable January 26, 1975, "G" litter produced the white and orange Gaulois, who had a successful show career but was little used at stud, as all the bitches in England were so closely related to him. Gavotte and Garland went to Philip Haas in Denmark; Gabrielle and Gallant to Elizabeth Streeter in America. At home, Gino became the first of Jeff and Heather Bunney's Zadal Kennel and Gitane went on breeding terms to Mesdames Harvey and Gurney and, as such, representing the "J" litter. On April 30, 1977, after mating her to Windsor, Jeannemart was born and offered to Evan Roberts of Varon Bassets as his first BGV.

Two years later, Nicholas Frost joined Clipperdown, having first seen the breed in the '70s while working in Holland at an Afghan show kennels. As Joan Wells-Meacham's kennel-man Nick's role in caring for Jomil, Varon and his own Dehra hounds kenneled together, led to their pedigrees becoming inextricably entwined. This was due mainly to the two corner-stones of Nick's breeding; Varon Zorro and, later, the imported Dan. Lux. Ch. Salto de Crislaure of Morebess.

Meanwhile, Jomil hounds became a success both at home and abroad and, in Switzerland, judge Hubert Desamy was surprised to find that he had awarded top honors to a dog bred in England and not France!

Joan found that the early Jomils had good bone, square bodies and good sterns, though some were a little heavy, particularly in head. Here their next import, the white and grizzle Arilica Otello provided that all-important out-cross. Otello's sire was a top French show and field winner, World Ch. 1976, Int. It. Ch. Untel de la Bougrière, his dam Junon de Fin Renard. He arrived in quarantine on January 3, 1979, from Rita Rossi, who had established a line on pure *petit* breeding with a strong emphasis on René Tixier's de Fin Renard hounds.

Over the next few years, Jomil started many new enthusiasts onto the path of success, including Giselle Taylor's White

Right: Arilica Otello of Jomil. (photo Pearce) Below: Bernie Skerritt with Jomil Sirène of Monkhams (Jomil Mistral ex Jomil Gitane) and Carolyne Bett with Dehra Armand Brumeux (Jomil Larbi of Varon ex Mistinguet at Dehra), 1984. (photo Gascoigne)

Webbs line with Myrhha (Arilica Othello ex Fauvette), Howard and Joy Blake with Rolande, Bernie and Linda Skerritt with Sirène; and Jim and Margaret Makin with Zinnia.

Early Shows and Formation of the Club

When they were introduced to the show scene, BGVs shared the same fate as all new "rare" breeds. Before 1977 breed classes were scarce, so dedicated exhibitors of roughies or griffs, as then called, entered the Variety or Not Separately Classified (NSC) classes. In 1969 and the early '70s, the Wells-Meacham/Seiffert partnership, and Nickie Hunt and Joan Walker with their hounds, were the prime ambassadors.

Guildford was the first Canine Society to provide classes for the breed when, in 1974, Mrs. Rossi awarded Rigolo de la Vrignaie BOB. Subsequently, several hounds made their mark on the show scene, notably Fauvette who won Reserve BPIS at Guildford in 1975, then BPIS at Dunstable. In 1976, Gaulois made breed history by winning BIS under Terry Thorn at Guildford, having gone Best "Rare Breed." The Houndshow was the first championship show to recognize BGVs when, in 1975, basset breeder Betty White judged the entry of nine and Rigolo won yet another BOB.

On February 19, 1978, at Hemel Hempstead, Hertfordshire, John Evans chaired the inaugural meeting of the BGV Club. Joan Wells-Meacham was elected to the chair, Mildred Seiffert as vice-chair, Peter Baker as secretary, and Evan Roberts as treasurer. The committee included Monica Baker, Ruth Brucker, Sally Edwards, Zoe Pearce, Joan Walker and Clipperdown kennel-man Mark Sandwell.

The Kennel Club agreed to the carefully chosen club name as, although only Petits were then in the U.K., this provided for Grands to later become established under the auspices of the same club.

That year membership grew to 38 and, in May 1979, the BGV Club held the first of four annual shows in conjunction with Hertfordshire Agricultural Show. By 1980 David Dunbar and Richard Gilbert were enthusiastic committee members and Richard succeeded Peter Baker as club secretary from 1981 until 1985.

On April 23, 1983, Terry Thorn judged the club's first independent Open Show at Little Gaddesden, near Clipperdown. From 61 dogs (many of whom were entered in more than one class, making a remarkable total entry of 116), he awarded Best Puppy and BIS to the outstanding Jomil Rigolo, born July 18, 1972, (Varon Zorro ex Jomil Leda).

Sharing Experiences

In the BGV Club's first newsletter in 1978, George Johnston (Sykemoor Bassets) shared his experiences of French shows and hound kennels. The best shows were the Spéciale Vénerie exhibitions and the Club du Griffon Vendéen Spéciales. He recalled the Spéciale at Gueret when he was fortunate to be a *juge assesseur* with Hubert Desamy. All the *anglaises* there identified those they would have loved to purchase but, as Joan Wells-Meacham discovered before them, buying a prospective good hunter from a Frenchman was like extracting teeth from a hen!

With *la chasse* almost as important as *la table* in rural France, George found that, during the hunting season, it was impossible to travel far without seeing hounds working or being assembled for hunts. Invariably many were Vendéens. The huntsmen would sell without hesitation the "pursued," rabbit, hare, deer, wild boar, pheasant, but definitely not the "pursuer!" By visiting some kennels, he realized that not many French breeders kept the type of hound pictured mentally by the English when they saw the word "basset" in the breed name.

Establishing Type

George's words rang true. Work continued on the preparation of a PBGV breed standard for submission to the Kennel Club but, meantime, its absence complicated matters. Kennels began to produce their own preferred type, or form, of PBGV. However, with only a loose translation of the French Petit and Grand standards to go on and the breed just called Basset Griffon Vendéen, there was no real need or incentive to breed to a particular size. Even first bitch import Orée's lines stemmed from de Coeur Joie and de la Brèche des Charmes French kennels, renowned for their Grands Bassets. Understandably, until stabilized by generations of breeding, size and features of progeny from imported stock could not be guaranteed. Consequently, enormous variation in size and type appeared in the showring.

Being unfamiliar with the breed, British judges often favored the larger, longer and heavier hounds. Though not necessarily preferring the Grand type, they associated the word "basset" in the title with the traditional Basset Hound. Few appreciated that *"basset"* signified height in relation to the other GV breeds.

In Europe there was talk of a "British BGV," neither Petit nor Grand but somewhere in between. If asked to officiate in England, foreign judges found it particularly difficult as, although lovely, few were of true type. Cessation in France of inter-breeding between Grand and Petit eased matters slightly.

As type stabilized, the draft British standard mirrored the French one, augmented slightly to highlight the PBGV's virtues. Only six hounds were registered in 1980 but, by 1981, club membership rose to 71, with 59 hounds registered and a

Thirteen years after the first CCs, George Johnston judging PBGVs at Darlington Championship Show, September 1998.

further 44 in 1982. In tandem with working towards a breed standard, in 1981 the club first applied to the Kennel Club for championship status. This, too, was approved in 1983, with the first Challenge Certificates to be awarded at Crufts, February 10 1985.

Foundation Breeders and Influential Hounds

Leading up to and following establishment of the name, breeders did all they could to promote the PBGV. None bred excessively. Steady and careful reproduction provided a sound basis for new kennels and in establishing type.

Each breeder has his or her special place in development of PBGVs in Britain. Charting the period 1969 to 1985 (when CCs were first offered) shows how the main, early advocates were instrumental in helping others. Most are still fully committed.

Huntersbrook

A Jomil Bourbon – Danielle breeding produced Huntersbrook March Capers, born March 21, 1974, followed by Topaz and Tomahawk, born March 15, 1975 (Windsor ex Danielle); all shown regularly by Nickie Hunt. From the same litter, Ivanhoe went to Mrs. Lacey. Born December 21,

Jomil Bourbon of Huntersbrook, Crufts 1974. (photo Garwood, Dog World)

1976, Huntersbook March Rain (Tomahawk ex March Capers) went to Peter and Monica Baker (Dawbak).

Nickie's hounds had many AV Sporting NSC wins but Jomil Bourbon holds a special place. In 1974 he became the first Basset Griffon in 58 years to be shown at Crufts, gaining a 2nd in NSC. She recalled that, in the beginning, with the breed such

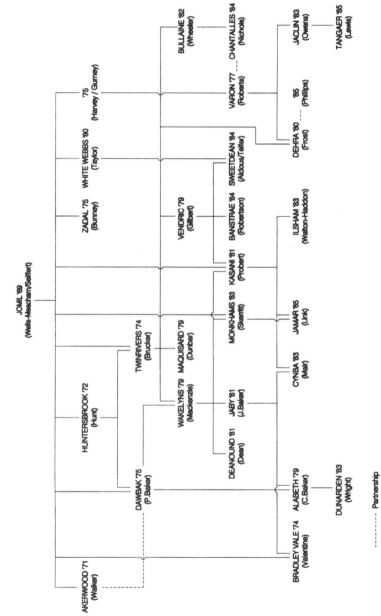

FOUNDATION OWNERS / BREEDERS - 1969 to 1985

an attraction at shows, all-rounders like Joe Braddon often commentated by loudspeaker on the winners. Times may have changed but, since then, Nickie has remained a staunch supporter, exhibitor and respected judge of the breed.

Akerwood

Joan Walker imported Windsor von Schloss Isabella, born December 27, 1972, (Fr. Int. Ch. Titus de la Réote ex Nina de la Réote), from Mr. Richartz of Luxembourg, who also owned GBGV and Basset Fauve de Bretagne.

Windsor von Schloss Isabella. (photo Pearce)

Although never used widely at stud, Windsor proved a great strength behind breeding programs in Britain. Several noted stud and show dogs carried a strong line back to him. Jomil Larbi, Best Dog at the first BGV Club show in 1979; Ch. Jomil Rigolo, one of a remarkably successful litter; and Twinrivers Herspereus at Dehra, born September 9, 1983 (Varon Zorro ex Twinrivers Alouette).

From 1973–74, Joan showed Windsor successfully, with her first import, half-sister Vloret, born September 2, 1972, (Fr. Int. Ch. Titus de la Réote ex Fr. Ch. Salée de la Bougrière). Joan's first litter from her imports, born March 29, 1975, included Akerwood Athol (who went to Philip Haas in Denmark), Alpha (to Marianne Ranåker-Månsson in Sweden), Astra, André and Amos. With March Rain and Jomil Kiekie (Armand of Jomil ex Jomil Fauvette), Amos formed the foundation of Peter and Monica Baker's Dawbak Kennel.

Dawbak

With Joan Walker, Peter Baker also acquired Pacha des

Peter Baker and Pacha des Barbus d'Entre Lac

Barbus d'Entre Lac, born May 17, 1979, (World Dutch Lux. Ch. Loy du Val d'Orbieu ex Mireille de Kweb), from Thelma Vlas in the Netherlands. His sire was Dutch top dog All-Breeds 1978. By 1980, he himself became top PBGV in England and an influential stud, siring many successful hounds including the Mackenzie's Dawbak Panique, born July 6, 1980, out of Jomil Kiekie.

At Crufts 1981 Pacha and Gaulois took part in a cavalcade. Peter Baker and Evan Roberts donned traditional Vendéen costume and emerged furtively, embarrassed at what people would think of their strange attire. Overcoming the momentary crisis when their banner collapsed, the quartet paraded round the main ring, creating much interest in the rare breed. A memorable day for Pacha, who lived to the astonishing age of 17-1/2.

Alabeth

In 1978 March Rain's small face gazing over a fence met Chris Baker when visiting brother Peter. "Her name was Fluff. I have had dogs from mongrels who sat on my bicycle crossbar to doing obedience classes with various breeds. But from the moment I saw Fluff, I was smitten and she was soon living with us. I joined Peter in the BGV Club and have good memories of those times."

On August 8, 1981, Fluff had a litter by Pacha, and Chris' Alabeth Audace ("Boot") was born. This stylish white and orange campaigner did much to familiarize the breed. Six years later, at the August 1987 Houndshow, he became a champion. Boot was the first of many strong Alabeth hounds, notably Alabeth Astre ("Wellington") and Altesse, born September 23, 1983, (Alabeth Audace ex Dawbak Petitesse of Alabeth), who went to Miss Jean Wright in Scotland.

Ch. Alabeth Audace.

Chris' Alabeth H'Ortensia and H'Aras, born September 14, 1990, (Alabeth Astre ex Vendric Venus of Alabeth) were successful campaigners. Litter sister H'Oulette, together with Kasani Rapsodie of Barnspring (Rabbit Trapper of Kasani ex Ch. Galaxie of Kasani) introduced Roy and Iris Dykes to the breed and in 1995 Roy joined the committee. Chris too had served on the committee from 1983–89 and, to this day, remains committed to the breed.

Dunarden

Sheep and deer outnumber humans in Jean Wright's part of the world, Pitlochry, Scotland. In the early '70s people marveled at her Afghans. Then Jean came under the spell of the little "ruffian" hounds. In 1983 Alabeth Altesse, the first PBGV to cross the Border, created much curiosity, becoming the popular "wee French hound."

Her first litter, born January 22, 1986, by Gambit of Kasani, produced Chris Baker's second champion, Dunarden Fleur of Alabeth; also John and Elma Clark's Ch. Dunarden Fifine of Kirghiz, BIS winner at the BGV Open show in 1988 and 1989. The second, born January 9, 1989, by Cynba the Dazzler, produced John and Adele Walton-Haddon's Criquette of Ilsham and Clairon of Kasani. This dog made his name in England with

All-rounder Joe Braddon with one of the winners at an inter-club show, Verona, Italy, 1978.

Sylvia Probert before succeeding in America with Valerie Link.

On November 6, 1991, Kirghiz Petite Fleur was born (Alabeth H'Aras ex Fifine). As foundation bitch for basset breeder Anne Holdsworth's Iveson Kennels in West Yorkshire, Fleur soon became a champion. Ann first saw the breed in France in 1969 and was so enchanted, she became an early member of the BGV Club. Although she delayed entering the breed, her son worked for a while at Rita Rossi's kennels in Italy. Ann has many memories of personalities, who always livened up proceedings both in and out of the showring, especially at multilingual European inter-club shows.

Twinrivers

With Flambard and Farandole, Ruth Brucker showed her other foundation bitch, Huntersbook Mystery, litter sister to Topaz and Tomahawk, followed by Twinrivers Alouette (Windsor ex Farandole) from her first litter, born December 13, 1976. This breeding also represented the Jomil "I" litter. Ixia of Jomil went to Sweden then, in March 1977, Jomil Isabella became the first PBGV in Finland, going to pioneer of the breed, Eeva Virpio. Isabella gained many titles, soon becoming a Finnish and Swedish champion.

From a Flambard – Mystery breeding came Twinrivers Babette, born January 12, 1978, BOB winner at the first BGV Club Show in 1979 and, from a repeat mating, Richard and Carol Gilbert's Twinrivers Clothilde at Vendric, born January 18, 1979.

Ruth, who had the distinction of breeding Danielle, the first PBGV champion, recalled the early years of showing with great affection. With few shows giving classes, not even the judges had any idea what the dogs were. It was not unknown to over-hear the judge whispering, *"What is it?"* to the steward.

Many of the older Basset fraternity viewed the BGVs with suspicion and even disapproval. Some diehard hunting enthusi-asts felt owners would follow their forebears and crossbreed with Basset Hounds. At one Albany Basset meet an elderly lady accused Ruth of trying to ruin Bassets by breeding those "hairy things." Ruth said the last thing they wanted to do was to spoil BGVs by putting in Basset blood! Thankfully, this attitude was not wide-spread and devotees received much help from pack master John Evans.

Rebecca Gilbert-Jackson, 1984 Junior Handler of the Year with Vendric Vagabond. (photo Hartley)

Vendric

Twinrivers Clothilde at Vendric became dam/ grand-dam to the first three breed champions in Canada and, during that time, sev-eral Vendric hounds helped to establish the breed both in the U.K. and North America. Tilly's litter sired by Pacha des Barbus d'Entre Lac, born July 28, 1981, included the Gilbert's Vagabond and Vanity and Vanessa, who became one of Sylvia Probert's foundation bitches. Valeria went to Anne Snelling in Canada.

From a later litter (Jomil Rigolo ex Twinrivers Clothilde at Vendric), born July 30, 1983, came Venom, owned by the Gilberts' daughter Rebecca. Rebecca did much to promote the breed when, in January 1984 with Vagabond, she won the prestigious Junior Handler of the Year award and a trip to New York and Westminster Kennel Club Dog Show.

Sweetdean

Born June 7, 1984, Vendric Ariadne (Arilica Otello of Jomil ex Vendric Vanity) became a champion for Pam Aldous and Graham Telfer. White Webbs Wrodeo Rider, bred by Giselle Taylor and later owned by Pam and Graham, was a consistent BOB winner. In 1987 he sired Ch. Wakelyns Chasseuse. A later champion, bred by Pam Aldous, was Soloist, born March 10, 1990 (Ch. Jomil Zadok ex Sweetdean Passion), who carried several strong lines including White Webbs. In 1998 Dehra Yasmine, one of the successful mating between Ch. Chantalles Asticot at Dehra and Dehra Oisive, became the latest Sweetdean champion.

Maquisard

Twinrivers Danielle, born June 8, 1979, (Jomil Flambard ex Twinrivers Alouette) was basset breeders Barbara and David Dunbar's foundation bitch at their Maquisard Kennels near Winchester, Hampshire. Mated to Pacha, on March 18, 1981, she produced their Chantal Gamine, who inherited Danielle's sound construction, straight front and dark eyes.

In 1980 Barbara joined David on the BGV Club committee, serving on it for nearly 12 years, latterly as newsletter editor. On March 2, 1982, Gamine's litter by Zorro included their Maquisard Clouseau, top-winning PBGV 1984. A later mating between Clouseau and Gamine gave Ch. Maquisard Poil Rouge, born September 17, 1985.

On July 11, 1983, from Danielle's litter by Belgian import Gourou, Bonnechance became basset breeder Barbara Golding's foundation bitch at Beacontree and mother of Mattisse, the third PBGVCA champion. Later a mating between Sylvia Probert's Gambit and Maquisard Champenoise gave the Dunbars Ch. Mesmerienne, born November 27, 1987. She was dam of Linda Millar's Ch. Maquisard Le Barbu, born December 15, 1990, sired by Ch. Rillaton Solace at Trebloclin. And a Zadok – Champenoise puppy introduced David and Judy Currah (Kykesow) to the breed with Martine, born March 1, 1989. Both became strong supporters, with David joining the committee in 1993, becoming vice-chairman three years later.

For the Dunbars, without doubt it was Danielle who gave them their finest moment when, at Crufts 1985, out of an entry of 51 PBGVs, she won the Bitch CC and BOB.

Wakelyns

Anne and Sandy Mackenzie saw their first BGV at a local agricultural show in May 1979. Twinrivers Duchesse, Danielle's litter sister, joined them soon after. By the 1986 Houndshow Duchesse became the second bitch champion.

Known as "Musette," or "Nosewet" as their granddaughter christened her, Duchesse was the center of attention. One day, soon after she arrived, peace was

Sandy Mackenzie with Belgian-bred Gourou of Wakelyns, 1983.

shattered. A hare raced away through the spring barley, hotly pursued by Nosewet giving tongue, followed equally closely by Anne, also in full cry. Nosewet had discovered what generations of her forebears had been bred to do; and Sandy realized Anne was smitten. By 1982 he joined Anne on the committee and, when Joan Wells-Meacham became president in 1985, he took over as chairman.

In 1982 Ruth Brucker had traveled to Belgium with the Mackenzies to collect a stud dog. Though never used widely outside his home kennel, Gourou, bred by R. Noel and born February 6, 1982, (Echo ex Calina del Doppo Réal) left his mark through his daughters when mated back to the original Flambard/Farandole line.

In those important early days the Mackenzies also introduced many to the breed. From a Pacha des Barbus d'Entre Lac – Twinrivers Duchesse litter, born January 27, 1981, Jan Baker's Wakelyns Adele won Best Bitch at the club's first independent show in 1983; Anis went to Marjorie (Bunty) Evans (Huntswold); Anique to Yvonne Dean (Deanound) in Sussex; and Annette became one of Sylvia Probert's foundation bitches at Radlett, Hertfordshire.

In terms of breed history for Americans, perhaps the most important of this litter was Angelique, who went to Mrs. Noreen Beasley in Canada. On June 14, 1983, Angelique whelped Alexander, whose charms captivated America and helped spark interest in the breed. From a repeat of the 1983 Gourou – Duchesse mating, which gave Bernie and Linda Skerritt Wakelyns Willow, another success was Noblesse, born August 1, 1984, the PBGVCA's first breed champion.

Consistent winners of the strong Wakelyns type have since flowed from this kennel, now in Herefordshire, with Bunty Evans' Ch. Wakelyns Traquer and the Mackenzie's Ch. Trompette born November 13, 1988, (Twinrivers Ivor of Wakelyns ex Huntswold Trefle of Wakelyns), Ch. Wakelyns Chasseuse, born July 27, 1987, (White Webbs Wrodeo Rider ex

Twinrivers Duchesse of Wakelyns) and Ch. Wakelyns Countess, born February 6, 1993 (Ch. Trompette ex Ch. Chasseuse).

On January 7, 1995, Countess whelped a successful litter by Marion Hunt's Dehra Ypres of Bondlea (Ch. Jomil Zadok ex Ch. Dehra Lalique), who himself became a champion. Escort went to founder member Sally Edwards and, following in the Mackenzie's own Ch. Echo's footsteps, by 1997 Empress was also a champion. She was foundation bitch at Betty Judge's Plushcourt Kennels. After a visit to France, Betty started introducing into the U.K. de Fin Renard lines from René Tixier, including the first black and tan, Mystic de Fin Renard. He made his debut in the showring at the Houndshow 1998, judged by John Miller.

Deanound

From a mating with Varon Zorro, on August 29, 1983, Anique's litter included Deanound Mystique. She became a multiple Group, multiple BIS and Crufts BOB 1986 winner for Yvonne Dean (BGV club secretary from 1988) and Claire Gutherless. At the 1994 Welsh Kennel Club Championship Show at the grand age of nearly 11, Mystique became a champion. From a mating with Eng. Dan. Lux. Ch. Salto de Crislaure of Morebess, Deanound Pourquoi was born on July 8, 1987, who also gained her crown in 1994. Breedings between Carolyne Bett's Dehra Armand Brumeux and Anique produced the "N" and "O" litters, born October 25, 1984, and May 20, 1985, including Nocturne for Yvonne and Odette for Joyce Miley-Woodfin in California, who already had Monkhams Django.

Over the years Deanound has introduced newcomers to the breed, many of whom have become keen advocates. Nomade went to the Deleurs in Sussex and, on June 10, 1994, a mating between Kathryn Moulding's first PBGV Deanound Quelsey (Zadok ex Mystique) and Ch. Morebess Haveloc at Dehra produced the striking Ch. Nykarth Groundsel, the first Griffkin BGV for Steve and Bernadette Redgate in Derbyshire. Success has continued in the showring for Yvonne and Claire with Ch. Dehra Amourette at Deanound (Ch. Anoroc Eire at Dehra ex Varon Ulema) born July 8, 1992, and, from a Halistons Dameret – Amourette mating, a young dog, Uriage, born December 12, 1997.

Kasani

Sylvia Probert's three foundation bitches (Wakelyns Annette, Vendric Vanessa and Jomil Revelry) soon attracted others, notably Mrs. Cynthia Mair and John and Adele Walton-Haddon, who respectively had litter-mates Kasani Clochard and Charité, born March 21, 1983, (Jomil Larbi of Varon ex Vendric Vanessa of Kasani). In 1984 Vanessa produced a litter by Varon Zorro, having gone BIS at Luton that March.

The following year Sylvia became acting club secretary when Richard Gilbert's professional commitments prevented him from continuing. She became secretary in 1986. Keen to improve her own stock and increase the country's small gene pool, Sylvia imported Salto's half-sister, Ristourne de Crislaure (Noiro de l'Égalité ex Nanouche de Crislaure), in whelp to Dan. Ch. Ursins des Rives de la Garonne. From the resulting litter, born in quarantine on November 20, 1984, Gaffeur went to Audrey Benbow's Sirhan Kennels in Canada and Gamin to

Sylvia Probert with her PBGVs.

Colin and Dianne Poole (Peterstown). Sylvia kept two; Galaxie, who was a champion by December 1988, and Gambit, who earned two CCs and became an influential stud in his short life, siring champions Kasani Karelia and Korister, born October

10, 1987 (ex Twinrivers Hortense of Kasani). In 1988 litter brother Kraftsman joined Valerie Link in the States.

In 1987 Sylvia's other import, Chouan Katzenjammer Kid of Kasani, born May 2, 1986, (Dan. Ch. Chouan Hen's Dream ex Dan. Ch. Morebess Nadia de Cahors), arrived from breeders Gunnar Nymann and Holger Busk. Shown sparingly, in July 1989 she passed to Nickie Hunt and subsequently had two litters.

While living in Gloucestershire, Sylvia supported the hunt and her Rabbit Trapper of Kasani (Chantalle's Officer ex Future Amnesty) spent time with Nick Valentine's pack. Following Sylvia's ill health, Helen Bamforth in West Yorkshire took over her Kasani stock. Thankfully, after moving to Surrey in 1996, Sylvia could renew her lively interest and, in 1998, was voted back on the committee. That year at the BGV Club Show she saw Helen's Helensfield Osprey (Ch. Jomil Zadok ex Helsensfield Mimosa) win Best PBGV, Reserve BIS and become a champion. Mimosa is by Kasani Voyageur ex Ch. Kasani Roulette of Helensfield.

Cynba

Kasani Clochard helped Cynthia Mair to spread the news about PBGVs in Scotland after moving from Luton, England in 1985. Until then there was just a handful north of the border, with only Joan Robertson's Vendric Aphrodite at Banstrae (Arilica Otello of Jomil ex Vendric Vanity) and Jean Wright's Alabeth Altesse being exhibited.

Cynthia's Folly Acre

Cynthia Mair with (l–r) Cynba The Attraction, Folly Acre Buttercup from Piplaurie and Cynba The Dazzler.
(photo David Freeman)

Buttercup from Piplaurie (Jomil Flambard ex Wakelyns Adele) had been mated to Varon Zorro and produced seven puppies, the first litter in Scotland. She kept a dog and a bitch, Cynba The Attraction and Cynba The Enigma.

Cynthia's many successes included those with Jaby Flax (Ch. Alabeth Audace ex Wakelyns Adele), also Ivelsyde Baroque at Cynba (Ch. Jomil Zadok ex Dehra Eloise of Ivelsyde), bred by Geoff Place. Her dogs' distinctive names became well known in the showring and, although not now active in the breed, her breeding carries through many of today's pedigrees.

Ekoz

Cynba The Classic, born June 26, 1986, (Cynba The Attraction ex Flummery and Bittersweet of Alnehills) carried strong lines back to Jomil Flambard. She became Jim and Margaret Makin's first PBGV in Stirlingshire, Scotland. A year later Jomil Zinnia joined them, born January 13, 1987 (Eng. Dan. Lux. Ch. Salto de Crislaure of Morebess ex Jomil Reverie). She gained 4 CCs.

Their most successful PBGV, whose sire and dam were both progeny of Salto, was the white and sable Ch. Dehra Xenephon

Jim Makin with Jomil Zinnia, winning her third CC, judge Nick Frost, Sylvia Probert with Dunarden Clairon of Kasani, Dog CC, BIS, Third BGV Club Championship Show, October 1990.

at Ekoz, litter brother to Ch. Dehra Xato. Robbi gained a total of 15 CCs, his distinguished career including being short-listed for the Hound Group at Crufts 1994 and going BOB Crufts 1999.

Jaclin

Lynne and Jack Owens' first PBGV was Varon Xanthia, born July 6, 1983, (a repeat of the Arilica

Otello of Jomil – Jeannemart of Varon mating that, in 1980, produced Varon Zorro). She became foundation bitch of a long line of successful Jaclin PBGVs and, in 1988, was their first champion.

Jaclin Apocalypse Now, born September 26, 1985, (Dehra Armand Brumeux ex Ch. Varon Xanthia for Jaclin), was brother of the PBGVCA's fourth champion, Jaclin Indecent Obsession. Although never becoming a champion himself, he gained a remarkable twelve BIS at Open Show level and over 100 BOBs. Lynne's

English breed record-holder Ch. Jaclin Cards on the Table at Junastar. (photo Martin Leigh)

outstanding white and sable Ch. Jaclin Cards on the Table at Junastar, born December 6, 1990, (Eng. Dan. Lux. Ch. Salto de Crislaure of Morebess ex Ch. Varon Xanthia for Jaclin) who, ironically, was sold then taken back in, became breed record-holder with 17 CCs.

Tangaer

Jaclin Noli Me Tangere, litter sister to Apocalypse Now, became Linda Lewis' successful foundation bitch in Wales. Having had Irish Setters since 1963 and being used to their elegance and glossy coats, Linda found PBGVs quite a contrast. Her first litter

Mary Lewis with a young Tangaer Crême Caramel, 1996. (photo Gibbs)

whelped October 31, 1988, (sire Jaclin All You Need is Love, co-owned with her mother, Maureen Jones) resulted in Ch. Tangaer Joie de Vivre. White and orange Yvette produced three litters and two champions for Linda; L'Amour, born May 13, 1994, (sire Ch. Dehra Xato) and Crême Caramel, born April 28, 1995, (sire Ch. Jomil Zadok), who carries strong lines to Salto. To date "Cyril"'s stunning show career has notched up 10 CCs, all with BOB, including BOB at Crufts 1998 where a daughter, Barbara Cole's Clunebrae Surya at Crynllis, won the Bitch CC.

In 1998, like several before her, Linda used the relatively new Balai Directive, thus avoiding quarantine. She imported a young male from Jolanda Huisman in Holland, Garwedd du Greffier du Roi (Dan. Fin. Ch. Magic des Rives de la Garonne ex Dutch Ch. Autre Chose du Greffier du Roi).

Varon

To go full circle and find the strongest links with America, we must return to the early days at Clipperdown and Evan Roberts' and Nick Frost's interest in the breed.

Like other basset fanciers, Evan keenly visited French shows. Following the July 1984 Festival Chiens Courants at Mouchamps, he remarked how surprisingly well owners showed their dogs considering the event was oriented primarily towards *"la chasse"* rather than *"la beauté."* He added it was always a source of confusion for the *anglaises*, when a doubtful specimen's faults were excused on the grounds of great qualities as a hunter.

Evan's first PBGV, Jeannemart of Varon, had a distinguished show career. She resembled her mother Gitane; so much so that, in

Jeannemart of Varon.
(photo Pearce)

the atrociously muddy conditions of the club's first joint show with Hertfordshire, they became mixed up. Unbeknown to judge George Johnston, Jeannemart appeared as Gitane in the Open class. They only realized their mistake when the mud had dried off!

Arilica Otello's influence was passed down through Jeannemart's two litters by him. The first, born July 13, 1980, included Zach, Zero, Zorro; and Zuleika, who in December 1981 went to Canada. Zero was tragically killed on the road but, fortunately, Evan and Nick managed to buy back Zorro after seeing him advertised for sale in a newspaper! The second litter, in 1983, was all bitches, including Ch. Varon Xanthia for Jaclin and Varon Xio, who went to America in whelp, producing only one puppy.

Chantalle

Diana Nichols' first PBGV was Bullaine Mon Prefère de Chantalle, bred by Ida Wheeler. Born May 3, 1984, (Wumberlog Flute of Thatchwood ex Twinrivers Ghislaine of Bullaine), this young bitch went BPIS first time out. By 1985 Diana formed a partnership with, then married, Evan Roberts; and Evan moved his dogs from Clipperdown to near Tenterden, Kent.

Varon Wanton de Chantalle (Salto ex Twinrivers Gabrielle) and Jomil Wuzzle de Chantalle (Salto ex Reverie) joined their kennels and for the next six years Varon and Chantalle PBGVs succeeded in Britain, America and Canada. Then, in 1990, Evan's work took him to Amersham, Buckinghamshire.

Keeping the close connection with Dehra, Diana's small kennels—for a while in Ireland then returning to England—bred successfully from Dehra Brioche of Chantalle (Varon Zorro ex Dehra Urfa). A May 11, 1995 litter (Ch. Dehra Xato ex Brioche) produced Diana's Chantalle's Allumeuse, Nickie Hunt's Armand of Huntersbrook and Julie Shelton's Ch. Asticot at Dehra, owned for a short time in partnership with Nick Frost and then with successful basset breeders, Phil and Jo Freer.

Dehra

Alongside his own line, Nick continued the Varon breedings until 1985 when Evan moved to Kent. Also that year, Joan Wells-Meacham moved from Clipperdown into town nearby; and the last Jomil litter (the "Z") was in 1987. Thereafter, Joan and Nick bred some Fredwell litters and, from the time Vivien Phillips joined Nick at Clipperdown late 1985, he bred several Dehra litters in partnership with her.

The Wrattens bred Mistinguet at Dehra, born May 10, 1981 (Jomil Mistral ex Mondalis Zeta). On going BPIS at Border Counties Hound Club Championship Show later that year, she was the first real success for Dehra and for British PBGVs. However, it was Nick's first PBGV, Varon Zorro, who started the true Dehra line. Owned jointly for a while with Evan Roberts, the beautifully headed, white and orange Zorro sired countless successful Dehra PBGVs, many of which were to become the foundation stock for American breeders. Early on, Nick also acquired Akerwood Babette, born January 1, 1978, (Windsor ex Vloret von Schloss Isabella), helping to save an early line that was nearly lost in Britain.

Some particularly good bitches produced by Zorro bred well with Nick's first import. In 1984 he was fortunate to obtain from Per Knudsen one of Europe's most influential stud dogs, Dan. Lux. Ch. Salto de Crislaure of Morebess. Salto was bred in France by Bernard Beaulieu and born on January 14, 1981 (Noiro de l'Égalité ex Musette de Crislaure). A heavily-coated, particularly sound dog with a striking head, he produced well for Per before arriving in the U.K.

Owned jointly for a spell with John Moore, by 1986 Salto became a British champion. He then made breed history when he topped a 1989 Championship Show Veteran Stakes in a magnificent line-up including three Crufts BIS winners. In 1991, aged ten, he went BOB at Crufts under Mildred Seiffert. Salto's greatest legacy was as a stud dog. He had a profound influence on the breed, passing on his effortless movement. Remarkably, at one time he was top producing sire in Denmark, the U.K. and America!

Jeannemart's third litter, by Salto, resulted in two pups. Although having a level bite, the superb Varon Ulema remained and produced well. Aged nine and fit as a fiddle, Jeannemart produced her final and most successful litter of five by Salto. Born June 23, 1986, it included a trio of champions: Tachet for Diana Nichols, Tapette and Tamburlaine for Nick. Tamburlaine placed consistently in Groups and top awards at Championship Shows and was, for some time, the breed record-holder.

Adele Walton-Haddon with Alabeth Ballivernes of Ilsham Dog CC, and Nick Frost with Eng. Dan. Lux Ch. Salto de Crislaure of Morebess, Reserve Dog CC, Crufts 1988.

The next important contribution was the importation from Per Knudsen of a Salto daughter, Dan. Fin. Ch. Morebess Oleine de Biars, in whelp to Morebess Élégant de la Baule, a line-bred Rives de la Garonne dog. Diana Nichols' Hagar de Chantalle and Nick's Helga and Haveloc at Dehra (who became a champion in 1991) were born in quarantine February 22, 1987. Both the latter produced well and when Helga was bred back to her grandfather Salto, on July 27, 1990, she produced Ch. Dehra Urio, an exceptional sire in his own right.

Ch. Dehra Xato was born on July 22, 1991, from a Ch. Dehra Urio and half-sister Varon Ulema mating. At Bath 1994 he became the first British All-Breed Championship Show PBGV BIS winner and was breed record-holder until he left for America. Xato himself sired many sound PBGVs, including

(l–r) Zorro, Salto, Tamburlaine, Ultra, Zadok, Rigolo. (photo Pearce)

Kevin Anderson's Ch. Finaud (ex Ch. Anoroc Tempo at Dehra), Vivien Phillips' and Joan Wells-Meacham's Ch. Fredwell Mireau (ex Ch. Fredwell Cocarde at Dehra); and Dehra Larroche (ex Dehra Psyche), who became the first New Zealand PBGV champion.

With Vivien Phillips, Nick made two further imports; Ch. Galant des Ajoncs de l'Aulne from Pierre Salaün (Fr. Ch. Baldo de la Côte d'Olhette ex Axelle), born March 10, 1991, and Hardi des Rives de la Garonne (Dach de la Côte d'Olhette ex Urbine des Rives de la Garonne) who provided useful out-crosses. Their progeny produced champion offspring when bred back to Urio or his offspring.

From a Ch. Galant des Ajoncs de l'Aulne – Dehra Urfa mating, John and Barbara Clifton in Lincolnshire started their

Nick Frost with BIS Ch. Dehra Xato. (photo Johnson)

successful Famecliff Kennel of PBGVs with Dehra Guinevere, born November 6, 1993, also Ch. Dehra Egrillard, born May 31, 1993, from a repeat Ch. Dehra Urio – Varon Ulema mating. An early champion for them in 1996 was Jester Jac, born August 20, 1983 (Haveloc ex Jaclin Look Who's Laughing). Famecliff Chemin de Fer with Afterglow followed, born October 11, 1997 (Famecliff Fourquett ex Guinevere). Owned by top handler, Mike Gadsby, and shown by Joan Robertson's son, Gavin, he soon progressed towards his title.

Bred to Zorro daughters, Salto sired some of his best progeny, one of which, Ch. Jomil Zadok, born January 16, 1987, (ex Jomil Reverie) produced several of the breed's most prestigious and successful hounds. They include Ch. Dehra Celestine, born March 21, 1993 (ex Dehra Psyche), Ch. Tangaer Crème Caramel, Marion Hunt's Ch. Dehra Ypres of Bondlea (ex Ch. Dehra Lalique), Keith and Rose Phillips' Ch. Halistons Dameret (ex Femme Fatale at Dehra) and Helen Bamforth's Ch. Helensfield Osprey.

In 1995 Nick moved to the United States, taking with him many prominent dogs. He left breeding stock behind and Dehra Oisive (Ch. Galant des Ajoncs de l'Aulne ex Ch. Dehra Lalique) whelped some successful PBGVs, bred in partnership with Julie Shelton (Pommeraie). From a breeding with Ch. Chantalles Asticot at Dehra, the December 13, 1996, litter produced Julie's Yorrick, Pam Aldous' Ch. Yasmine and Yo-Yo, who in 1999 made a name for himself in America.

Debucher

From the nucleus of stock remaining at Clipperdown, which included Zadok, Ch. Fredwell Cocarde and Fredwell Mireau, Vivien Phillips continued the Fredwell line in partnership with Joan Wells-Meacham. She also applied for her own affix (Debucher) and alongside her main love, the GBGVs, worked hard to rebuild this leading PBGV kennel. In May 1997, under the Balai Directive, she imported from Jolanda Huisman Édition Limité du Greffier du Roi, whose sire carries strong de la Garonne lines and dam goes back to Varon Tapette. At home, Debucher PBGVs started to gain recognition in the showring and, following a breeding between Édition Limité du Greffier

du Roi and Halistons Basilia, on January 18, 1998, L'Ange Bleu was born. She went to Kitty Steidel and Sandy Weinraub to become a successful show Petit in the U.S. With Dehra Larroche, Debucher Mise En Scène introduced New Zealand to the breed.

However, it was at Crufts 1997 that Vivien's early recovery from depletion of stock was truly evident when her young Debucher C'Est Ça, born August 28, 1995, (Ch. Jomil Zadok ex Hamanda des Rives de la Garonne) went BOB. Judge Barbara Dunbar felt that his extrovert, lively

Vivien Phillips with Debucher C'Est Ça, Hound Group winner Crufts 1997. (photo Russell Fine Art)

Making UK history—First set of CCs, Crufts 1985. Barbara Dunbar with Twinrivers Danielle of Maquisard, Judge Bobby James, and Lt. Cdr. Howard Blake with Jomil Rolande à Cochise.

bearing would serve the breed well in the big ring and, to her delight, he did just that, winning the Hound Group and giving the soon-to-be champion a place in PBGV history.

Turning back the clock, in 1985 it was Barbara Dunbar herself who took the limelight when her Danielle won BOB. All-rounder judge Bobby James wrote that he found the breed was settling down well with comparatively even type, but that too many had little or no forechest, spreading feet, or were soft-coated. On the credit side, he found outlines, toplines and quarters reasonable, heads lovely, particularly in the bitches and, most important of all, delightful temperament. By September that year both his CC winners were champions.

And it is perhaps fitting to reflect on the club's first Championship Show, which took place on October 29, 1988, in its tenth anniversary year. A truly international occasion with visitors Per Knudsen from Denmark, Finn Margareta Grandqvist, Jolanda Huisman from the Netherlands and Heidi Winkelmann from Germany. It was the proudest day for basset enthusiast May Bews when judge Renaud Buche, president of the French Club du Griffon Vendéen, awarded BIS to her young dog Kasani Joufflu of Bewmay, born October 13, 1986, (Gambit of Kasani ex Twinrivers Hortense of Kasani), who became a champion at Crufts the following year.

"Chers Amis Griffoniers!"
Judge Renaud Buche
awarding BIS to May Bews'
Kasani Joufflu of Bewmay,
first Club Championship
Show 1988. (photo Gibbs)

Significantly, thanks to Terry Thorn who awarded Jomil Gaulois BIS when the breed was in its infancy, Joan Wells-Meacham acquired some medals from him; and the club's Best in Show Trophy is fashioned from one presented to Mabel Tottie at Alexandra Palace in 1900.

The 1988 British BGV Club Committee at the first club Championship Show: (l–r) back row, Sandy Mackenzie, Lynne Owens, John Walton-Haddon, Anne Mackenzie, Chris Baker, Barbara Dunbar, Evan Roberts; front row, Sally Edwards, Yvonne Dean, Bunty Evans, Ruth Brucker. (photo Gibbs)

CHAPTER SIX

CROSSING THE

ATLANTIC

New things are made familiar, and familiar things
are made new.
—Dr. Samuel Johnson (1709–1784)

For many American PBGV enthusiasts, the story of Alexander has become something like an enchanting children's tale, and Alexander will always hold a special place in their hearts.

In 1983, when George and Betty Barth of Philadelphia were on a family vacation in Alexandria, New York, they noticed a pen of irresistible puppies for sale in the petting area of a zoo. The sign read "Basset Griffon Vendéen – Registered." Not knowing the breed, or where these puppies were registered, they investigated. The breeder's daughter, who was caring for them, told them about PBGVs and explained that the sire and dam,

Belray Alexander Gebeba.

Jomil Pascal and Wakelyns Angelique, came from England. Owner Noreen Beasley (Belray) of Canada had imported several PBGVs from there.

Intrigued, the Barths left the zoo and continued on their vacation but were unable to get those dogs off their minds. On the last day of their visit, they returned to the zoo, and bought their first PBGV. This, of course, was Alexander and the start of the Gebeba Kennel in Pennsylvania.

A week later history was made. The Professional Handlers Association/Owner Handlers Association (PHA/OHA) sponsored "The Supermatch," the first of its kind. Not only were AKC recognized breeds entered, but rare breeds were also invited. It was a highly publicized match with a judging panel of AKC judges, professional handlers and top breeders from around the country. The New Jersey show brought an entry of over 3,300 dogs, with prize money of $1,000 for Best in Match.

Betty Barth later said, "By the time Best in Match was to be judged it was getting dark and the ring was illuminated by car headlights. In true PBGV fashion Alexander, who had just won the heart of the rare breed group judge, went into that ring undaunted by the lights and the cheering crowds and won Best Puppy in Show."

The following week the Barths were inundated with calls from dog magazines, photographers, newspaper columnists, all wanting to know who he was and where he came from. *Dog World* magazine featured Belray Alexander Gebeba and his story was told in newspapers across the country. The breed came to the attention of many who were to become involved in the early '80s and who became influential founders of the Petit Basset Griffon Vendéen Club of America.

Forming the PBGVCA

A year after Alexander captivated the dog world in America, the AKC held its Centennial Celebration show in Philadelphia, bringing together many of the people interested in the breed. On

November 19, 1984, the first meeting was held in the Exhibition Hall, and the PBGVCA officially formed.

Those present at this inaugural meeting were Kitty Steidel, Sue and William Barton, Louisa (Appie) Myers, George and Betty Barth, Geraldine Cross, Anne Snelling, Barbara Cromley, Heidi Martin, Mary Jo Shields, Jackie Balog, Sally Sweatt, Marc Delanier, Barbara Wicklund, Barbara Galbraith and Patricia Fellman-Gellerman. Although not present at the initial meeting, Bob Booth was to become an important figure in the club.

Kitty Steidel, acting secretary (subsequent first president and driving force behind the club's education program), explained that the purpose and philosophy of the club was "to protect and promote the PBGV in America by setting up a network of communication among fanciers; for the purpose of educating and informing interested individuals so that top quality dogs would be imported for breeding and exhibition." Since there was already much publicity and interest, the goal was to protect and educate, rather than promote.

Despite efforts to slow down the frenzy for the new hound, publicity and interest had reached a high and many had begun to contact European breeders, import dogs and join the newly formed PBGVCA, not only to learn about the breed but to be part of its foundation. Membership grew to 53 by the end of the first year. As in England, many were basset breeders.

The first standard was written by a committee consisting of Betty Barth, Bob Booth, Barbara Cromley, Appie Myers and Kitty Steidel. Their proposed standard then went to the board of directors for input before going to membership vote. It was based on the French and English standards; the latter having just been put into place after ten years' work. Wording was augmented as they felt temperament and character should be included, aspects then lacking from the French standard. It was also clear that the dogs in the United States were not going to be used primarily as hunting animals. In many ways this, and the subsequent 1991 AKC adopted standard, was superior to those of Europe since more detail and guidance were provided. However, there were divergences from some physical attributes of the French and FCI standards.

One difference was inclusion of an upper height disqualification. Another was that the American standard accepted a slight rise over the loin (which appeared in the French standard of the Grand Basset), whereas the French standard called for a straight loin. These inconsistencies led to some dissatisfaction with the newly adopted North American standard.

By this time the PBGVCA had also written a constitution and adopted bylaws, and set up a national registry and studbook. The club declared its intention to work towards AKC recognition and, from December 1986, club approved point shows were held, allowing PBGVs to amass points towards becoming a club champion.

Early member Mollie Williams (Braebrook) recalled, "When Rick and I joined in 1985, the club was in its infancy. There was a tremendous correspondence between all PBGV owners, and enthusiasm for the breed was thrilling. I remember taking the rare breed standard with me to matches in hopes that it would

be studied, though I must admit that many a time Agatha would go Best in Match on her cuteness alone! The club worked hard to comply with AKC requirements for recognition. We all showed as

Rick Williams with Huntswold Javott, known as "Agatha," (Gourou of Wakelyns ex Fixed Asset of Huntswold) in 1986. (photo Bruce Harkin)

often as possible and proved there was a viable contingent of enthusiasts out there. What a thrill it was to see the first PBGV shown at Westminster."

The Early Imports

In January 1972, long before the wave of interest in the breed, Hubert Desamy helped Finn and Mary Louise Bergishagen from Michigan arrange to import a bitch in whelp. This never materialized because, sadly, the bitch died, so shortly after they acquired a dog, Jomil Aiglon, from the first litter to be born in England (Rigolo le la Vrignaie ex Orée). He, too, suffered problems, making them wonder whether this perhaps was not the breed for them.

Following this and Elizabeth Streeter's early Jomil imports, some of the first PBGVs to arrive in the country were Alexander's littermates. In the early '80s, Barbara Oxholm (Polygor) saw a slide show by noted canine writer Louise Shattuck, which included a BGV. Barbara immediately started looking for one. When she saw Alexander at The Supermatch, she surprised George Barth by saying she recognized the breed. George told her where they had bought Alexander and, borrowing all the cash she could from doggy friends, Barbara jumped into her car and drove upstate to buy a Belray dog and bitch. The latter, Belray Polygor Foxy, became her foundation bitch.

Another early arrival was Oaktree's Pepperhill Pistache (Can. Ch. Vendric Déjà Vu ex Vendric Valeria), which Jeffrey and Barbara Pepper of Putnam Valley, New York, bought from Anne Snelling in Canada in November 1984. Jeffrey remembered, "She immediately won our hearts. We were so enamored with Pistache that we talked to Richard Gilbert in England, the breeder of both her sire and dam, and asked him to send us a dog and a bitch. These imports, Vendric Bravo and his littersister Butterfly (Gamin of Kasani to Peterstown ex Vendric Vanity) arrived late 1985."

Bravo completed his Canadian championship, became the first male PBGVCA champion and sired the first American-bred Canadian PBGV champion, Pepperhill's Domaine Chandon. From Butterfly came the first American-bred PBGVCA champion, Pepperhill's Chardonnay (co-owned with Gerry Roose and William Doyle of California).

Gerry Roose with Pepperhill's Chardonnay and Judge Linda Skerritt, California, 1988. (photo Fox and Cook)

Visiting Denmark in spring 1984, Kitty Steidel was fortunate to spend time with some of the top Danish PBGV breeders. With Mogens Hansen (Axmo) and Per Knudson (Morebess) she saw PBGVs en masse and learned much about the breed. Describing her first impressions as "captivated, fascinated and intrigued," she made arrangements to import the following year.

Two puppies arrived from Mogens Hansen in April 1985: Kitty's Axmo's Babette de la Garonne, born September 21, 1984, (Tonus des Rives de la Garonne ex Neiges des Rives de la Garonne) and litter brother, Balzac, who went to Bob and Mary Jane Booth in Texas. Three other Axmo's were imported, Don Camillo de la Garonne, Don Diego and Don Ranudo (Dan. Ch. Ursins des Rives de la Garonne ex Turaine des Rives de la Garonne)—foundation stock of Barbara Wicklund and Pat Fellman-Gellerman, Mary Jo Shields and Tom Underhill respectively.

Early import and PBGVCA registered #1 Axmo's Babette de la Garonne.

Soon there were imports from England, at this time primarily from Jomil, Vendric, Varon and Wakelyns, and further dogs from Denmark and Sweden. Even at this early stage of the breed's development, the influence of Eng. Dan. Lux. Ch. Salto de Crislaure of Morebess was apparent. Within a short time of coming out of quarantine in England, Salto sired many of the early imports to America.

Barbara Galbraith (Lacebark) remembered seeing the breed for the first time while on vacation in Scotland 1984. There, at a dog show, she saw "an entire row of PBGVs, tails wagging. I fell in love with the breed. Having had Irish Wolfhounds for years, we wanted a smaller dog." That year she imported Wakelyns Noblesse (Gourou of Wakelyns ex Twinrivers Duchesse of Wakelyns) from the Mackenzies.

Affectionately known as "Jackie" or "Grandma Jack," Noblesse became a multiple Specialty winner and, in January 1988, the first PBGVCA breed champion. Despite only having one litter when bred to another of Barbara's imports, Wakelyns Javelot (Twinrivers Ivor of Wakelyns ex Huntswold Trefle of Wakelyns), she produced Lacebarks Lydia, born July 6, 1988, owned jointly with Debbie Perrott and Shirley Knipe (Hootwire). Lydia became one of the top winning, top producing bitches in the breed's history and the foundation of many American kennels.

In 1985 Appie Myers (My Lu), from Spicewood, Texas, imported littermates, a dog and a bitch, from French breeder

Debbie Perrott with Int. Am.
Can. Mex. Ch. Lacebarks Lydia.
(photo Alex Smith Photography)

Gilbert Pène. Born on August 25, 1984, Venise and Venus des Rives de la Garonne had all the attributes Appie was looking for in a breeding program. Unfortunately, both disliked showing, though Venus displayed true hunting prowess and eventually went to live and work with a Beagle pack. The following year Venise was bred to Bob and Mary Jane Booth's Danish import Axmo's Balzac de la Garonne, which, on July 7, 1986, produced Appie's "A" litter, the first PBGVs to be born in America and registered with the PBGVCA. My Lu's Amérique became foundation bitch for Mary Jo Shields (Kazoo), Michigan, and My Lu's Armand went to Appie's good friend, Het Garwood. The litter included Albert, Alphonse and Antoine.

The legendary and much-loved Alexander lived to the grand age of 15-1/2. Although not used at stud himself, during his life he saw George and Betty Barth begin a successful breeding program. In 1985 Turenne, bred by Pierre Salaün, joined them from Elizabeth Streeter's Skycastle pack. His pet name, "Warrior," belied his stature. He was 13.5 inches (34

My Lu's Amérique. (photo
Imagemasters)

cm) at the withers, quite compact, with short ears and tail, which made him a very small dog who looked out or place compared to those being shown at the time. Mrs. Streeter's assurances that he was, in fact, very true to type proved well-founded as, until his death in 1997, Turenne continued to influence many pedigrees and bloodlines through his progeny. In July 1991 he became an AKC champion.

Betty said, "Warrior would always rather be out hunting, but did enjoy the occasional romp in the showring. He was a strong, healthy, active dog, the foundation stud dog for our kennel and every PBGV we have bred goes back to him."

In late 1985, in partnership with Joyce Miley-Woodfin and Jackie Cresswell, well-known Clumber Spaniel breeder/judge Betty Young (Cypress Woods), California, imported several dogs from England—Monkhams Django (Dan. Lux. Ch. Salto de Crislaure of Morebess ex Wakelyns Willow of Monkhams) from Bernie and Linda Skerritt, Varon Vamp (Wumberlog Flute of Thatchwood ex Twinrivers Gabrielle) from Evan Roberts and White Webbs Wood Nymph (Dehra Berceuse of White Webbs ex Jomil Myrhha of White Webbs) from Giselle Taylor.

Shortly after, Mike and Arlene Dickinson (After-Ours) in White City, Oregon, acquired Beacontree Monet (Maquisard

Ch. Turenne (Oslo ex Nanou) winning Veteran Dog at the 1996 Regionals, having won Veteran Dog at the National. (photo The Standard Image)

Clouseau ex Maquisard Bonnechance of Beacontree) from English breeder Barbara Golding; and litter brother Mattisse (who later transferred to Kitty Steidel) joined Betty at Cypress Woods. "Bets," as she was fondly known, also imported a bitch from Lynne Owens—Jaclin Indecent Obsession (Dehra Armand Brumeux ex Ch. Varon Xanthia for Jaclin).

Also in late 1985, Ruth Balladone and Marianne Paulsson (Balmar) of Northern California imported a dog and bitch, Edeängs Fridolf and Trogens Värmlands Jänta from Sweden, and, in June 1986, a Danish bitch, Morebess Charlotte de St Florent. It was a mating between Fridolf and Charlotte that truly established the Balmar breeding program and, ultimately, many others who began with this line, including Ann Kresse and her Balmar's Mignonnette, the foundation of her successful Elan PBGVs.

By the end of 1986 many of today's well-known PBGV kennels were on their way. Breed advocates had begun their own breeding programs and were continuing to import. Debbie Perrott and Shirley Knipe with Belray Sirhan Braconnier, born September 27, 1985, (Can. Ch. Jomil Pascal ex Can. Ch. Belray Princess Puff); and Lawrence Terricone and Jennifer King with Wakelyns Eloise, born April 5, 1985, (Gourou of Wakelyns ex Dawbak Panique of Wakelyns) from the Mackenzies. Other importers were Paul and Donna Kovar (with Mary Macquiddy) owning Jomil Xenobia, born November 12, 1985, (Eng. Dan. Lux. Ch. Salto de Crislaure of Morebess ex Jomil Tamarisk) from Wells-Meacham and Seiffert; and, from Ruth Brucker, Nancy Trucker's and Bets Young's Twinrivers Gabrielle who, in June that year, was imported in whelp bred to top winning British dog, Jomil Rigolo. This litter, born July 22, was the first sired by a foreign dog and the first at Cypress Woods.

For Larry Terricone, the attraction was not only the physical attributes but, more importantly, "What's between the ears—the gray matter. A mind that never quits." Although he and Jennifer King first saw the breed at The Supermatch, it wasn't until 1985 when Larry judged at a Rare Breed show and fell in love with Barbara Galbraith's Jackie that they weakened. With the arrival of Wakelyns Eloise from England that year came the foundation of their Clarion Kennel.

In 1988 Eloise was bred to Arlene and Mike Dickinson's Beacontree Monet and produced her only litter. This included PBGVCA Am. Ch. Clarion's Rumpole, Ch. Madcap Elvira, Ch. Cordelia Gray and Maud Silver. That year Eloise also became a PBGVCA champion. Achievements in the showring continued alongside an immensely successful diversion into agility in the '90s, and in 1992 Jennifer bought Ch. Agrid'Or Blanche du Greffier du Roi, imported from Jolanda Huisman by friend Jim Heard, who showed her to her championship. In 1994, she started a new breeding program under the kennel name, "Dubois," using Dutch and French bloodlines. She and Helen Ingher imported Shamblewain's d'Outre Mer, bred by Marion Quaedvlieg, from Holland in July 1997.

Valerie Link (Jamar) returned to America in 1986 with two young bitches, Monkhams Hannah, born November 5, 1984, (Jomil Larbi of Varon ex Jomil Sirène of Monkhams) and Kasani Honette, born January 5, 1986, (Gambit of Kasani ex Kasani Élégance). Valerie's interest in the breed grew from first seeing PBGVs in 1981 at Newmarket, a year after arriving in England. Her introduction of Kasani bloodlines to the American gene pool proved important as Sylvia Probert had not exported widely to North America, her only other exports being Honette's litter sisters, Harmonie and Hilarité, to Harry and Geraldine Jeffries (Tecknique) in Canada.

In subsequent years Valerie imported four more hounds from Sylvia: Kasani Kraftsman in February 1988; Eng. Ch. Dunarden Clairon of Kasani and daughter Kasani Nectaire (the latter co-owned with Melissa Grueninger) in March 1993; and Eng. Ch. Kasani Ravissant in July 1996. Jaclin Love Me Do (Eng. Dan. Lux. Ch. Salto de Crislaure of Morebess ex Jaclin All About Eve), co-owned with Frank and Judith Barnett

(Fitzcap) in Illinois, arrived in 1990.

Although Honette (Pippa) was already seven years old when Clairon (Nimrod) arrived in America, it was the breedings between these two that proved most successful for Jamar. The first litter, born July 25, 1994, gave a dog and two bitches. Jamar's Olly Olly Oxen Free went to Melissa Grueninger in Illinois, then to junior handler Billy Ellis in Florida, who put him in the top ten PBGVs in 1998. Catch the Spirit became foundation bitch for Marion Schwilk's Merci Kennels in Ohio. Kindred Spirit remained with Jamar. In 1996 she was bred to Ch. Elan's Cartouche de Qubic and produced Devils Advocate, an influential stud dog co-owned with Pete Ammon, DVM, in Illinois.

Valerie Link with Ch. Jamar's Kindred Spirit and Judge Michael Sosne. (photo Booth Photography)

The second litter in April 1995 consisted of three bitches. Miss Behavior went to Fitzcap; Miss Demeanor to Charlotte Day in Atlanta; and Class Action stayed at Jamar. Another 1996 mating, this time between Class Action and Ch. Charlen's For Your Eyes Only, resulted in a "dream litter" of seven. The Shakespeare litter included top winning puppy McDuff, As You Like It and Much Ado About Jamar.

March 13, 1987, saw the club coming into its own. The first PBGVCA National Specialty was held in Louisville, Kentucky,

Right: Morebess Charlotte de St Florent, foundation stock for Balmar.

Below: Kasani Honette, foundation stock for Jamar. (photo Pearce)

and, from the entry of 24, top awards went to imported hounds. Winners Dog and Best of Breed was Tom Underhill's Axmo's Don Ranudo de la Garonne. Winners Bitch went to the three-year-old Wakelyns Noblesse. In his critique, hound expert William Barton said, "This was a thrilling experience and an historic moment for our breed. As an engineer, I have to know how all the pieces fit together to make a balanced piece of equipment. This is how I judged. I was looking under the skin to see how the pieces of the dog fit together."

His overall criticisms were, "I found some heads a little large, some light eyes, overly long bodies and silky coats. Few had prominent sternums. However, most of the headpieces were good, and I found good bites, straight movement and straight fronts." Praising his win-

Tom Underhill with Axmo's Don Ranudo de la Garonne, Judge William Barton.

ners, he described BOB, Axmo's Don Ranudo de la Garonne, as "an excellent type of dog, in coat and body conformation. Compact body, well balanced, excellent mover." His Winners Bitch was "well balanced, with excellent conformation and movement." From this show, a few dogs emerged who historically would be remembered as having a major impact on the breed's development.

Barbara Galbraith with Wakelyns Noblesse in 1988.

Across the Border

Anne Snelling (Oaktrees) saw her first PBGV at Crufts in 1981. She was riding up an escalator but was so intrigued by the breed disappearing into the distance that she immediately got on the down escalator. "And there they were—tails wagging, looking around and being pleased with themselves!" She could not stop thinking about them. Back in Canada, Anne contacted the Canadian Kennel Club for help and advice. They were very supportive and provided information to see the breed through to full recognition. Unlike the AKC, there only had to be seven PBGVs in the country to apply for full status.

In 1983, after long hours studying the breed and a return visit to Crufts—where Anne tried unsuccessfully to get Sylvia Probert to part with Vendric Vanessa—she imported litter sister Valeria, in whelp to Varon Zorro, from Richard Gilbert. Valeria had six puppies, so there they were—all seven for full status. Another requirement was for the breed to be in three provinces. More people became involved and the search began to trace every PBGV in the country.

Even in mid-Canada, from Saskatchewan to Manitoba, PBGVs were tracked down, some imported by people who did not continue with the breed, others by stalwarts like Noreen Beasley, the first in Canada to breed a litter. By 1985, there were about 35 PBGVs registered in six out of the ten provinces. This assisted acceptance into the Miscellaneous class, effective March 1 that year. Entry into the Hound Group followed shortly after, on May 1. With a three-day show starting at Niagara Falls, Ontario, that very day, what better way for PBGVs to make their debut? Harry and Gerry Jeffries' Oaktrees Hercule at Tecknique went BOB.

With Audrey Benbow (Sirhan), Geraldine Cross, Karen Fyke, Pam Sutherland and, by 1985, Muriel Popkin (RareGems), Harry and Gerry of Montreal were early advocates of the breed. Their Oaktrees Hercule at Tecknique, who truly put the breed on the map in Canada, came from a breeding between Anne Snelling's July 1983 imports Vendric Déjà Vu, who later became a champion, and Vendric Valeria. Herky, however, took the honor of becoming the first Canadian PBGV champion, and with handler Sandy Fletcher he then traveled from coast to coast accumulating Specialty and numerous Group wins.

More importantly, he was a great ambassador for the breed on both sides of the border. Since many Americans were traveling to Canada to show their PBGVs, Herky became well known. He was used extensively at stud in Canada, and also on American-owned bitches. In 1987 a mating between him and Valerie Link's Monkhams Hannah produced a dog and a bitch, Jamars Hot Gossip and Jamars Milton Bradley, who became two of the top winning hounds in Canada in the late '80s.

When asked what attracted him to the breed, Harry Jeffries simply replied, "Sylvia Probert!" Harry first saw PBGVs in 1979 at the Hammersmith Show in Wood Green, London, when he was visiting the UK. Then, in 1983, he and Gerry met Sylvia and visited her Hertfordshire home. With her enthusiasm and guidance, he was converted. In 1986, three English imports joined Tecknique. From Chris Baker, Festoon Around Bryony (Jomil Flambard ex Wakelyns Adele), whom Chris had taken on from breeder Jan Baker. Bryony, born March 10, 1983, became the Jeffries' foundation brood bitch, her progeny starting many Canadian kennels. And from Sylvia came the two long-awaited Kasanis.

Below: Foundation bitches for Tecknique, Can. Ch. Festoon Around Bryony, and the two youngsters Kasani Harmonie and Hilarité.

Above: Can. Ch. Oaktrees Hercule at Tecknique in 1986. (photo Mikron Photos)

Since the PBGV was still considered a rare breed in the States, for Americans it was not simply a case of entering a show and crossing the border into Canada. As the breed was not AKC registered, the PBGV somehow had to be registered with the CKC, which was not an easy task. Valerie Link's Monkhams Hannah was helped towards her Canadian champion status by being imported via Canada and CKC registered en route to America. For others, either tattooing or a nose-print had to be submitted with any CKC application, which also, of course, needed a Canadian address. This resulted in many dogs being co-owned between American and Canadian fanciers.

While still awaiting Miscellaneous status, the late '80s saw a frenzy of activity for the PBGV and the PBGVCA. Many American exhibitors made their way across the border to Canadian circuits as well as heading south to Mexico. At this time two of the breed's most enthusiastic devotees were Debbie Perrott and Shirley Knipe of Southern California. They set off on their travels with Braconnier (Poacher) and imported a bitch from Diana Nichols, Chantalles Hispa (Varon Zorro ex Varon Wanton de Chantalle). Attending most major circuits in British Columbia, international shows in Mexico and Rare Breed

shows in California, they soon put the word out about Petits. In 1989 with scores of 184, 177.5 and finishing at Long View-Kelso Show in Washington with a 188, Poacher was the first to gain an obedience CD following acceptance into Miscellaneous classes and the first AKC title holder. He later finished his Mexican Obedience title and became an Int. Mex. Can. Am. champion.

Int. Mex. Can. Am. Ch. Belray Sirhan Braconnier CD. (photo Fox and Cook)

The Introduction of Dehra and Other European Lines

In 1988 Nick Frost first visited America and the beginning of great changes for PBGVs both in England and America began. Linda Skerritt, 1988 PBGVCA National Specialty Sweepstakes judge, had persuaded Nick to accept the invitation to judge the Regular classes. The San Rafael, California, entry of 54 included the only two PBGVCA champions at that time, Wakelyns Noblesse and Vendric Bravo. Winners Dog and Best of Breed was Barbara Galbraith's Wakelyns Javelot; Winners

Bitch, Bets Young's Jaclin Indecent Obsession.

Here the Peppers met Nick. Although he was not over-complimentary about their dogs, they spent time together and became friends. Jeffrey recalled, "We realized that we could improve on the type of dogs we had. We really needed to start over again with dogs more correct in type." In the summer of 1989, Jacobin at Dehra, born July 27, 1988, (Morebess Haveloc at Dehra ex Jomil

Jeffrey Pepper with Jacobin at Dehra. (photo Ashbey)

Reverie) arrived from Nick, beginning a new Pepperhill blood-line.

Keen to learn more about the breed, the Peppers visited Nick and Vivien Phillips at Clipperdown Cottage in 1990. There they were surrounded by many PBGVs and also attended shows. One especially caught Jeffrey's eye—Fredwell Birribi of Dehra, from a repeat Haveloc – Reverie breeding. This young bitch went with him to join Pepperhill in New York.

Another major influence on the breed's development was Jomil Ultra. Born November 17, 1984 (Dan. Lux. Ch. Salto de Crislaure of Morebess ex Jomil Leda), his unexpected arrival in the United States became one of the most important factors in the early days. Jeffrey said, "Adam's purchase was unplanned. I went to England in January 1991, just after the breed was fully recognized in America. Nick asked me to show Adam in the Open Dog class at Crufts, which he won. I was impressed with him and asked Nick if I could have him. He kindly agreed and Adam flew home with me that week." Handled by Ellen Weiss-

Frost, Adam repaid Jeffrey's confidence in him by promptly going BOB under judge Mrs. Lee Canalizo at that year's National Specialty.

As the Peppers gradually imported more dogs from Europe, their breeding program began. Jacobin, who became a Can. Am. champion, was mated twice with Vendric Butterfly, and Ultra with Birribi. Then, early in 1992, Nick asked the Peppers to whelp a litter for him. Eng. Ch. Varon Tapette was in the Netherlands where she had been bred to Galant des Ajoncs de l'Aulne, whom Nick had recently bought from Pierre Salaün in France. Not wanting the bitch to whelp in UK quarantine, Nick asked Jolanda Huisman (Du Greffier du Roi) to take Tapette to New York. There, on October 3, 1992, she had ten puppies. Since an American must own the whelped litter for it to be registered with the AKC, this became the first of many co-bred Pepperhill-Dehra litters.

With Jolanda in the States, the Peppers had the perfect opportunity to send a bitch back to Europe to be bred, thus introducing a new bloodline to North America. Birribi was mated to a French dog, Ch. Hans du Camp des Garrigues, and two Du Greffier du Roi bitches, Be Seen and Bisou, were sent to the Peppers in New York. Birribi remained in the Netherlands until her next season, when she was bred to Per Knudsen's Dan. Ch. Morebess Obelix de Nîmes (Urio des Rives de la Garonne ex Morebess Jezabel d'Evreux). She returned to New York and became the cornerstone of the Peppers' breeding program.

Birribi whelped in December 1993. From this Pepperhill "O" litter, one went to Holland, one to Japan. Both became champions. The rest remained in America. Owned by Anne Esperance and Onnie Martin, Orville became a champion for Pandan Tu in California, and the Peppers' O'Henri achieved #3 PBGV in the country in 1996.

Ch. Varon Tapette was mated twice more, to Ch. Fredwell Comete at Dehra, born October 6, 1990 (Eng. Dan. Lux. Ch. Salto de Crislaure of Morebess ex Jomil Reverie), owned by

Kitty Steidel and Christine Dresser; and, in 1994, to Ch. Dehra Urio. Born September 15, 1994, the one bitch in this second litter, Ch. Pepperhill-Dehra Charmaine, became #1 PBGV in the country 1997 (All-Breed points) and 1998 (All-Breed and Breed points).

Ch. Pepperhill-Dehra Charmaine with handler Clint Livingston, first American to win Crufts Junior Handling, 1988.

At that time, Charles and Helen Ingher (Charlen) of Putnam Valley, New York, owned a successful boarding kennels in partnership with the Peppers. They had been involved in dogs for over 30 years and, in 1986, Helen began working as a professional handler. Having become familiar with PBGVs, that year their first one arrived from Anne Snelling—Oaktrees Taiaut, born May 27, 1986 (Jomil Pascal ex Vendric Valeria).

Meanwhile there were other imports, including Dehra Heebie, born September 12, 1987, (Eng. Ch. Jomil Rigolo ex Varon Ulema); Dehra Nuance, born February 24, 1989, (Varon Zorro ex Morebess Helga at Dehra); and an adult bitch from Evan Roberts, Varon Willful of Pauntley, born May, 1, 1985, (Dan. Lux. Ch. Salto de Crislaure of Morebess ex Twinrivers Gabrielle), affectionately called "Truffles." Soon Helen became one of the leading breed advocates and most influential breeders in the country.

On July 1, 1988, a Taiaut – Truffles breeding produced Charlen's Amulet. "Amy" was one in a million. Co-owned by the Inghers, she was a gift to Marilyn Crownsberry of Chicopee, Massachusetts, who knew she was special. By 1990 Amy had completed three obedience titles within a year—CD, CDX, and the final, most amazing achievement, a UD. In

Oaktrees Taiaut, first PBGV to arrive at Charlen.

August 1991, Amy gained her show championship, becoming the first dual-titled PBGV.

Helen imported dogs from Denmark after becoming friends with Gunnar Nymann and Holger Busk in 1990. On June 6, 1991, a breeding between the first arrival, Dan. Ch. Chouan Pretty Flamingo (Blake de la Baracine ex Rosette de la Baracine) and Ch. Dehra Nuance, resulted in the first of the Charlen-Chouan litters, including Charlen's Isis of Chouan and Charlen-Chouan Instant Replay. Dan. Am. Ch. Pretty Flamingo was bred once more to Nuance before returning to Denmark.

In 1992 the Danish BIS winning Petit and multiple champion, Chouan Gimlet, arrived in America on lease for a limited time to Helen Ingher and Carol Strong (Bihar Kennels, Cazenovia, New York). He made a lasting impact in the showring but, more importantly, through his progeny. That year, Gimlet's first breeding in America to Randy Weaver's Dehra Hester—litter sister to Ch. Heebie—became Randy's foundation stock in Ohio. Bred to several bitches, both line-bred and out-crossed, Gimlet benefited the breed at a time when it needed it most. He consistently passed on his small, correct size, harsh coat and overall type, not least in a breeding with Ch. Isis, which, on December 26, 1993, produced Am. Can. Ch. Charlen's For Your Eyes Only, known as "Sean." Co-owned with Linda Kendall and handled by Peter Green and Helen, Sean was the Pedigree Award Winner (Top Dog in Breed Points) 1996, becoming as influential a stud dog as his sire.

Next, on May 17, 1994, came Charlen's Paradox (Fin. Dan. Can. Am. Ch. Morebess Sur-Moi de Fontenay ex Charlen's Balkhr Hollywood), co-owned with Loren and Jeanie Shapiro.

Also a Pedigree Award winner, Paradox won the 1997 National Specialty, breeder/owner handled to BIS.

When talking about Paradox, Helen said, "He was so different from others being shown. His show attitude gave him that little extra ring-presence, making the judges notice his small features indicative of the breed." Bred to outside bitches, both Sean and Paradox

Am. Can. Ch. Charlen's Paradox.

have sired some of the top-winning PBGVs that have influenced or been the foundation of other kennels, including Takako Tezuka, the leading PBGV breeder in Japan. There over the past few decades, the Japanese Kennel Club, formed in 1948, has done much to turn the Japanese into a Western-fashion, dog-loving community, now having over 166,000 members and registrations totaling over 400,000 dogs a year.

The Inghers made their first of many trips to France and the Club du Griffon Vendéen Exposition Nationale in 1994. Helen was particularly taken with the soundness of the French hounds. After studying the pedigrees over many generations, she found the health of the lines, including mental and physical working abilities, unparalleled.

The year 1996 saw the arrival of the first French imports for Charlen from René Tixier's de Fin Renard Kennels—first

Am. Can. Ch. Charlen's For Your Eyes Only. (photo Ashbey)

Merle and Magnifique, then Loden in 1998, following a visit to the French Club show. Although shown sparingly, Magnifique has been used extensively in the Charlen breeding program. When bred to Charlen's Isis of Chouan, thus combining the French and Danish lines, he sired the 1998 Specialty winning Charlen's La Femme Nikita, born October 10, 1997, who exemplifies the soundness and type strived for in the de Fin Renard bloodlines.

The Inghers' dedication to the betterment of the breed is demonstrated by three times achieving #1 PBGV in the country: 1993, multi-champion Chouan Gimlet; 1996 home-bred Am. Can. Ch. Charlen's For Your Eyes Only; and 1997 home-bred Ch. Charlen's Paradox.

Gaining Recognition

By the end of 1988, 27 litters were registered with the PBGVCA. These included first litters of well-known kennels such as Balmar, Charlen, Clarion, Hootwire, Jamar and Pepperhill, all of whom produced dogs that would make a significant impact in the years to come.

In January that year, an early attempt had been made to gain admittance into the Miscellaneous class when the PBGVCA board of directors was invited by the AKC to put forward their presentation. At that time, the PBGVCA had 108 members, with only 100 dogs registered. Although a very young club, they felt the breed was ready. The AKC thought differently and entry was denied. James Crowley, Director of Dog Events, explained that although the club had "done an excellent job in overseeing the development of the breed in the United States," it was still in its infancy. Combined with low membership, small numbers of dogs and uneven distribution throughout the country, this counted against them.

Barbara Wicklund, original board of director member and then secretary, masterminded the first and subsequent applications for admittance. She wrote and organized the breed presentation that was eventually approved in February 1989, effective July 1, 1989, and made further efforts for full-breed recognition into the Hound Group. By this time there were over 150 PBGVs registered and 32 American-born litters. These dogs were issued an Indefinite Listing Privilege (ILP) number for eligible entry to Miscellaneous class (conformation) competition, as well as for any obedience and tracking trials.

During the next 18 months, Miscellaneous classes from coast to coast were full of Petits. Many were also taking part in obedience and tracking events and the first CD and TD dogs, Belray Sirhan Braconnier CD and Can. Ch. Monkhams Hannah TD, were crowned that same year. The PBGVCA continued to hold Specialties and offer points for club championships.

On August 20, 1990, Andrea McE. Field, club registrar, received a letter from AKC Secretary James Derringer. He told her that, at its August 1990 meeting, their board of directors authorized the opening of the AKC Stud Book to PBGVs in the Hound Group, effective December 1, 1990. It was official! All current PBGVs became eligible for full registration as foundation stock and entitled to enter regular shows from February 1, 1991.

First Miscellaneous Class of PBGVs in Southern Oregon, July 1989: (l-r) Shirley Knipe with Belray Sirhan Braconnier; Arlene Dickinson with Beacontree Monet; Clarion's Rumpole; Valerie Link with Jamar's Likely Lad; Kasani Honette. (photo Animal World Studio)

A Series of Firsts

Soon after the breed's full status with the AKC, things happened quickly. That month, at the first weekend of shows following eligibility, Barbara Wicklund's and Sarah Whalen's Axmo's Fagin de la Garonne (Dan. Ch. Chouan Hen's Dream ex Axmo's Altair de la Garonne) won the Hound Group at the Cape Cod Kennel Club show. Handled by Elliot Weiss, Fagin was the first to complete his AKC championship in just three shows, less than one month after recognition. Soon after, his show career ended and he took on the role of family pet with the Whalens. Sara felt that showing was meant to be a fun sport and that the aim was not necessarily to breed show dogs. She foresaw the day when this delightful breed would be over-bred and end up in animal shelters, adding, "I didn't want to be part of the problem."

The first All-Breed BIS came less than a year later on January 18, 1992, when the Ingher's Ch. Varon Willful of Pauntley won at the Saratoga Kennel Club under all-round judge Dorothy Nickles. Helen will long remember the excitement, cards of congratulations and flowers from people around the country.

As the prestigious Westminster is a champions-only show, 1992 was also the first year that the breed was eligible to compete at Madison Square Garden, New York City. Thirty-three

First BIS winning PBGV, Ch. Varon Willful of Pauntley. (photo Ashbey)

PBGVs were entered and, judging by the number of non-owner spectators (including TV crews) crowding the ring, they created a great deal of interest. One New York television station devoted a three minute segment to the PBGV on their 5 p.m. newscast.

It was Ch. Jomil Ultra who stole the day and the hearts of many by winning BOB. Other Petits to subsequently shine at Westminster included Ch. Chouan Gimlet in 1993; Ch. Foxmead's La Belle Sauterelle in 1994 going on to a Group 2; Ch. Kallista Christian Dior in 1995; Ch. Elan Vogue d'Mont Jois in 1996; Eng. Am. Ch. Dehra Celestine in 1997; Ch. Pepperhill-Dehra Charmaine in 1998 and 1999. The winning Petit also went to Hound Group 2 in 1996–97 and '99.

It is not often that one breeder and one owner does a double at a National Specialty, thus demonstrating uniformity of type of the hounds and consistency of judging. In May 1993, at the PBGVCA National Specialty, held in Windsor Locks, Connecticut, this almost happened twice. It drew 116 PBGVs, the largest entry to date of writing at any Specialty. Patricia Fellman-Gellerman, Hound Group judge and one of the first to import a PBGV into America, chose Ch. Chouan Xcept When I Laugh (Sealand Lucky Kristian ex Chouan Ornella) for her

Judge Patricia Fellman-Gellerman with 1993 National Specialty winner Ch. Chouan Xcept When I Laugh and handler Kathy Kirk. (photo Tom DiGiacomo, Dog Show Photography)

Father and daughter, Eng. Am. Ch. Dunarden Clairon of Kasani and Ch. Kasani Nectaire. (photo Tom DiGiacomo, Dog Show Photography)

BOB. BOS was Gimlet. Both dogs were bred by Gunnar Nymann and Holger Busk, who had owned them jointly with Helen Ingher. Carol Strong also co-owned Gimlet. Winners Dog/Best of Winners was Eng. Ch. Dunarden Clairon of Kasani, Valerie Link's import from Sylvia Probert. Winners Bitch went to Clairon's daughter, Kasani Nectaire, bred by Sylvia, and owned by Valerie and Melissa Grueninger.

Establishing Other Kennels

Although the foundation of many kennels was based on imported European lines, several of today's well-known breeders began with North American-bred dogs from original breed advocates: Chien Blanc, Lacey (Deux Amies); Elan (Balmar); Fitzcap (Jamar); Huntahare, JanVan (Hootwire); Ivytree (After-Ours and Jamar); Jubilee (Jamar and Weavers); Oakhaven (Ivytree); Pandan Tu, Pathos (Pepperhill); Polygor (Belray); and Redfeathers (RareGems and Jamar).

If the saying "If it ain't broke, don't fix it" has ever applied to a breeding program, it has with Anne Kresse's Elan PBGVs. In 1991, she bred her first litter—a mating between her top-winning bitch Ch. Balmar's Mignonnette and English import Ch. Dehra Requin (Eng. Ch. Jomil Zadok ex Dehra Astre Brumeuse at Bareve), owned by Matthew and Marian Bonnefond. This, and two repeat breedings, produced 13 champions, including three of the top winning PBGVs to date. Their offspring won a cumulative total of four BIS awards, BOB and a Group 2 at Westminster, a National Specialty BIS and, amazingly, in excess of 230 Hound Group placements.

Ch. Balmar's Mignonnette winning the Brood Bitch class at the 1993 National Specialty with her sons Elan Vogue d'Mont Jois and Elan Cartouche de Qubic, then seven months old.

The first litter, born September 11, 1991, produced Ch. Elan Vogue d'Mont Jois. Throughout his early show career, he was owned by Sylvia Selcer and Christen Lubinski, but in 1994, Wendy Culbertson (Redfeathers), from Caseyville, Illinois, took the dog to a higher level. Handled by either Wendy or professional handler, Dennis Lautire, "Quinn" won 23 Hound Groups with three All-Breed BIS. In 1996, he became #1 PBGV in America and took a Group 2 at Westminster.

Anne's second litter, born September 15, 1992, produced her second top-winning hound Ch. Elan's Cartouche de Qubic, co-owned by Mary Anne Brocious, Tim Ninnis and Mary Beecher. As a puppy "Nate" showed great promise, having gone Reserve Winners Dog at the 1993 National at eight months of age. Judge Patricia Fellman-Gellerman confidently called him, "one of the all time greats." Always handled by Mary Beecher, he won his first BIS at Northeastern Indiana Kennel Club in 1994. He gained eight Group 1s and, in 1994 in Scottsdale, Arizona, under Kitty Steidel, he became the first American-bred Petit to win a National Specialty.

Ch. Elan's Christmas Surprise, "Woody" was also from this second litter. Owned by Patricia Diehl and her son Daniel, he won 11 Group 1s and BOB at the 1996 Regional Specialty. He went BOS at the PBGVCA National Specialty the same year. Above all, however, he was Daniel's pet and, whenever possible, Daniel would accompany him to the shows.

Deux Amies Astre, born September 12, 1988, (Can. Ch. Sirhan Enfant Terrible ex Can. Ch. Belray Princess Puff) became foundation bitch for Lacey Kennels. Bred by Brenda Lee Vidinha and Audrey Benbow, Astre's excessive barking necessitated a change of home so Juli Lacey-Ames, living surrounded by woods in Connecticut, took her on. Co-owned with Christine Ingalls, Astre proceeded to win BOB from the American-bred class at the 1990 Regional Specialty under Renard Buche.

Juli Lacey-Ames' Deux Amies Astre winning BOB at the 1990 National Specialty. (photo Barber Photos)

Bred to Ch. Dehra Nuance, on August 12, 1990, she produced five puppies, including the true foundation for the Lacey's breeding program, Alox de Corton, who was soon a champion. On his second American judging assignment in 1991, Nick Frost awarded litter brother Lacey's Auxey Duresses BOB at the supported entry with the Albany Kennel Club. One of the top ten PBGVs for 1991, Auxey went on to be a BISS champion for Juli and Russell Ames.

Dorothea Garrett also started with Deux Amies bloodlines after spotting the breed in the '80s when managing a pet care center. The Shupans (Fallingrock) were regular customers so she saw and learned about the breed. After attending many Rare

Breed shows, sometimes traveling hours to see just one PBGV, Dorothea fell in love with youngster Sirhan Enfant Terrible (Jomil Pascal ex Jomil Urette), in her opinion "a beautiful dog with flawless movement." She promptly put a deposit on a puppy. It took time but a bitch puppy eventually arrived. Deux Amies Jasmine, born March 16, 1990, was out of an Enfant Terrible son, Deux Amies Artifisje (litter brother to the Lacey's Astre), and Balmar's Pernilla Pia.

Not turning out to be the type Dorothea wanted to begin a breeding program, son Matthew took Jasmine under his wing in his role of junior handler and Dorothea acquired another bitch from Brenda Reynolds, this time sired by her favorite Can. Ch. Enfant Terrible. Bred by Brenda, the stylish white and orange La Belle Fleur, born December 7, 1990, (ex Balmar's Pernilla Pia) took on the kennel name of Chien Blanc and became the true start of a successful line.

In time Fleur was line bred to Ch. Foxmead's Marquis des Taches (Ch. Sirhan Diablotin ex Ch. Sirhan Étoile Filante), bred by Jane Chesmel, and litter brother to Ch. Foxmead's la Belle Sauterelle, then #1 Petit in the country. A car killed Fleur in '93 when the puppies were just 12 weeks old, leaving her daughter Chien Blanc C'est Si Bonne (named after the old Eartha Kitt song) to carry on. And carry on she did. "Sissy" finished her championship easily, was awarded many Group placements and an Award of Merit at the Westminster Kennel Club.

In 1997 a breeding with Am. Can. Ch. Charlen's For Your Eyes Only resulted in two success stories for Chien Blanc. Born September 9, 1997, April in Paris was only eight months old when she went Winners Bitch at the 1998 PBGVCA National Specialty, making her a champion; litter brother D'Artagnan was Reserve Winners the same day and Best of Winners at the following day's Regional Specialty.

The Breed Progresses

Although still small in numbers, the rustic little hound soon began to show evidence of AKC recognition. With many professional handlers anxious to become involved, signs of over-grooming became apparent. The club and dedicated breeders/owners/handlers started the tough, ongoing battle to keep the breed natural. The theory that grooming was acceptable as long as it was a natural trim, as if by hunting in thorn and thicket, was difficult to support. Then, and even now, few have seen the "natural" coat of a hunter, therefore, such a trim was an unknown. Some grooming was expected and necessary, but allowing shaping and trimming of the PBGV's coat was completely unacceptable in the eyes of breed enthusiasts.

Almost two decades after arrival in the States, the breed was firmly established. One judge back from England commented that the consistency in type and quality of the American dogs now surpassed that of transatlantic hounds. Problems that plagued the breed in the early days such as incorrect fronts and *grand* features, appeared to be a thing of the past. It seemed the pendulum had swung.

The early days' issue of hounds being too large had also come full circle, some now feeling PBGVs were being bred too small. The strong, muscular hound had been forgotten for a more *petit* show dog on the smaller end of the scale. In his article "Judging the Veteran Dog," AKC judge and breed aficionado Dan Smyth referred to the new style of PBGV. "Overall size has become too important in our breeding programs. Proportionate adherence to the standard must replace the need to show smaller dogs. Petit means small—but only in the sense that it is the smallest of the four levels of Griffon Vendéen hounds. We seem to be giving up some of the qualities necessary to the hound— the strong hindquarters; prominent sternums; long, strong neck; fronts that can take a self-inflicted pounding with elbows close to the body. Much of this is lost in the smaller, more compact hound."

It was also realized that, with such a vast country, PBGV type varied from coast to coast. There was an "East Coast" and a "West Coast" type—a style clearly defined by breeders and kennels that had made a major impact on the breed. West Coast hounds tended to be larger and "houndier" with, typically, less grooming for the showring. East Coast PBGVs appeared smaller, more compact and refined.

Despite some considering that American PBGV quality was now surpassing that of overseas neighbors, breeders were continuing to import dogs from European countries and, for the first time, in significant numbers from France. Following Canadian breeder Muriel Popkin's (RareGems) importation from René Tixier of littermates Filou in 1993 and Fritou de Fin Renard in 1996 (Int. Ch. Ciron de Fin Renard ex Int. Ch. Vinie du Mont des Saules), it seemed destined that more French imports would follow.

Multi-champion Fritou de Fin Renard BC.

Born January 1, 1990, Fritou soon added Am. Can. to his Belg. Lux. Int. champion and BC titles. For RareGems, these and Coni de Fin Renard, who was imported in whelp to Int. Ch. Beloskar de Fin Renard BC, one of M. Tixier's top winning French hounds, became a turning point. Muriel said, "The de Fin Renard imports certainly refined my stock. They not only have true petit features—muzzle, ear length, topline, scale of leg to height of body—but are able to produce them. The physical and mental qualities I've come to love in this breed are the result of many years of careful breeding by dedicated individuals in France—dogs with superior physique, instinct and temperament."

The late 1990s saw many French hounds arriving in America, adding to the development of the breed and gene pool. Several de Fin Renard dogs were imported, including those becoming dominant in the Charlen breeding program: Nancy Dorsey's and Debbie Perrott's Nestor de Fin Renard (Fr. Ch. Igor d'Iparla ex Fr. Ch. Hawai de Fin Renard) and Nancy's Goldorak de Fin Renard, considered to be the first black and tan in the country. Before moving to America, Goldorak's successes in Europe had given him the titles of French and International champion. He earned several hunting certificates, sired more French champions than any other French-bred hound to date and is grand-sire of the Ingher's Magnifique. Other French imports include Jan Willis' Noe de la Belle Musique (Igloo de la Belle Musique ex Gipsy de la Belle Musique) from the Mounacs in Alsaces and Nook des Ronciers de la Mainecrie (Mann du Terroir des Ducs ex Fleur des Ronciers de la Mainecrie) from Jean-Claude Raymond and his wife in Les Eperlecques.

Having had Whippets for some years and being involved with lure coursing, it was a natural transition to the little rough-coated scenthound for Frank and Linda Zaworski of Minnesota. Their first bitch, from Jan and Van Willis and Debbie Perrott, was Ch. JanVan Turtle Sundae, born December 17, 1994, (Ch. Morebess Ursins de Saumur ex Ch. Hootwire's Head of the Class). Then, in 1997, they traveled to the French Exposition Nationale in Saint-Germain du Puy to study the breed. There they were taken with a dog, Belg. Lux. Ch. Item de Fin Renard BC (Despote des Ajoncs de l'Aulne ex Dosca de Fin Renard). He had won the Travail (Working) class in both 1996 and 1997.

After speaking to owner Mme. Véronique Gilbert-Ortegat, arrangements were made to breed Turtle Sundae ("Myrtle") using chilled semen. On January 8, 1998, a litter of six was born, the first sired by a foreign dog using this means. Linda recalled, "It was nerve-racking to say the least. We did the progesterone testing on Myrtle and when the vet said, 'Go,' we called Véronique. She collected the semen at about 2 p.m. our time, by midnight it was in Ohio, and at 9 a.m. the next morning, I picked it up in Minneapolis! With time-factor so crucial, the worst part was hoping everyone knew his/her role and that the paperwork was in order." Runamok Snow Bunny, co-owned by Jan Willis, Margie and Dennis Haarsager, came from this litter and just over a year later she gained her title.

Dehra Moves Stateside

In 1995 Nick Frost left England to marry Ellen Weiss and settle in North Carolina. Ellen was a professional handler he had first met when she was working for the Peppers, handling both Pepperhill and Dehra PBGVs. Ellen visited Clipperdown Cottage on many occasions and also showed some dogs for Nick while in England.

When he left the UK, Nick took with him a wealth of expertise, countless successes, and his beloved piano (having taught music for years). Many top-winning British hounds went too, and less than two months after his arrival, success continued. At the 1995 PBGVCA National Specialty in Eureka, Missouri, Ellen handled

Nick Frost at the 1995 PBGVCA Specialty with Dehra Eminent.

Ch. Anoroc Eire at Dehra, owned by the Peppers, to BOS. Winners Bitch was the superb Celestine and Winners Dog Xato. Urio was best Stud Dog, having sired the Winners Dog. Next day at the Club's Regional Specialty, Anoroc Eire was BOB and Winners Dog was a new hound, Dehra Eminent (Urio ex Varon Ulema). These hounds finished their championships quickly.

Outstanding achievements followed and Ch. Pepperhill-Dehra Charmaine became the most successful PBGV to date in America, amassing more BIS wins than any other PBGV. Ch. Dehra Querelle, a BIS and multiple Group winner, is another success story.

The long line of Dehra champions, now on the century mark, indicates that this consistent breeding has come a long way from the early days at Clipperdown. Two beautiful Dehra bitches, Francesca at Boxwood (Dehra Zip-a-Dee-Doo-Dah ex Dehra Neige) and Hallelujah (Dan. Fin. Am. Can. Ch. Morebess Sur-Moi de Fontenay ex Dehra Psyche) are now making a name for themselves, while Dehra Yo-Yo, bred in England in partnership with Julie Shelton, has become another Dehra All-Breed BIS-winner.

There are currently about 2,500 PBGVs registered with the AKC and interestingly, of those registered between 1995–97, 847 (27 percent) became champions. Looking back over the important years that have shaped the breed since its introduction to North America, it is apparent that the PBGV has become firmly established and of more defined type.

Influential Hounds

Throughout these formative years many PBGVs have crossed the Atlantic and become a great influence on the breed's development. However, few have the distinction of making a significant impact in both their country of origin and in North America. We finish this chapter with a look at those whose names will long be remembered on both sides of the Atlantic. (Pedigrees are provided in the appendix.)

DANISH, GERMAN, VDH, DUTCH, CANADIAN, BERMUDAN, AMERICAN CHAMPION CHOUAN GIMLET

Born October 11, 1983. Breeders: Gunnar Nymann and Holger Busk.
Owned by Gunnar Nymann and Holger Busk.
Imported into America 1992, handled by Helen Ingher.
Owned in the U.S. by Gunnar Nymann and Holger Busk, Helen Ingher and Carol Strong.

To date, Gimlet has been the most influential PBGV imported into the United States. In 1992, at the age of eight, having already achieved many European titles, he won 30 CACIBs and BIS at the World Show 1989 in Copenhagen and been named Dog of the Year All-Breeds (Denmark) 1989. He soon became a champion in both America and Canada, and picked up his Bermudan title before returning to Denmark. His wins in the States alone included BOB Westminster 1993, 84 Group placements, 25 Hound Group 1, three BOB at PBGV Specialties and four All-Breed BIS awards. He made a significant impact as a stud dog and his progeny have

continued not only his winning ways but also the very typical PBGV characteristics so desirable in the breed. Gimlet died on October 28, 1999.

ENGLISH AND AMERICAN CHAMPION JOMIL ULTRA

Born November 17, 1984. Breeders: Joan Wells-Meacham and Mildred Seiffert.
Owned in England by Nicholas Frost.
Imported into America by Jeffrey and Barbara Pepper in 1991.

"Adam" won his first CC at Three Counties Championship Show in 1988. His second came that same year at Welsh Kennel Club and, in 1989, he gained his British Championship with his third CC at Hound Association of Scotland. He was also

(photo Pearce)

awarded five Reserve CCs. On importation, Adam soon made a name for himself in the USA. He was BOB at the 1991 PBGVCA National Specialty and, that same year, #1 PBGV; 1992 BOB winner at Westminster Kennel Club; BOB winner at the Eastern Regional Specialty 1993; gained 40 Group placements, including seven Hound Group 1. A wonderful ambassador for the breed, who introduced many people to the world of PBGVs. Adam died in May 1996.

ENGLISH AND AMERICAN CHAMPION VARON TAPETTE

Born June 23, 1986. Breeder: Evan Roberts.
Owned in England by Nicholas Frost.
Imported into America by Jeffrey and Barbara Pepper in 1992. Co-owned with Nicholas Frost.

Tapette won her first CC at the BGV Club Championship Show in 1988 under French judge Renaud Buche. Her second came at Crufts 1989 and, later the same year, she gained her title at Scottish Kennel Club. She won one more CC, two Reserves and was BOB at Crufts 1990. In 1992 Tapette was sent from the Netherlands to the States in whelp to Galant des Ajoncs de l'Aulne. She completed her American championship the same year. Her co-ownership between Jeffrey and Barbara

(photo Pearce)

Pepper and Nicholas Frost started the successful combined Pepperhill-Dehra prefix.

Tapette had two more litters, both line-bred to imported Dehra stock. Her last litter, when bred to Urio, produced Ch. Pepperhill-Dehra Charmaine, winner of the 1998 PBGVCA National Specialty, BOB Westminster 1998–99 (the latter with Hound Group 2) and current record holder with, to date, 13 BIS wins and 65 Group 1s.

ENGLISH AND AMERICAN CHAMPION DUNARDEN CLAIRON OF KASANI

Born January 9, 1989. Breeder: Miss A. J. Wright, Pitlochry, Scotland.
Owned in England by Mrs. Sylvia Probert.
Imported into America by Valerie Link in 1994.

"Nimrod" (meaning gallant hunter) began his show career in England with Sylvia Probert. Top Puppy 1989, both within the BGV Club and with Our Dogs/Pedigree Petfoods, received his Junior Warrant at nine months and, at 19 months, was awarded his first Challenge Certificate and BOB at the BGV Champion-

ship Show under Nicholas Frost. He went on to win another six CCs and four Reserve CCs and was #1 PBGV in the breed in Britain 1991.

Six weeks following his arrival in America, Nimrod went Winners Dog and Best of Winners at the 3rd annual PBGVCA National Specialty. Not being heavily campaigned in the showring, his most significant contribution came as a stud dog.

ENGLISH AND AMERICAN CHAMPION DEHRA URIO

Born July 27, 1990. Breeder: Nicholas Frost.
Owned in England by Nicholas Frost.
Imported into America by Nicholas Frost in 1994.

Urio won his first Challenge Certificate in England at Three Counties Championship Show 1992 under French breed expert Renaud Buche. He went on to win another three CCs and four Reserve CCs before arriving in America. He soon became an

AKC champion and received an Award of Merit at the 1995 PBGVCA National Specialty. Although never campaigned to any great extent in the showring, he became a very important stud dog. Bred to Ch. Varon Tapette in 1994, he produced Ch. Pepperhill-Dehra Charmaine, currently the top winning PBGV in the history of the breed in the United States.

ENGLISH AND AMERICAN CHAMPION DEHRA CELESTINE

Born March 21, 1993. Breeder: Nicholas Frost.
Owned in England by Nicholas Frost.
Imported into America by Nicholas Frost in 1995.
Co-owned with Ellen Frost, Paul and Donna Kovar.

"Tina" won her first Challenge Certificate in England at

Three Counties Championship Show 1994. She gained her second at Driffield in 1994 and was made into a champion at the 1994 BGV Club Championship Show under John Miller, where she was BOB. She has a further four Reserve CCs. On her arrival in America in 1995, Tina was Winners Bitch at that year's PBGVCA National Specialty, then BOB at the following year's National Specialty. She went BOB at Westminster Kennel Club 1996 with a Group 2 and won a total of 51 Group placements, including 17 Group 1s and two All-Breed BIS wins.

(photo Sabrina)

CHAPTER SEVEN

POPULARITY IN OTHER COUNTRIES

Genius is of no country.
—Charles Churchill 1731–1764

As the PBGV started to gather devotees in England, its popularity also spread to other countries outside France.

Denmark

Founded in November 1968, Denmark's Beagle and Basset Club began with 73 dedicated owners and breeders. It continued successfully until January 1982, when the Beagle members decided to start a club of their own and the Danish Basset Club was formed to continue alone. Chairman Per Knudsen was lucky to have an enthusiastic, dedicated board of directors, who did much to establish a strong club, encompassing the six *basset* breeds: GBGV, PBGV, Basset, Bleu de Gascogne, Artésien-Normand and Fauve de Bretagne.

Today with well over 500 members, it is active in conformation and working events including *Schweisswork,* where the hounds search for game that has been shot or injured. This requires concentration and calmness, attributes not normally associated with the PBGV! Training begins with obedience and tracking and progresses to working in the forests and state parks. Following the blood trail (or *Schweiss,* meaning scent or sweat, as it is euphemistically called), hounds give tongue to alert hunters to where the wounded animal has fallen.

On successful completion of a *Schweisswork* test, the hound is certified in tracking and its name added to a register. If an animal is wounded, for example being hit by a car or shot, the hound can then be called out to hunt for it. The huntsman must therefore be licensed to carry a gun, in case he needs to kill the injured animal.

The first Basset Griffon Vendéen was registered with the club in 1976. At that time no clear division had been made between Petits and Grands in Denmark. In fact, one of the first PBGVs to become a Danish champion turned out to be quite a nice Grand Basset! His name was Arlequin (Hubbestad Harrrods ex Akerwood Alpha). Bred by Marianne Ranåker-Månsson in Sweden, he arrived in 1977 to join Countess Anne Lise Scheel's other early imports and was owned jointly by her and Sysse Petersen. Sysse later took Arlequin as her kennel name.

In 1974 Countess Scheel had been to France with her daughter-in-law Birte, who spoke French fluently. She managed to buy three dogs and a bitch; Ivoire and Ibis de la Vrignaie from one litter, Jago and Isabelle from two others. These were the first in Denmark.

Unfortunately, the countess' original French and Swedish imports had no progeny past the first generation. However, Phillip and Jytte Haas' Gavotte, Garland and Akerwood

Dan. Ch. Jomil Hotspur.

Athol and Per Knudsen's Jomil Hotspur became the foundation for Danish stock. Hotspur, in particular, had a major impact on the breed's development.

After thorough research, in the late '70s Per Knudsen planned

to import dogs systematically, one or two at a time, from France. With the French reluctance to sell, Per realized that improving his French would help. However, his interest in hunting undoubtedly helped establish his bona fides in France. He corresponded for two years with Hubert Desamy before successfully importing the first PBGV from a French breeder. This was the first of many regular visits to France to obtain high quality hounds, not only for himself but for other enthusiasts— and so began the Danish breeding program.

At that time, knowing that French breeders were unwilling to sell their good hounds, North American fanciers were hesitant to go directly to France—and French breeders seemed to deter those who did. Consequently, in the mid '80s Americans turned instead to other European countries, such as Denmark, where English was spoken freely and breeders were more willing to export. The Danish breeders had already acquired a name for the best quality PBGVs outside France, a reputation closely guarded to this day.

From an entry of 28 PBGVs at the 1985 World Show in Amsterdam, judge Hubert Desamy awarded most of the top honors to Danish bred PBGVs. This was a testimony to the high standard of Danish breeding. Best of Breed, CAC and CACIB was Axmo's Altair de la Garonne, bred and owned by Mogens Hansen; Best of Opposite and Youth Worldwinner with CAC was Mrs. Jacqueline Hiemstra's Chouan Ink Street; Worldwinner with CACIB and Reserve CAC multiple champion Chouan Gimlet who, at that time, was with Claus Holberg.

Since these early days, the names Axmo, Morebess and Chouan have been familiar to English and Americans alike. However, in the '90s, Axmo ceased breeding PBGVs and another kennels came to the fore. Connie and Bent Rasmussen started their Newgrif stock on Morebess lines in 1981 when Ultra le Parlementair joined them. Wanting to start breeding themselves, they bought their first bitch, Chouan Hippie Girl, in 1984. Considerable success followed, and they won the title

Breeder of the Year in 1993, 1994 and 1997.

Axmo

On one of his visits to France, in 1982 Per bought Neige des Rives de la Garonne (Laron du Val d'Orbieu ex Jenny du Grangeot de Callou) for Basset breeders Mogens and Axel Hansen, the foundation bitch for Axmo.

The following year, a visit with Mogens resulted in brother and sister Ursins and Urfa des Rives de la Garonne (Rabio des Rives de la Garonne ex Perine du Clos Garnachois) arriving in Denmark from Gilbert Pène's kennels. Both had good harsh coats, which helped to improve this feature in Danish breeding, and in 1984 Ursins, who easily became a Danish champion, sired his first litter (ex Morebess Nadia de Cahors), producing the successful Chouan Ink Street.

At the Specialty in Le Puy-en-Velay that year, the Hansens bought a dog and a bitch, Tonus and Turaine des Rives de la Garonne (Poly ex Ch. Noisette des Rives de la Garonne). The first litter by Tonus was out of Dan. Ch. Neige des Rives de la Garonne; he was also mated to a daughter of Neige, Axmo's Altair de la Garonne, whose sire was the outstanding Salto. Turaine had one litter sired by Ursins, with puppies from these three litters being exported to Sweden and America.

Meanwhile, litter brother Axmo's Aramis de la Garonne became a Danish and Nordic champion and, in 1984, he himself sired a litter by Fin. Ch. Beacock Jezebel, owned by Miss Nina Harju. Jezebel's littermates, Jeremias and Jugurth (Swed. Ch. Nounours des Barbus d'Entre Lac ex Beacock Helka), also became champions.

However, without doubt, many breeders in the States were grateful to Kennel Axmo for giving early, sound foundation to their breeding program and, in 1989, they were pleased to welcome Mogens when he judged the Regional Specialty in Kansas City.

It was perhaps fitting that at the previous day's Nationals, top score in Obedience went to Pat Gellerman's, Al and Barbara Wicklund's Axmo's Ghostwriter (Dan. Ch. Chouan Hen's Dream ex Dan. Nor. Ch. Axmo's Altair de la Garonne).

Morebess

In 1977 the Morebess prefix was registered and Per Knudsen's first litter of Basset Hounds was born. The following year, Per and Philip Haas imported Mignonnette de la Belle Musique (Uron de la Belle Musique ex Jira de la Belle Musique) from France. Mignonnette became a Danish champion in three shows. Per subsequently took over Mignonnette, and Jomil Hotspur also arrived from England and won his Danish title the same year.

From a Hotspur – Mignonnette mating came the first Morebess Griffons Vendéens litter in 1979. Per kept two dogs and one of them, Raymond le Rebelle—the PBGV upon whom the Club of America's logo was later based—went Best Puppy in Show at an International in November that year. He continued to win, picking up his Danish, German and Dutch titles and gaining two BIS and Runner-up Dog of the Year All-Breeds in Denmark 1980 along the way.

In 1981 Per made one of his regular visits to France. He returned with half-brother and sister Salto and Ristourne de Crislaure, bred by Bernard Beaulieu. Both were pure-bred Petits for several generations and made a tremendous impact on the breed. Salto produced very typical, sound PBGVs with good pigmentation, though some coats tended to be a little soft. In 1982 a mating between Salto and Morebess Thérèse la Tranqueuse produced Dan. Fin. Ch. Morebess Oleine de Biars. The following year Thérèse went to the Idolens Kennels in Sweden to become an important bitch in Martina Hoffman's breeding program and a multi-champion.

In 1984 Per allowed Dan. Lux. Ch. Salto to go to Nick Frost's Dehra Kennels in England and the following year Per bred his first litter in English quarantine when Ristourne went to Sylvia

Probert.

Three years later, in 1987, after 12 years on the Danish (Beagle and) Basset Club committee, the latter seven as president, Per retired to concentrate on his breeding program with the aim of improving overall quality in Denmark. Apart from his Salto offspring, Per decided to leave his old bloodlines behind and follow Gilbert Pène's lines, which he felt carried all the important characteristics. He obtained a Urio des Rives de la Garonne daughter at the French Specialty. A second Morebess litter born in quarantine in England that year (Morebess Élégant de la Baule ex Dan. Fin. Ch. Morebess Oleine de Biars) gave Nick Frost valuable breeding lines for England.

From Finland, Margareta Granqvist with her Longbody's Bassets joined Per in 1988 and the next year, in France, Per bought Echo, son of top stud dog Urio des Rives de la Garonne. Although a sickly puppy, Echo became a proven tracking dog and slowly outshone others in the ring, especially under breed specialists, becoming a Danish, Finnish, German, Dutch and International champion. Colombe des Rives de la Garonne, a typy Petit, arrived in 1990. It had taken Per a year to persuade Gilbert Pène to let her go and it took another two for her to come in season! In 1991, M. Pène parted with two more PBGVs—Vendée, the most consistent winner at the French Specialty for many years, and Urio, born August 1983, whose progeny went to other European countries and America. At one time 50 percent of top Danish dogs were Urio's offspring!

In 1993 one of his sons, Morebess Obelix de Nîmes (ex Morebess Jezabel d'Evreux) went Top Dog All-Breeds, having gone BIS at three shows

Morebess Obelix de Nîmes.

before the age of two and before being old enough to become a Danish champion! At three months of age, Obelix had been sold to a Swedish breeder, remaining in Denmark to await abolition of Swedish quarantine. Meantime, Per decided to show him and he was successfully used at stud by most breeders. The top bitch in Denmark for four years (1994–1997) was Morebess Sirène de Fontenay, a Urio daugher.

Urio's position as top stud dog was taken over by Obelix in 1995. Top show dog was Dan. Fin. Ch. Morebess Sur-Moi de Fontenay (litter brother to Sirène) who, in 1993, went to America to become an American and Canadian champion. Used successfully at stud, he returned the following year. In December 1997 he went to Nick and Ellen Frost for a year.

In 1996 Per lost Urio, who was 13. However, that year he managed to buy a Urio grandson (Dan. Fin. Ch. Magic des Rives de la Garonne), which gave an interesting addition to his breeding program. With other breeders having a similar interest in him, Magic already has offspring in Finland, Sweden, Denmark, Germany, Holland and America.

With such strong stock behind him, Per consistently breeds

Below: Dan. Fin. Am. Can. Ch. Morebess Sur-Moi de Fontenay.

Above: Per Knudsen with Dan. Fin. Ch. Magic des Rives de la Garonne.

true, typy 13-inch (33 cm) bitches and 14-inch (35–36 cm) dogs, which continue to be forceful ambassadors for the breed that he loves and promotes.

Chouan

Gunnar Nymann and Holger Busk visited their first dog show in 1980. Gunnar had become attracted to a rare breed of Mastiff called the Broholmer, which was being exhibited at the Danish Kennel Club All-Breed show. At the time, he and Holger were on the waiting list for a puppy. Holger had never owned a dog in his life and they were both fascinated with the whole concept of dog shows. In fact, they found it all quite ridiculous! However, they were intrigued enough to stay for Best in Show. The line-up included a Maltese (who eventually won) and a PBGV, Per Knudsen's Raymond le Rebelle. When they saw this cute, scruffy little dog, though not really knowing what it was, they looked at each other and immediately agreed, "Forget about the Mastiff, we'll have one of them!"

The following week Gunnar called Per, asking about puppies. He said he had a litter, but none of show quality. Gunnar had absolutely no interest in showing, so a pet puppy was fine. Shortly after, Morebess Uron Comme Grand-Père (Dan. Ch. Jomil Hotspur ex Dan. Ch. Mignonnette de la Belle Musique) came to live with Gunnar, and Holger and was the beginning of Chouan.

Morebess Uron Comme Grand-Père ("Griff") with progeny.

Several months later Per telephoned Gunnar and asked him to take "Griff" to a show since the rest of the litter would be there and it was a good opportunity to see all the pups. Reluctantly, Gunnar agreed. Not knowing the first thing about showing or grooming, he bathed Griff and set off to the show by train. He was placed last.

On the way home from the show he and Holger admitted they enjoyed showing. However, they had competitive natures and never wanted to repeat the experience of not only coming last, but also of being totally embarrassed. They agreed to give it five years. If at that time they didn't have a formidable, winning kennel of hounds, they would quit.

"PBGV" number two arrived in 1981, bought for them in France by Per. Unfortunately, Tenor grew to 17 inches (43 cm) at five months so, as a replacement from Per, in 1982 they acquired Morebess Nadia de Cahors (Dan. Lux. Ch. Salto de Crislaure of Morebess ex Morebess Rosamonde la Reine), who became the foundation bitch for Chouan. At the time, Gunner and Holger had an apartment in Copenhagen and on weekends they travelled to shows by train.

Nadia's—and Chouan's—first litter, sired by Griff, born October 11, 1983, produced two males; Gibson, and one of the great dogs of all time, Gimlet. His success in the showring was unprecedented. By 1988 he had numerous titles, having been top winning PBGV the two previous years (which continued through 1990). In 1989 he was Dog of the Year (All-Breeds), also awarded Best in Show at the World Show in Copenhagen, a first for a Petit. Still a force to be reckoned with, in 1991 he was Senior of the Year. After a very successful stay in America between early

Holger Busk and Gunnar Nymann with Gimlet after winning the World Show in 1989.

1992 and fall 1993 (with a visit to Bermuda with his owners, where co-owner Carol Strong handled him to his championship title), he returned home to win Veteran of the Year 1994.

In 1984 Gunnar and Holger imported the four-year-old Rosette de la Baracine (Negus du Rocher de la Mer ex Nigelle) from France. Already mated to Poker D'Heyhartz Garaya (Noe de la Belle Musique ex Urlette de Fin Renard), in August that year she produced the "H" litter. Chouan Honey Bee went to Germany as foundation stock for Heidi Winkelmann's Vom Escalup Kennels; Hippie Girl to Connie and Bent Rasmussen's Newgriff Kennels and Hen's Dream remained at Chouan. Rosette herself proved to be an outstanding brood bitch, having the type Gunnar and Holger wanted to reproduce in their breeding program. Although not shown much, she was placed twice in the final BIS line-up and, at her first show in Denmark, went BIS3.

The year 1984 also saw a breeding between Ursins des Rives de la Garonne and Nadia, which resulted in one male puppy, Chouan Ink Street. He went to join Jacqueline Hiemstra's d'Équipage d'Ancien Pays PBGVs in the Netherlands. Another single puppy litter was the "K" on November 3, 1985, from a Chouan Hen's Dream – Nadia breeding, resulting in Kentucky Woman. (A subsequent repeat mating in 1986 produced Katzenjammer Kid, who went to Sylvia Probert in England).

From a 1989 mating with Axmo's Grison de la Garonne, Kentucky Woman later whelped Chouan Vera's Vinter

Danish Ch. Chouan Hen's Dream with Holger Busk.

Gunnar Nymann with the young Chouan Kentucky Woman.

Vin, who joined Terri Rand, Helen Ingher and Cheryl Perrone in America.

At the end of their initial five years, Gunnar and Holger found they were now committed to the world of PBGVs, breeding and exhibiting. The hounds of Chouan were, indeed, making a name for themselves. Both became involved with the Basset Club. At varying times, Holger acted as secretary and Gunnar as vice-president. Outstanding achievements followed, resulting in being named Breeder of the Year six times in succession from 1987–92.

From a litter born on May 11, 1987, out of Rosette and Gimlet, came Chouan Nikoline Nielsen. At the 20th Anniversary Show of the Danish Basset Club, at only one year old, she was BOB under respected hound judge and breeder of Basset Artésien-Normand from Holland, Lydia Erhart. The following year she won the breed at the Club Specialty in conjunction with the World Show. Unfortunately, attempts to breed from Nikoline proved unsuccessful so, after a stunning but short show career, she joined a family to take on the equally important role as companion and pet at the age of four.

The Chouan Kennels, appropriately named after the Vendée rebels of the Revolution, have continued to concentrate on correcting faults far too common in the breed—soft coats, crooked fronts and, most importantly, size. Over the years their dogs have gone to other European countries and the States. In Europe, Chouan bloodlines began the popularity of the breed in the Czech Republic and Poland.

Gunnar commented on the Eastern European countries, "Funny thing, one would think they had no dogs worth looking at there but surprisingly, with many breeds, they have very good dogs, with dedicated breeders. Our dog from Poland, Carlos (Complement Idée Fixe) is really Danish bred out of Chouan and Morebess. He is a Danish champion and #9 All-Breeds 1998." Carlos is a grandson to Am. Ch. Chouan Vera's Vinter Vin and a Gimlet and Morebess Raymond le Rebelle great-great-grandson.

By the mid-'90s the influence of Chouan dogs in America proved an important factor in the development of the breed. Xcept When I Laugh (Sealand Lucky Kristian ex Chouan Ornella) went BOB at the PBGVCA National Specialty 1993 and 1995; Pretty Flamingo (Blake de la Baracine ex Rosette de la Baracine) began the successful Charlen lines of Charles and Helen Ingher; others were Indiana Jones (Morebess Obelix de Nîmes ex Chouan A Little Night Music); Georgie Girl (Newgriff Eager Beaver ex Chouan We'll Meet Again) and Lucky Luke (Chouan Indiana Ink ex Chouan Xplosive Stuff). Xplosive Stuff, an American import herself, returned to Denmark so that Gunnar and Holger could have one litter from her. She gained her Danish championship there.

Chouan has not imported much new stock over the years, concentrating more on their own lines. Gunnar and Holger know that all dogs have faults, but they work toward improving and establishing sound type all the time. They are uninfluenced by what others import, but have their own clear type in mind, particularly regarding quality of head, which is admittedly their penchant. Gunnar said, "If the puppy has a good head with correct proportions, I will usually run it on. The other parts must be correct, too, but I do tend to be partial to head and expression." By striving for and breeding to such ideals, the success story for Chouan is certain to continue.

The Netherlands

The BGV appeared in the Netherlands as early as 1948. Little is known other than he was a French import named Xatan. Mrs. Gondrexon-Ives-Browne of the du Toutonier Bassets Artésiens-Normands in Remmerstein had a great interest in *vénerie* and, although evidence is sketchy, it seems that in the early 1950s she imported two BGVs, Ali Baba and Delurée des Rechercheurs, also both from France. Except for the odd appearance of nondescript rough-coated hounds, apparently there was little further interest in the breed until the early '70s when the PBGV was truly introduced.

One advocate was Basset enthusiast Carla Gerber (Hollandheim) who, in early 1973, imported Delice from the Jomil "D" litter in England. The previous year Mr. and Mrs.

Gerard Vlas with a meute *of PBGVs.*

Van de Broek (Kweb) imported a bitch called Neruska. She was a typical PBGV, who did much winning and even became a World Winner, despite the general lack of knowledge of the breed at that time. By 1975 two further imports had arrived. All visually of correct *petit* type, they produced both Grands and Petits, a legacy of their forebears' interbreeding.

In 1973 Thelma Vlas was on vacation in France with her husband Gerard, daughter Yolande, and their beloved show Basset. While there they visited a dog show and, for the first time, saw BGVs. This resulted in Idée and Ibis joining their household from Raymond Rousseau's des Genêts Roux Kennels. Both became Dutch champions. The dog, Idée (Pacha de Coeur Joie ex Roquepine du Marais de Riez) was small, yet with typical *grand* characteristics. A breeding between him and Ibis (Ugo ex Simonette) gave Jolanda Huisman (du Greffier du Roi) Nana des Barbus d'Entre Lac, a very influential hound in the early development of Grands in the Netherlands.

Thelma Vlas with Loy du Val d'Orbieu.

As Thelma's interest and knowledge grew, so, too, did her desire to educate people in the distinct difference between the Grand and Petit. To achieve this, she bought two hounds—Loy du Val d'Orbieu as a puppy and, at the 1975 French Specialty in Biars-sur-Cere, Juliana de la Bougrière. Again, both became Dutch champions but, although visually of true *petit* type, Thelma knew only too well that matings would produce "the Grand surprises—the charms of breeding these dogs; a double challenge for the breeder." Two other imports were also introduced to the des Barbus d'Entre Lac bloodlines: Vesta and Urbain des Rives de la Garonne. The progeny of these two proved most successful and influential in many Dutch bloodlines, especially Bassilia des Barbus d'Entre Lac, who was the foundation for Anneke Ossebaar's Quelderings Kennels.

Idée des Genêts Roux (left) with M. Vlas and Ipie du Grangeot de Callou (right) with M. Tixier, March 1975.

In 1989 Thelma's decision to stop breeding and cease her involvement with PBGVs caused concern. She was the biggest, most influential breeder in the Netherlands at that time, so how would this affect the breed? It seemed it would be left to other advocates, such as Jacqueline Hiemstra, Anneke Ossebaar and Jolanda Huisman.

However, Yolande Vlas decided to continue with her mother's breeding program. The retired Juliana, who went to live with her at the age of nine, was her first PBGV. Dutch Ch. Taquine (World Dutch Lux. Ch. Loy du Val d'Orbieu ex Pétula de Fin Renard), who had won the CAC at the French Nationale d'Élevage, and Chiquita des Barbus d'Entre Lac followed and Yolande began to breed in her own right. Out of Chiquita's first litter, when mated to the home-bred Bertrand, came Elle-Belle, Yolande's top bitch and her pride and joy in the field. Chiquita and her daughter both became Dutch and International champions, but it was Elle-Belle's excellent hunting abilities that made her such an outstanding bitch. She excelled at her first Brevet de Chasse held in Huest, France, in 1995 with 145 points (just slightly below Excellent) and remains the highest pointed Dutch PBGV at a French Brevet de Chasse.

At the same event, with Marie José Van de Pol and Marjon Ploeger, Yolande had Best Meute from the entry of 27 over the three-day event with Elle-Belle, Riesling des Burettes, Ici Stefanie des Marais Sallants and Belg. Ch. Idole Jouette de Fin Renard, whom Yolande imported from René Tixier in 1993.

Now breeding under the Chibella's prefix, Vesta des Rives de la Garonne joined Yolande in 1994 and, more recently, Olotte de Fin Renard—a continuation of importing hounds from René Tixier to achieve expansion of her bloodlines. Although active in showing, Yolande stressed it is the complete package. "I keep my dogs at home as pets but train them for show, obedience, agility and, of course, hunting. The most important thing for me is the character, anything else the dogs do well in is extra!"

Jacqueline Hiemstra and her daughter Madeleine began their

Three generations: Dutch Int. Ch. Chiquita des Barbus d'Entre Lac (left); her dam Dutch Ch. Vesta des Rives de la Garonne; and daughter Dutch Belg. Int. Ch. Elle-Belle des Barbus d'Entre Lac. Owner, Yolande Vlas.

d'Équipage d'Ancien Pays Kennel with a bitch from Thelma Vlas—Patachou des Barbus d'Entre Lac (World Dutch Lux. Ch. Loy du Val d'Orbieu ex Mireille de Kweb) born May 17, 1979, litter sister to Pacha, who went to Joan Walker and Peter Baker in England. This line provided foundation stock for many kennels, yet Madeleine's research of the pedigree has shown that there were equal numbers of Grands/BGVs and Petits going back five generations.

Further acquisitions were Rebecca des Barbus d'Entre Lac, born September 1980 and, in 1981, French import Sorgo des Rives de la Garonne. On September 9, 1982, from a Sorgo – Patachou mating, their first litter arrived. Madeleine said, "Sorgo can be found in almost all our dogs' pedigrees. He was, and still is (though no longer with us), the prototype of the breed—short, compact, with a marvellous character."

With the help of Hubert Desamy, in 1984 their breeding program was further strengthened with imports Ulla and Unique du Clos Garnachois from France; and, from Denmark, Chouan Ink Street arrived from Gunnar Nymann and Holgar Busk. In 1988, Fr. Ch. Brack de Fin Renard BC came from René Tixier in France.

Sorgo was titled Best Dutch PBGV in 1984 while Ink Street, known as "Jensen," was a World Youthwinner and Best Dog at the 1985 World Show and a CAC winner in France. An effective breeding program combining the Sorgo/Brack lines with several French bitches produced the Hiemstra's successful Vivienne and Lionne d'Equipage d'Ancien Pays.

Sorgo's great-great-granddaughter, Lionne d'Equipage d'Ancien Pays, aged three. (photo M Hiemstra)

The Club du Griffon Vendéen des Pays-Bas was founded in March 1985, beginning with 60 members. It was finally authorized by the Dutch Kennel Club in 1988 to function as the only Special Breed Association in the Netherlands, being open to all four Griffon Vendéen breeds, but with the PBGV still the most popular.

Club members are conscientious concerning breeding. Before producing a litter of puppies, a bitch must win two placings of "Very Good" at a licensed show. The club will then grant permission for the breeding and offer help in selling puppies. A male does not require any awards before being offered at stud. While there are many who show in exhibition, in the Netherlands the PBGV's most common role is that of family pet.

Although hunting is allowed in Holland, land restrictions abound and permits are needed for legality. These are valid for one year, then have to be renewed. Legal hunting may only take place by obtaining permission from the landowner (or from the state, if the land is state-owned) and from any other huntsman who already has permission. Marie José Van de Pol said, "Yolande and I are very lucky. We have permission to hunt on state-owned forest land five minutes from my house. It is ideal for training the dogs and working them regularly."

However, countless protected species, such as the hare, cannot be hunted, and the major restriction is the widespread view that hunting is more of a novelty than acceptance of a long tradition. Artificial scent work is done, which many feel looses the dog's natural instinct to hunt for prey, and enthusiasts who wish to hunt their hounds for pleasure or for trials have difficulties. Consequently, keen huntsmen travel to France or Belgium to work their hounds, which most prefer to do in woods on rabbit.

During the mid-'80s, interest in PBGV hunting trials increased. Since then, the number of successful Dutch *meutes* travelling to France to compete at the Brevet de Chasse has increased steadily. At the 1998 trial in Huest, hosted by the Club du Griffon Vendéen, from the second day's entry of 13 *meutes*, Jannie Dekker's and Nancy Ruiten's four PBGVs went Best Meute that day, with one of their dogs the highest scoring on 140 points. This mother and daughter team had only hunted in trials for a year, with this only their second visit to the French Brevet de Chasse.

René Huisman, owner of nine PBGVs, is an avid huntsman who travels to France to hunt, but not in trials. He explained, "It is a normal way of hunting there—not for display or show. There are many people who have a pack of hounds and hunt for the love of them and for food on the

After a successful hunt, Nancy Ruiten with Judge Armelle Combre.

table. Sadly this splendid, informal occasion is seldom seen by anyone, yet it is the true spirit of hunting."

René works closely with a few others to improve breeding stock, believing it is best to go to France to retain and improve quality. "It is my goal to breed into the old lines as much as possible as, by out-crossing too much, such quality and working traits can be lost." He occasionally enters the showring with his dogs at select events under French judges or at the French Nationale d'Élevage, but is vehement that the main reason he owns the dogs is for hunting and "just simply being out in the fields with a small pack." He added light-heartedly that a PBGV likes to walk on five legs—four legs and his nose!

Sweden

The first Basset Griffon Vendéen arrived in Sweden in 1973 from England. Gerd Flyckt-Pedersen (then Ohm), wife of hound expert Geir and an authority in her own right, bought the dog on a whim after seeing him and his brother (Harrods Perrine) in Harrods, Knightsbridge, London. Bred by Joan Wells-Meacham and Mildred Seiffert, from the November 30, 1972 Rigolo de la Vrignaie – T'Arlette "D" litter, it seems the pups passed first to basset owner Jackie Davies-Aldridge in Cornwall, who had Dandini and Desirée and also leased

Hubbestad Harrods.

T'Arlette on breeding terms. They then went to the well-known pet department, possibly because they were among the many males in the early days for which suitable homes were hard to find. Sold with papers but no name, Gerd's purchase became Hubbestad Harrods. Although judges were unfamiliar with the breed, she showed Harrods with some success and, in time, he became a champion.

On moving to Norway, the Flyckt-Pedersens left Harrods, who used his voice rather too freely, with veterinarian Marianne Ranåker-Månsson. Harrods sparked her interest in the breed, and in 1976 Akerwood Alpha arrived from Joan Walker in England, followed in 1978 by Nounours des Barbus d'Entre Lac (World Dutch Lux. Ch. Loy du Val d'Orbieu ex Juliana de la Bougrière) from Thelma Vlas. Meanwhile, a Harrods – Jomil

Isabella mating produced Finnish champions Beacock Honey, Helka and Heero for Eeva Virpio and, significantly for Denmark, the first of the two matings between Harrods and Alpha (the first Swedish-born litter), included Countess Scheel's Arlequin.

Early Swedish import Ixia of Jomil, who became a Nordic, Dutch, International champion.

During the late 1970s Martina Hoffmann (Idolens) imported Jomil Elisette, who was sadly killed in an accident. Ixia of Jomil, then Jomil Kasmira (Armand of Jomil ex Jomil Fauvette) followed, thus helping the breed to gain popularity in Sweden. In 1980, Martina bred her first litter of Idolens PBGVs out of her English imports. From this a bitch, Idolens Atrice, went as foundation stock to Kerstin Jernberg (Trogens), who became one of the breed's greatest advocates in Sweden. From a mating between Marianne Ranåker-Månsson's Nounours and Alpha, Kerstin also obtained Copin. Becoming one of the most famous Swedish-bred dogs, Int. Nordic Ch. Copin can be found in most Swedish pedigrees today. Similarly influential were Martina Hoffman's Danish imports, Morebess Moustache de St. Foy and Morebess Thérèse La Tranqueuse, who arrived from Per Knudsen in 1983.

In late 1987 Kerstin imported more PBGVs who were to make a major impact on the breed—from England, Jomil Zebedee (litter brother to Eng. Ch. Zadok) and Morebess Per (litter brother to Eng. Ch. Morebess Haveloc at Dehra) and, eventually, from Denmark the famous Axmo's Aramis de la Garonne. She was also the first to import a dog directly from France with Fr. Ch. Ulysse Du Terroir des Ducs.

A mating between Int. Nordic Ch. Copin and Idolens Atrice in 1982 produced Kerstin's first litter, including Trogens

Int. Nordic Ch. Copin with
Kerstin Jernberg.

Sweden's first triple champion,
Trogens Thyras.

Thyras, the first PBGV to become a triple champion in Sweden in conformation, tracking and working. Thyras subsequently became the kennel name for owners Ingrid and Mårten Lindström when, in 1985, they bred their first litter sired by him.

The active PBGV Club of Sweden was formed in 1992. Current membership is around 200. They host a yearly Specialty and Hunting Test, have a dedicated health committee and offer competitions for game tracking and show PBGV of the Year. Today the older, established, top Swedish kennels of Idolens, Trogens and Thyras have been joined by other recognized breeders such as Vilauddens, Rainstone and Väntans, who counted among the 1998 winners: Top Working Dog, Vårforsens Jum-Jum, owned by Yngve Gustafsson; Dog of the Year, Rainstone Jubiler, bred and owned by Monica Anderson; and Top Winning Bitch, Inge Hansen Pettersson's home-bred Väntans Enda E-vita.

Inge's first PBGV in 1987 was Edeängs Ilisa, from Caring Yngvesdotter Krook (breeder of Edeängs Fridolf, foundation stock for Balmar, California). Inge has been dedicated to the breed ever since. She hunts her dogs and, not only does she

Working/tracking Dog of the Year 1998, Vårforsens Jum-Jum.

Show Petit of the Year 1998, Rainstone Jubiler.

Sweden's Top Winning Bitch 1998, Väntans Enda E-vita.

boast several Top Hunting PBGVs, but she has also owned the Top Winning Show PBGV 1989, 1992, 1993 and 1996. Her Danish import, Checkstar's Pax, 1996 titleholder, sired Rainstone Jubiler. Added to the top honors awarded by John Miller at the 1996 Danish Basset Club Show, Pax also won that year under English breeder Diana Nichols at the Petit Club Show.

Seen initially in the conformation showring in the 1980s, nowadays Sweden's approximately 3,000 PBGVs are not kept primarily as pets, but rather as hunters of rabbit and fox, occasionally pheasant and partridge and, popularly, of deer. Most breeders will therefore sell only to huntsmen or those who will work the dogs.

However, many do show their dogs in conformation at championship level but, in line with other working breeds, PBGVs must also demonstrate natural instinct and hunting abilities. Before show championship can be granted, working free in the forest for at least four hours and a second prize (Very Good) at a tracking competition is necessary.

Of the two different hunting tests, tracking in *Schweisswork* fashion involves laying a scent trail, usually of blood, or dragging the foot of a deer simulating the search for wounded game. The other hunting test is similar to those in France, where the dogs are free to hunt in woods and forests for rabbit and other small game. These two tests ensure that the popular tradition of hunting is maintained in Sweden and that PBGVs are kept first and foremost as hunters.

CHAPTER EIGHT
THE PBGV STANDARD

We must touch his weaknesses with a delicate hand.
There are some faults so nearly allied to excellence,
that we can scarce weed out the fault without eradi-
cating the virtue.
—Oliver Goldsmith 1728–1774

A breed standard is a written picture of the ideal dog in any particular breed. It describes, part by part, those characteristics that make up the whole animal and set that breed apart from another. Every breed recognized by an official kennel club must have a written standard and it is to this standard that breeders strive to produce the ideal, near-perfect dog. It is the judge's duty to learn and apply this standard when officiating at shows.

When a breed enters a new country, the land of origin standard is naturally turned to as a basis for production of that country's own standard. This should ideally mirror the original. A committee of breed experts appointed by the breed club writes the standard, which is then submitted to the governing body, the country's own kennel club, for approval and acceptance. Inevitably there may be slight nuances in translation of some points and, following introduction, many place their own interpretation on what the ideal should be.

Founded in 1911 and recreated in 1921 after the World War I, the Fédération Cynologique Internationale, based in Belgium, works closely with affiliated countries (America and Britain are not currently members). The FCI recognizes only one governing body in each affiliated country and one of its many functions is to accept all breed standards submitted. Its own standards commission adapts these into a common format, although decision on breed criteria remains strictly with the country of origin.

Characteristics of the Breed

By considering in turn the parts that make up the whole, we can begin to fit the pieces of the ideal dog together. First, what are the essential characteristics? According to Anna Katherine Nicholas in *The Nicholas Guide to Dog Judging*, there are five essentials that make the complete dog: type, balance, soundness, style and condition.

Temperament, being such a critical factor in today's world of show dogs and pet ownership, perhaps should be considered a sixth essential.

In referring to **type** we look at the combination of distinguishing features that makes each breed unique. Until the eye is familiar with a breed and can identify these features, individ-

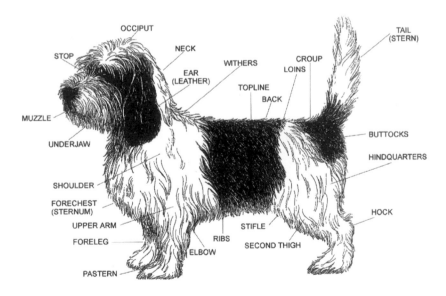

uals look very much alike and no amount of knowledge of dogs in general will enable a person to appreciate the finer points of a particular breed.

Nicholas states that breed characteristics and type are of equal importance. A dog said to be "typy" must be strong in all points or features considered by the written standard to be characteristic of the breed. Dogs are judged by evaluating, point by point, virtues and failings; thus finding the more typical specimen of the breed. A "typy" dog catches the expert eye on sight.

It is experience, and experience alone, that teaches appreciation of those small differences, and how to learn by comparison to distinguish true type. Although all dogs of the same breed are basically the same type, we have seen that slight variations within a breed, such as small differences in features, create subdivisions within the one family.

In his *Theory and Practice of Rational Breeding*, Everett Millais wrote, "Nevertheless I must candidly admit that the word 'type' is a difficult one to define; it is a word of considerable subtlety, and very doubtful if a benefit; but we have only to thank the paucity of the English language that it is so, and that it remains to us as a bugbear and a pitfall to many. In one word 'type' means 'form.'"

A. Croxton Smith further illustrated this in *British Dogs, 1903*. "We would say of the Scottish Highlanders, they are of Celtic type; but the term would not be used to describe some minute difference that may have been observable between the Clan Macgregor and the Clan Macdonald."

In other words, while adhering to the breed standard, each breeder produces their own 'type' (form or style), which may be something as simple as preferred color.

Balance, according to Spira (*Canine Terminology*), is "the pleasing, harmonious and well blending-in of an animal's parts and features, resulting in a final, composite effect of total symmetry." The various features in relation to one another—height to length; head to neck and body; neck to back; length and

The typical, balanced movement of a PBGV. (photo by Gay Glazbrook)

width of skull to foreface—all combine to create a well-balanced dog conforming to the written standard.

However, a balanced animal is more than one that looks pleasing standing still. It is a combination of the individual features as a whole that enables the dog to move effortlessly and perform with ease. In other words, by bringing together the parts that conform to the standard with the dog's ability to use those parts harmoniously, you have balance.

Spira defines **soundness** as "construction, both physical and mental, that enables a dog to carry out duties for which it was originally designed." A sound dog is one free from any disability that would affect its movement; one that moves well, travels correctly in accordance with the breed requirements and is able to do its job with the least amount of effort.

Style is something that comes from a combination of many attributes. Along with the overall balance, the elements of showmanship and deportment create a pleasing picture. The comment "he was born with it" is also true of the dog. A show dog that moves freely around the ring, or the hunting dog making all the right moves in the field with a sense of achievement and confidence, adds style to the animal.

Condition is the overall well being of the animal—the weight it carries; the muscle tone; a well-kept, full, healthy coat; bright and inquisitive eyes. It is what instantly makes the dog appealing to the eye.

Temperament is of great importance in today's world of dog ownership, whether it is in the showring, in the field or as a family pet. Temperament *must* be sound. There is nothing worse than an aggressive dog or a cowering one frightened of its surroundings. This may be inherited or due to upbringing, a bad experience, or an unknown factor. Such dogs need a caring, patient owner who will cope with any problems.

Sound temperament is a quality that the PBGV is renowned for. The breed is happy, outgoing, inquisitive, full of life, with personality plus. Head up, tail up, saying "Look at me!"

It is a combination of these six qualities that a judge will take into account when assessing a dog and comparing the individual to the written standard. Dogs should *not* be compared one to another, but rather judged against the requirements for the breed as set out in the official standard.

The Four Griffon Vendéen Hounds Defined

The Grand Griffon Vendéen, Briquet, Grand Basset Griffon Vendéen and Petit Basset Griffon Vendéen make up the group of rough-coated hounds from the Vendée region. Combined, they constitute the most popular group of hunting hounds in France. Their sizes vary tremendously and minor variations in acceptable height range have occurred over the years as standards have changed, yet the type and hunting style remain similar.

Grand Griffon Vendéen

The Grand Griffon Vendéen is a dog of great size standing between 23.5–25.5 inches (60–65 cm), with a strong frame without heaviness. He is well proportioned with a distinguished appearance. The coat, not excessively long, has to be thick and hard with an undercoat for full protection. The head is lengthened; supple ears are narrow and fine and set on low. The pre-

Grand Griffon Vendéen –
Lino du Rallye des
Combrailles, owner
Bernard Serange, France.

ferred color is pale fawn or cream on white, white and orange, or white and lemon. The darker markings, undesirable to hunters, are seldom seen in the Grand. Born to hunt great game such as wolf and wild boar, the Grand has to be hardy over rough ground for which he is so well suited. His intelligence and sense of smell are exceptional; yet, as typical of the other griffon-coated breeds, he is sometimes too independent and eager to kill.

Briquet

The sociable and good-natured Briquet is an athletic dog in appearance, with lively behavior. Average size is 19.5–21.5 inches (50–55 cm) at the shoulders. The structure is short and well proportioned, square and cobby in outline, and significantly lighter than the Grand.

With the original type of the Grand being preserved, the

Briquet – Iowa du Sentier
d'Aimeron, owners Jean-Claude
and Florence Leonard- Nolle,
France. (photo Thierry
Gauzargues)

Briquet is a superb, scaled-down version retaining admirable features such as elegance and hunting qualities. All features are refined. His head, rather short, gives the eyes a dark, intelligent and vivacious look. The ears are mid-length and angled inwards. The hair, hard and rough, must not be woolly. White is the dominant color, with the lighter markings such as white with orange or lemon being the most desirable.

The Briquet is the ideal companion for the hunter of large game because he is fiery, hardy and tough for all occasions and over all ground. He is the ideal hunting dog, being capable of working alone or in a small pack. The Briquet is also used to hunt the smaller game hunted by the Bassets Griffons Vendéens.

Grand Basset Griffon Vendéen

Slightly lengthened in structure, the GBGV is a well-balanced, medium-height hound. Descended from, and a proportionally reduced version of, the Grand Griffon, he is strong and active, capable of a day's hunting. The forelegs are straight and well boned; rear well muscled and strong. A beautiful and noble head supports a long, square muzzle with strong underjaw; domed skull; low-set, long ears reaching at least to the end of the nose; eyes surmounted by long eyebrows and lips covered with hair forming a beard and moustache.

Grand Basset Griffon Vendéen –
Debucher Le Barbu, owner Vivien
Phillips, England.
(photo Johnson)

Measuring 15.5–17 inches (39–43 cm) for females and 16–17.5 inches (40–44 cm) for males, the coat can be plain (light fawn, hare-grizzle, white or gray), bi- or tri-color. The Grand Basset is good-natured, elegant, tenacious, courageous and stubborn. He is the ideal companion for the hunter shooting in moderate ground, combining swiftness, stamina and spirit. The GBGV is the faster of the Bassets Griffons Vendéens.

Petit Basset Griffon Vendéen

Very slightly long-limbed, the PBGV has straight legs, long, harsh-textured hair, neither silky nor woolly. The head is well rounded without being too large, carried proudly, with large eyes, dark and vivid, covered by a fringe that curls forwards. As with the Briquet, all parts are refined. He measures 13.5–15 inches (34–38 cm). The coat can be bi- or tri-color (eight colors are authorized by the French standard, plus four traditional). He is good-natured, elegant, tenacious, courageous and stubborn.

Petit Basset Griffon Vendéen –
Amxo's Aramis de la Garonne,
owner Trogens Kennel, Sweden.

Although the ideal companion for the huntsman shooting in moderate ground, he is, unfortunately, likely to work himself into a frenzy while in the field. The PBGV is also stubborn and independent. He is the livelier of the BGVs.

When comparing the four breeds of Griffon Vendéen hounds, one theory is that the PBGV type most closely resembles the Briquet. This is not to say that it is a miniature version of the Briquet, but the structure, more refined features and coat indicate a closer relationship to, if not a derivative of, the larger hound. The GBGV, meanwhile, is probably derived from the Grand Griffon Vendéen, with a standard calling for a hound of overall larger proportions than the PBGV.

Before 1977, crossbreeding of PBGVs and GBGVs was still practiced. This was because many still considered them to be one breed with two height limits. The dogs were of *"grande taille"* or *"petite taille."* Also, following World War II there were so few dogs that breeders had little choice when trying to rekindle particular breeds with certain traits and selective breeding for size was out of the question.

From the Netherlands, 1980, Yolande Vlas with Nectar des Barbus d'Entre Lac, a top winning GBGV born out of two champion PBGVs.

In France in January 1997, the two breeds became officially separate and interbreeding between Grands and Petits was forbidden. They became two distinct breeds with separate standards. However, humans cannot control animals' genes! For many generations, Grands would appear in Petit litters and vice versa. Now, over 20 years since the distinction was made, it is unlikely a true Grand will appear in a PBGV litter. Nonetheless, Grand features such as longer ears, heavier coat, larger head, longer leg or heavier bone structure may still manifest.

The Relative Height Index of the Different *Basset* Breeds

Measurements are important primarily by the ratios they provide.
—Dechambre, French veterinarian, c1928

The basset is created by a growth anomaly called achondroplasia of which the main effect is to make the limbs shorter. In a *basset* breed, the height at the chest does not change. Only the length of the legs, thus the height at the withers, changes. This makes the use of proportions essential when judging the conformation of a *basset* breed.

At the beginning of the 20th century, the use of proportions for predicting suitability for a task was very much in vogue in French veterinary circles. As far as the *basset* (low to the ground) breeds are concerned, the two main proportions are what the French call the *indice de hauteur pectorale* (pectoral height index)—that is, the height of the chest (distance between the sternum and the withers) divided by the height at the withers; and the *indice de taille* (height ratio), the height at the withers divided by the length (shoulder to buttocks). American John Miller, a respected Basset Hound and BGV authority who has lived in France since 1966, studied the *basset* breeds in-depth, comparing the ratio between height and length, from the point of shoulder to buttocks and from withers to ground.

The characteristic feature of the *basset* breed is its height ratio, which is clearly lower than one. When a dog is said to be "too long" or "too short" in body, it is really a comparison of length to height. A *basset* breed must be longer than its height, otherwise it would not be a *basset*.

The physical attributes of the dog of normal conformation from which the basset is derived must be taken into account. One emanating from a long breed should logically be longer than one derived from a short breed. For example, Briquets are the shortest of the medium-sized hounds. Their structure is square, with height and length essentially the same. Mr. Miller concluded that if we were to transform a Briquet into a *basset*, we should find a dog with a height index of 0.75 (height=0.75, length=1). This measurement represents the upper limit of the height index for *basset* breeds.

During his research, Mr. Miller looked at the ratio between the height of a basset from withers to ground and its height at the chest (measuring the distance from the sternum to the withers). He studied known measurements for *basset* breeds over the past 120 years and took a representative sample of quality *basset* breeds at various shows. He found that the ratio (pectoral height index), was about 0.67 for all breeds and coat types; also that the distance between the ground and the sternum represented one-third of the height at the withers.

In a dog of normal conformation, the pectoral height index is close to 0.5; the height at the chest being half the height at the withers. Using the pectoral height index of a normal dog (0.5) and dividing it by that of a basset (0.67) the ideal ratio of a basset can be found. In the case of a *basset* breed in general (or PBGV in particular), this brings us to 0.75. In other words, a hound loses 25 percent of its height in becoming a *basset* breed.

The American standard states that the correct proportions for a PBGV should be 50 percent longer than tall. (A ratio of height to length of 0.67). Length is not measured in the same way, however. The hound is measured from sternum to buttocks (as opposed to withers to buttocks), and compared with withers to

Eng. Am. Ch. Dunarden Clairon of Kasani. Height: 13.25 inches (33.65 cm) Length: 19.85 inches (50.5 cm), from sternum to buttocks based on the U.S.A. standard. This makes him 50 percent longer than his height.
The same dog measured using John Miller's formula—Height: 13.25 inches (33.65 cm) Length: 17.65 inches (44.85 cm) from withers to buttocks. This gives him a 0.75 or 75 percent height index.

ground. Also, since many North American dogs have a more prominent sternum than those in France, the height:length ratio would be somewhat different giving the overall impression of a slightly longer animal. But by using both measuring systems on an English and American champion adult male PBGV, we interestingly enough came up with the same ratios.

Color

A good dog, like a good candidate, cannot be of a bad color.
—Thoughts upon Hare and Fox Hunting,
Peter Beckford (1740–1811)

In his 1942 thesis *"Les Chiens Courants de Vendée,"* veterinarian Dr. Jean Auger said in his critique of the hound standards at the time, "A standard has to be precise, complete, methodical, that is to say, drawn up according to a logical plan, written in accurate and as far as possible standard terms, because these have well-defined meaning." Nowhere is this more important than when discussing the subjective topic of color of a PBGV's coat.

The English language and individual perception are considerable barriers to objective discussion about color. The color we see in dogs results from two aspects. The first is the amount of pigment present in the hair. Complete pigmentation shows as solid black whereas absence of pigmentation shows as white. Anything in between is part of a spectrum, with the main identifiable colors of yellow and brown.

The second aspect is the type of coat—length, density, thickness, straightness and so on. This affects the amount of light in, around and reflected by the hairs. This influences the apparent lightness or darkness of the color and its appearance as matte or shiny. Therefore, a starting point for the PBGV is to take the colors identified in the standards in order of density of pigmentation:

White: A purist might consider this in terms of "absence of color."

Lemon: A light, pale yellow, lacking in depth of color and without any red or blue pigmentation.

Orange: A range of colors resulting from a mixture of red and yellow.

Black: Total pigmentation.

For the PBGV, it is best to think of these colors as primary ones. They represent understandable and definable colors based on the physical quantity of pigmentation in the hair. Other colors are more qualitative, representing mixtures of the primary colors and referring to their appearance in relation to the texture of the hair. These are:

White and Orange: Dan. Swe. Fin. Nordic Ch. Morebess Thérèse la Tranqueuse.

Sable This is ˙ an ambiguous term since it can mean either black (like a black, sheeny fur) or brown (as in the arctic animal). In the PBGV, sable is a blend of these two colors with the appearance of a silky sheen, or a complete integration of the two colors

White and Lemon: Am. Ch. Jamars As You Like It.

Black and Tan: Lutin de Fin Renard.

and their qualities, sometimes lighter.

Grizzled Grizzle means
gray or partly gray.
Grizzled therefore indicates
gray or gray with other
colors, mainly with the
grayness being an interrup-
tion to another color.

*White and Sable: Eng. Am.
Ch. Kasani Ravissant.*

Tawny This is brownish-
orange, yellowish-brown or
tan colored. It appears in
the latest French standard
as *fauve* in four combinations. The combination
with white confuses matters
in relation to the colors in
the U.K./U.S. standards as
this description is then
qualified as white and
orange. The traditional

*White and Grizzle: Eng. Ch.
Helensfield Osprey.*

"coat of hare" (tawny) listed separately, like the animal
itself, varies from one country to another (and from
season to season), thus leading to further uncertainty in
interpretation. Whereas the
old standard clearly stated
that solid *"fauve"* in a
PBGV was undesirable, the
new standard is silent on
the matter. (The only unacceptable color faults are
solid black and solid
white).

*Tri-color: Monkhams Tegan
Jamars.*

Tri-color is white with any
two other clearly identifi-

able colors. Whether the colors are solid and distinctly separate or blend into one another gives further uncertainty to the discussion on color.

Why, then, is color important? After all, a good dog is a good dog whatever his color. There seem to be two important aspects: functionality and fashion, in other words, aesthetic preference. Conforming to color standards in a breed is of prime importance, since these standards will inevitably be based on function, fashion and, hopefully, both.

PBGVs are fundamentally hounds bred for their ability to hunt small game and it should be borne in mind that, in France, color is thought to be mostly irrelevant, as hunting prowess is the main priority. However ownership is now worldwide and their role is no longer solely to hunt. They have established themselves in the showring and are widely accepted as domestic pets. There is clearly no relation between the function of domestic pet and color. It is in countries outside France where color has become a major issue and the showring is the area where color fashion is most controversial and personal preference most obvious. It is necessary, however, to consider color in relation to the breed's original purpose—that of hunting.

The varied terrain, thick brambles, bushes and shrubs of the Vendée (the *bocage*) is an ideal habitat for small game, particularly rabbit. When hunting, the hounds work in the shadowy undergrowth where they must be easily visible; first to their master who occasionally may be waiting to take a shot at the game and, secondly, in relation to the rest of the pack. Therefore, their color must stand out, being confused neither with terrain nor game. At the same time, they must not be too easily visible to the game itself. It is therefore important that the hounds show white to their master—sides, backs and haunches and tails—while their faces should be a mixture of colors not dissimilar to their prey—rabbit and hare.

The point about color and hunting is clearly made by an old

Vendéen huntsman who, when asked about color and whether he would use black and tan PBGVs in his traditionally colored pack, answered, "Regrettably, they could all too easily be shot." Another had similar views, "All colors are accepted (except *fauve*)—the black and tan is not happy. They are not easy to see in the brambles and then it is dangerous."

The functionality of color for hunting might not be important to those who want to show hounds in the ring. Since a hound cannot be disqualified on its color, fashion-led color combinations will be bred for a fashion-conscious market. Moreover, these colors will be perpetuated if they are based on the genetically dominant pigmentations at the expense of the traditional pied, or piebald, appearance of the PBGV, undoubtedly inherited from their rough-coated ancestors of the Vendée.

Standards over the Years

At the end of the 19th century the popular Basset Griffon Vendéen existed in France within the group of *basset* breeds ideal for hunting purposes. With breeders' reputations hanging on their ability to produce a quality hound of correct size and proportions, length of leg became important depending on type of game hunted. Also, although no distinction was made between the two varieties of BGV, many appeared to be a mutation, with shorter, crooked legs and a slightly longer body.

While the Société Centrale (subsequently French Kennel Club) was founded in 1881, it had no real effect on breeding until after reorganization in 1885 and establishment of its LOF (studbook). Although the Société Centrale had firm control over the administrative part of French canine activities, when exhibiting became an attraction, controversy waged over judging at the Société Centrale's own dog shows due to lack of breed standards. Attempts at standardization began.

With the Société Centrale encouraging formation of breed clubs, in 1896 the *Club du Basset Français* was founded, embracing the *basset* breeds. In 1898 the Basset Griffon

Français preliminary standard was adopted. This appeared in 1904, printed in four languages in *Dogs of All Nations* by Count Henry van Bylandt. Each language showed slight differences in interpretation between the various countries, giving no clear distinction between the different sizes in the breed.

Countries based their standard on the ideal visualized in the country of origin, and the English standard of that era gives an indication of the distinct differences between the Basset Griffon Français and today's Petit Basset Griffon Vendéen. The breed was judged against a standard of points—though the English one was simplified.

Point Values		
	France, Germany, Holland	England
General appearance/frame	20	10
Head and ears	—	20
Skull	6	—
Eyes	3	—
Ears	10	—
Nose	5	—
Neck	3	—
Body, including hindquarters	—	35
Chest	6	—
Ribs	8	—
Loins	10	—
Legs and feet	—	20
Shoulders and front feet	6	—
Thighs and hind feet	8	—
Tail	6	—
Coat	6	15
Color	3	—
Total	**100**	**100**

After formation of the Club du Basset Griffon Vendéen in 1907, President Paul Dézamy recognized the need for changes to the only existing standard. This first revision, which became official in 1909, encompassed the variation in height, with the only significant difference being in crook (or lack of crook) of front leg. The standard of points reflected a deeper appreciation of all parts of the hound.

Point Values – France 1909	
General appearance/frame	20
Skull	5
Muzzle	5
Nose	5
Eyes	3
Ears	8
Neck	2
Shoulders	3
Chest	8
Back	10
Forelegs	7
Thighs and hind legs	5
Feet	5
Tail	5
Coat	6
Color	3
Total	**100**

Continuing on from Paul Dézamy's c1922 standard, and the 1952 one, which recognized the PBGV as a breed in its own right, on October 29, 1966, the FCI issued a standard for the Small Griffon Vendéen Basset. Subsequent revisions, which also included the word Petit, were written by a committee appointed by the French Club and adopted by the FCI.

From 1969 onwards, as popularity in England grew and spread to America, standards there evolved from the original French, with the American standard seeking to provide greater and clearer detail. All were designed with the ideal dog of that era in mind.

PBGV Standards

Club du Basset Français – 1898

General appearance	A very powerful hound for his size, on short and strong legs.
1. Head 2. Skull	1. Large 2. Narrow but of good length, the peak well developed.
Muzzle	Strong; jaws long and powerful; a snipey muzzle and weakness of jaw are objectionable.
Nose	—
Lips	—
Eyes	Dark and not prominent; kindly expression and intelligent.
Ears	Set on low, of good length and of fine texture.
Neck	Strong, of good length and muscular.
1. Body 2. Chest	1. Massive, of good length 2. Large and very deep, the sternum prominent.
Ribs	Well ribbed up.
Flank	—
Shoulders	Sloping.
1. Limbs 2. Forelegs 3. Elbows 4. Forearm	2. Short and very powerful; very heavy in bone, either crooked or nearly straight. 3. Should lie against the sides of the chest, and should not turn out.
Pasterns	—
Back	—
Loins	—
Croup	—
1. Hindquarters 2. Hind legs 3. Thighs	1. Powerful and muscular 2. Rather longer than the forelegs; stifles well bent.
Hocks	—
Feet	Thick, well padded and not open.
Stern	Set on high, of moderate length and carried gaily.
Coat	Profuse, thick and harsh to the touch, with a

	dense undercoat. The coat may be wavy.
1. Color 2. Skin	1. Any recognized hound color.
Height	At shoulder, 10–14".
Gait	—
Weight	Dogs from 40–50lbs, bitches rather less.
1. Faults 2. Serious faults 3 Severe faults	3. Any weakness or slackness of loin—a bad fault.

Club du Basset Griffon Vendéen – 1909[1]

General appearance	Structure allongée; pattes droites ou demi-torses; fouet légèrement relevé sans retomber sur le rein; poil rude et long sans exagération, ne devant être ni soyeux, ni laineux, sur tout le corps sans exception; tête importante, allongée, bombée. Oreilles garnies de longs poils, assez longues et attachées bas, tournées en dedans. Le chien à pattes demi-torses doit être plus long que le chien à pattes droites.
1. Head 2. Skull	2. Bombé, allongé, pas trop large, bien évidé sous les yeux; cassure du front marquée; l'os occipital très développé.
Muzzle	Long, carré à l'extrémité; chanfrein légèrement busqué.
Nose	Noire, développée, ouverte et bien sortie.
Lips	Recouvertes de bonnes moustaches.
Eyes	Grands, foncés, sans blanc, de belle expression, intelligente et familière. Le rouge de la paupière ne doit pas être apparent. Les poils surmontant la paupière supérieure doivent revenir en avant sans cependant masquer l'oeil.
Ears	Longues, souples, placées très bas, jamais au-dessus de la ligne de l'oeil, couvertes de longs

---

[1] Because the translation of French 1909 standards into English has caused controversy over the years, we have chosen to include the French version without any translation.

	poils, tournées sans exagération en forme de papillotes.
Neck	Long et robuste; plus épais près des épaules; sans fanon.
1. Body 2. Chest	2. Ouverte, longue et profonde.
Ribs	—
Flank	—
Shoulders	Sèches, obliques, sans être tournées en dehors, bien soudées au corps.
1. Limbs 2. Forelegs 3. Elbows 4. Forearm	1. Ossature developpée. 2. Les genoux ne devant jamais se toucher. 4. Épais.
Pasterns	Même chez les sujets à jambes droites, le poignet doit être bien marqué.
Back	Long, large, droit ou légèrement arqué à la région des reins.
Loins	—
Croup	Bien ouverte et très musclée.
1. Hindquarters 2. Hind legs 3. Thighs	3. Fortement musclées.
Hocks	Larges, coudés et jamais complètement droits.
Feet	Très larges aussi bien devant comme derrière. Les pattes de devant droites ou tournées en dehors. Gros et serrés à la fois, secs, sole résistante; ongles solides. Les pieds doivent être tournés en dehors, mais sans exagération, et ce seulement chez les chiens à pattes demi-torses.
Stern	Planté haut, gros à la naissance, s'amincissant régulièrement jusqu'à son extrémité, épié; assez long; ne revenant pas sur le rein; porté en lame de sabre.
Coat	Dur et pas trop long, plat, jamais ni soyeux ni laineux. Les franges pas trop abondantes.
1. Color 2. Skin	1. *Unicolore* - Orange foncé, orange pâle, poil de lièvre, blanc gris, gris ardoisé. *Bi-colore* - Blanc et orange, blanc et noir, blanc et poil de lièvre, blanc et gris, noir et feu, blanc et ardoisé, blanc et feu.

	Tri-colore - Blanc, noir et feu; blanc, poil de lièvre et feu; blanc, orange et feu; blanc, gris et feu.
Height	Deux types sont reconnus: l'un de 0m 34 à 0m 38, le plus souvent à pattes demi-torses; l'autre de 0m 38 à 0m 42, devant toujours être à pattes droites. La taille de femelles doit être inférieure de 2 cms environ à celle des mâles.
Gait	—
Weight	—
1. Faults 2. Serious faults 3 Severe faults	1. Tête plate et courte; museau pointu; mâchoires inégales; oreilles plates et dépourvues de poil long, attachées haut; encolure trop courte; dos mou et plongé; pattes de devant se touchant aux genoux, en arc de cercle ou pliant sans pouvoir supporter le poids du corps; coudes décollés; poitrine ronde ou serrée; pieds plat ou gras; doigts trop écartés; jarrets trop droits ou serrés; gigots plats; fouet trop recourbé ou porté sur les jarrets; poil laineux, soyeux ou frisé.

BGV Standard c1922

(Translated from the original French)

General appearance	Lengthened structure. Legs straight or semi-crooked. Stern slightly raised without hanging down over the loin; hair rough and long without exaggeration, it must be neither silky nor woolly over the whole body, without exception; substantial head, lengthened, domed; ears furnished with long hair, sufficiently long, above all attached low.
	The dog with semi-crooked legs must be longer than the dog with straight legs.
1. Head 2. Skull	2. Domed, lengthened, not too wide, well defined under the eyes; defined stop of the forehead, occipital bone well developed.
Muzzle	Long, square at the end. Foreface very slightly aquiline.

Nose	Black, developed, open and protruding well.
Lips	Covered with good moustache.
Eyes	Large, dark, without white, with noble, intelligent and friendly expression; the red of the eyelid should not be visible. The hairs surmounting the upper eyelid should turn back in front yet without masking the eye.
Ears	Supple, narrow and fine, covered with long hair and ending in elongated oval, well turned inwards, reaching at least the end of the nose; attached below the line of the eye.
Neck	Long and sturdy, thicker near the shoulders, without dewlap.
1. Body 2. Chest	2. Expansive, long and deep in the subjects with straight legs.
Ribs	Rounded, particularly with the semi-crooked legs.
Flank	Full rather than extending downwards.
Shoulders	Lean, sloping, without being turned outwards, well joined to the body.
1. Limbs 2.Forelegs 3. Elbows 4. Forearm	1. Developed frame. 2. Straight or turned outwards, the knees must never touch each other. 4. Thick-set.
Pasterns	Even in subjects with straight legs, the pastern should be defined.
Back	Long, wide and straight, starting to curve at its junction with the loin.
Loins	Solid, well filled and slightly arched.
Croup	Well expanded and very muscular.
1. Hindquarters 2. Hind legs 3. Thighs	3. Strongly muscular, but not too rounded.
Hocks	Wide, bent and never completely straight.
Feet	Large and at the same time tight, lean; resistant pad, strong nails. The feet of the front limbs should be turned outwards, but without exaggeration and, this, only in dogs with semi-crooked legs.

Stern	Set high, large at the root, growing thinner regularly towards its tip, slightly offstanding hair (like ears of grain), fairly long, carried like a saber-blade or slightly incurved.
Coat	Harsh and not too long, smooth, never silky or woolly. Fringes should not be too abundant.
1. Color 2. Skin	1. Unicolor: More or less dark *fauve*; coat of hare; gray. Bi-color: White and orange, white and black, white and coat of hare, white and gray, white and tan. Tri-color: White, black and tan; white, coat of hare and tan; white gray and tan. 2. Fairly thick, often mottled in tri-colors, white and black, or white and gray subjects.
Height	Two types are recognized. One, from 0ᵐ 34 to 0ᵐ 38, the most often with semi-crooked legs. The other, from 0ᵐ 38 to 0ᵐ 42, must always have straight legs. The height of females should be about 2 cm less than that of males.
Gait	The walk should be easy at the three paces.
Weight	—
1. Faults 2. Serious faults 3 Severe faults	2. Head flat and short, nose scant or losing color; light eyes, sharp-pointed muzzle, unequal moustache, flat ears and without long hair, attached high; neckline too short, height not reaching the minimum or exceeding the maximum indicated; back weak and dipping; front legs touching at the knees, bowed or bending without being able to support the weight of the body; loose elbows; feet flat or heavy, splayed digits; hocks too bent or too straight, close or wide-open; thighs flat; stern too in-curved or carried on the hocks; coat woolly, silky or curly.

French Club du Griffon Vendéen – 1999
Translated from the original French

1. General appearance 2.Behavior/ Characteristics 3. Temperament	1. Small, busy and vigorous dog, with a slightly elongated body. Stern carried proudly. Coat rough and long without exaggeration. Expressive head, ears well turned, furnished with long hair and set below the line of the eye, not too long. 2. A passion for hunting, courageous, he loves brambles and undergrowth. 3. Easy-going but self-willed and passionate.
1. Head 2. Skull	2. Slightly domed, slightly long, not very wide, well cut away under the eyes.. Occipital bone sufficiently developed. Defined stop.
1. Foreface 2. Muzzle	1. Much shorter than in the larger Basset but nevertheless very slightly lengthened and straight. Square at the end.
Lips	Covered with ample moustache.
1. Jaw 2. Mouth 3. Bite	1&3. Scissor bite.
Nose	Well protruded and developed, wide nostrils, black except for white and orange coats, where chestnut-colored nose is acceptable.
1. Eyes 2. Expression	1&2. Rather large and intelligent expression, without white visible. The haw should not appear. The hair above the eyelid coming forward but should not cover the eye. They should be a dark color.
Ears	Supple, narrow and fine, covered with long hair, ending slightly in an oval, turned inwards and not quite reaching the end of the nose. Well set below the line of the eye.
Neck	—
Shoulders	Clean, sloping, and set well to the body.
1. Front legs 2. Forequarters 3. Forearm 4. Pasterns	3. Well developed. 4. Very slightly defined.
1. Body 2. Chest	2. Not too wide. Sufficiently developed in depth,

3. Ribs	reaching the level of the elbow. 3. Moderately rounded.
1. Back/Topline 2. Loins 3. Croup	1. Straight, topline well held. 2. Muscular. 3. Well muscled and rather wide.
1. Stern 2. Tail	1. Set on high, rather thick at the base, tapering evenly to the end, rather short, carried like a saber-blade.
Hindquarters	—
1. Thighs 2. Hocks	1. Muscled and not very rounded. 2. Rather wide, slightly angulated, never completely straight.
Feet	Not too large, hard pads, toes very tight, strong nails. A good pigmentation of the pads and nails will be looked for.
Gait	Very free and easy.
Coat	Harsh, but not too long, never silky or woolly.
Color	Black with white markings (white and black). Black marked with fawn (black and tan). Black marked with sable. Fawn with white markings (white and orange). Fawn with black coat and white markings (tri-color). Blackened fawn. Blackened sable with white markings. Blackened sable. Traditional names: coat of hare, coat of wolf, coat of badger, coat of boar.[2]
1. Height 2. Size	1. At withers, from 0.34 to 0.38 m (13.39–14.96") with a tolerance of 1 cm (0.394") plus or minus.
1. Proportion 2. Substance	2. Rather strong boned but proportionate to height.
1. Faults 2. Serious faults	1. All deviation with regard to the preceding must be considered a fault which will be penalized in proportion to its seriousness. Head: Too short,

---

[2] *Noir à panachure blanche (blanc et noir). Noir marqué de fauve (noir et feu). Noir marqué de sable. Fauve à panachure blanche (blanc et orange). Fauve à manteau noir et à panachure blanche (tri-colore). Fauve charbonné. Sable charbonné à panachure blanche. Sable charbonné. Appellations traditionelles: poil de lièvre, poil de loup, poil de blaireau ou poil de sanglier.*

foreface short, flat skull; ears set on high, long, insufficiently turned or lacking hair. Light eye. Crowded teeth. Lack of pigmentation on the nose, lips or eyelids. Body: Construction too long or too short, lacking harmony, topline insufficiently held, croup lowered, kinked stern. Limbs: Insufficient bone, lacking angulation, splayed feet. Coat: Insufficiently thick, fine hair. Behavior: Subject timid.

1 Eliminating faults 2. Disqualification	1. Lacking in type. "Vairon" eyes. Mixed color. Prognathism. Marked invalidating fault. Unicolor black or white coat. Anatomical deformity. Subject nervous or aggressive. Woolly coat. Stiff stern. Height outside standard. Limbs crooked or semi-crooked. Significant lack of pigmentation. Lacking fullness in sternal region, ribs flat-sided towards the lower part.

Note: Males should have two testicles of normal appearance fully descended into the scrotum.

British Kennel Club
Basset Griffon Vendéen (Petit) – 1997

1. General appearance 2.Behavior/ Characteristics 3. Temperament	1. A well balanced, short-legged, compact hound. Rough coated. With an alert outlook and a lively bearing. 2. Strong, active hound capable of a day's hunting with a good voice freely used. 3. Happy, extrovert; independent, yet willing to please.
1. Head 2. Skull	1&2. Medium in length, not too wide, oval in shape when viewed from the front. Well cut away under eyes; stop clearly defined; the occipital bone well developed.
1. Foreface 2. Muzzle	2. Slightly shorter than from stop to occipital point. Underjaw strong and well developed.
Lips	Covered with long hair forming beard and moustache.
1. Jaw 2. Mouth 3. Bite	2. Jaws strong with a perfect, regular and complete scissor bite i.e. the upper teeth closely over-

	lapping the lower teeth and set square to the jaw. Level bite acceptable.
Nose	Black, large with wide nostrils.
1. Eyes 2. Expression	1&2. Large, dark showing no white, with friendly intelligent expression. Red of the lower eyelid should not be showing. Surmounted by long eyebrows standing forward but not to obscure eyes.
Ears	Supple, narrow and fine, covered with long hair, folding inwards, ending in an oval shape; reaching to end of nose; set on low, not above line of eye.
Neck	Long and strong, set into well laid shoulders; without throatiness; carrying head proudly.
Shoulders	Clean and sloping.
1. Front legs 2. Forequarters 3. Forearm 4. Pasterns	1&2. Elbows close to body. Forelegs straight, a slight crook acceptable; thick and well boned. 4. Strong and slightly sloping.
1. Body 2. Chest 3. Ribs	2. Deep with prominent sternum. 3. Moderately rounded extending well back.
1. Back/Topline 2. Loins 3. Croup	1&2. Back of medium length; level topline with slight arching over strong loins.
1. Stern 2. Tail	1&2. Of medium length, set on high, strong at base, tapering regularly, well furnished with hair; carried proudly like the blade of a saber.
Hindquarters	Strong and muscular with good bend of stifle.
1. Thighs 2. Hocks	1. Well defined second thigh. 2. Short and well angulated.
Feet	Hard, tight padded, not too long. Nails strong and short.
Gait	The movement should be free at all paces, with great drive. Front action straight and reaching well forward; hocks turning neither in nor out.
Coat	Rough, long without exaggeration and harsh to the touch, with thick undercoat, never silky or woolly. Shown untrimmed.

Color	White with any combination of lemon, orange, tri-color or grizzle markings.
1. Height 2. Size	1. 33–38 cm (13–15").[3]
1. Proportion 2. Substance	—
1. Faults 2. Serious faults	1. Any departure from the foregoing points should be considered a fault and the seriousness with which the fault should be regarded should be in exact proportion to its degree. Knuckling over is highly undesirable.
1 Eliminating faults 2. Disqualification	—

Note: Male animals should have two apparently normal testicles fully descended into the scrotum.

American Kennel Club – 1990[4]

1. General appearance 2.Behavior/ Characteristics 3. Temperament	1&2. The PBGV is a scent hound developed to hunt small game over the rough and difficult terrain of the Vendéen region. To function efficiently he must be equipped with certain characteristics. He is bold and vivacious in character; compact, tough and robust in construction. He has an alert outlook, lively bearing and a good voice freely used. The most distinguishing characteristics of this bold hunter are his rough, unrefined outline; his proudly carried head, displaying definitive long eyebrows, beard and moustache; his strong, tapered tail carried like a saber, alert and in readiness. Important to the breed type is the compact, casual, rather tousled appearance,

---

[3] 1993 standard – height "34–38 cm (13.4–15"); *a tolerance of 1 cm (0.4") either way allowed.*" Amended 1994 to "33–38 cm (13–15")" to avoid conflict of 39 cm upper limit of PBGV with 39 cm lower height range of GBGV.

[4] American Kennel Club standard: approved August 14, 1990; effective February 1, 1991.

	with no feature exaggerated and his parts in balance. 3. Happy, extroverted, independent, yet willing to please.
1. Head 2. Skull	1. Carried proudly and, in size, must be in balance with the overall dog. It is longer than its width in a ratio of approximately 2:1. A coarse or overly large head is to be penalized. 2. Domed, oval in shape when viewed from the front. It is well cut away under the eyes and has a well developed occipital protuberance. Stop clearly defined.
1. Foreface 2. Muzzle	2. The length of the muzzle is slightly shorter than the length from stop to occiput. The underjaw is strong and well developed.
Lips	Covered by long hair forming a beard and moustache.
1. Jaw 2. Mouth 3. Bite	3. It is preferable that the teeth meet in a scissors bite but a level bite is acceptable.
Nose	Black and large, with wide nostrils. A somewhat lighter shading is acceptable in lighter colored dogs.
1. Eyes 2. Expression	1. Large and dark, showing no white. The red of the lower eyelid should not show. Surmounted by long eyebrows, standing forward but not obscuring the eyes. 2. Alert, friendly and intelligent.
Ears	Supple, narrow and fine, covered with long hair, folding inward and ending in an oval shape. The leathers reach almost to the end of the nose. They are set on low, not above the line of the eyes. An overly long or high-set ear should be penalized.
Neck	Long and strong, without throatiness, and flows smoothly into the shoulders.
Shoulders	Clean and well laid back. Upper arm approximately equal in length to the shoulder blade.
1. Front legs 2. Forequarters 3. Forearm 4. Pasterns	1–3. Elbows close to the body. The length of leg from elbow to ground should be slightly less than one-half the length from withers to ground. Viewed from the front, it is desirable that the

forelegs be straight, but a slight crook is acceptable. The leg is strong and well boned. 4. Strong and slightly sloping. Dewclaws may, or may not, be removed.

1. Body 2. Chest 3. Ribs	1. Muscular, somewhat longer than tall. 2. Deep, with prominent sternum. 3. Moderately rounded, extending well back.
1. Back/Topline 2. Loins 3. Croup	1&2. The back is level with a slight arch over a strong loin. Loin muscular and rounded about the lateral axis of the dog. 3. Viewed in profile, the withers and the croup should be equidistant from the ground.
1. Stern 2. Tail	2. Of medium length, set on high, it is strong at the base and tapers regularly. It is well furnished with hair, has but a slight curve and is carried proudly like the blade of a saber; normally about 20 degrees to the aft of vertical. In a curved downward position the tip of the tail bone should reach approximately to the hock joint.
Hindquarters	Strong and muscular with good bend of stifle
1. Thighs 2. Hocks	1. Well defined second thigh. 2. Short and well angulated, perpendicular from hock to ground.
Feet	Not too long, with hard, tight pads. Slight turnout of the front feet is acceptable. The nails are strong and short. Hind feet as in front, except that they must point straight ahead.
Gait	The movement should be free at all speeds. Front action is straight and reaching well forward. Going away, the hind legs are parallel and have great drive. Convergence of the front and rear legs towards his center of gravity is proportional to the speed of his movement. Gives the appearance of an active hound, capable of a full day's hunting.
Coat	Rough, long without exaggeration and harsh to the touch, with a thick shorter undercoat. It is never silky or woolly. The eyes are surmounted by long eyebrows, standing forward, but not obscuring the eyes. The ears are covered by long

hair. The lips are covered by long hair forming a beard and moustache. The tail is well furnished with hair. The overall appearance is casual and tousled. *Hounds are to be shown untrimmed.* Indications of scissoring for the purposes of shaping or sculpturing are to be severely penalized.

Color	White with any combination of lemon, orange, black, tri-color or grizzle markings.
1. Height 2. Size	2. Both sexes should measure between 13–15" at the withers, with a .5" tolerance in either direction being acceptable.
1. Proportion 2. Substance	1. Somewhat longer than tall. A correctly proportioned dog will be approximately 50% longer than tall when the entire body is measured from sternum to buttocks as compared to withers to ground. 2. Strong bone with substance in proportion to overall dog.
1. Faults 2. Serious faults	1. Any deviation from the ideal described in the standard should be penalized to the extent of the deviation. Structural faults common to all breeds are as undesirable in the PBGV as in any other breed, regardless of whether they are specifically mentioned. 2. Any tendency to knuckle over.
1 Eliminating faults 2. Disqualification	Height over 15.5" at the withers.

Interpretation of the Standard

Over the years much attention has been given to aiding interpretation of the standard to ensure there is no misunderstanding on any point. As a result, the standard has become longer.

An overview of the standards in this chapter helps draw together commonalties and highlights specifics, such as height:length comparison and length of tail (taken from the American Kennel Club standard for the breed).

General Appearance

A sturdy dog, rough and ready, with tousled appearance created by a rough coat. Not refined in outline in any way. This is an essential feature of correct breed type. He is neither quiet nor demure-looking, but rather appears as pent-up energy, noticing and making a comment on all he sees or meets. He is extremely balanced, with no feature exaggerated.

Size, Proportion, Substance

In referring to the PBGV as a working (hunting) dog, the conclusion is actually that he "should appear" capable of a day's hunting. Whether or not the animal is a "hunter" is irrelevant, but he must be strong and well muscled with the appearance of a working hound. He is between 13–15 inches, with a tolerance of half-inch either way (according to the American standard) at the withers and an average weight of between 25–38 pounds. Although great emphasis is put on size, it is not a case of "the smaller, the better." *Petit* means small; *but only by comparison with the family of other Griffon Vendéen hounds.*

More importantly, any dog within the correct range must be in complete balance in order to conform to the standard on all points. As a compact hound, the compactness should come from a short loin, combined with a good length of rib. The length of leg is not the sole determinant of what makes a Petit because, as the height increases, so do lengths of tail, ear, body and muzzle.

Head

The head is in balance with the compact body. It is a proud head carried high and with confidence. It is not long and is an oval shape. The length of muzzle is slightly less than the distance from the stop to occiput. The stop should be clearly defined. The expression is friendly, not in any way harsh. The ears are narrow and fine, folding inward to hold scent. They are set low, not above the line of the eye. The tip of the leathers should always be found when measuring for length, as the hair or furnishings can give them the appearance of being overly long.

Neck, Topline, Body

The same head, which is so often held and carried proudly, can be dropped with ease for scenting and following a trail. The neck must be long and strong, and set well into the shoulders. Viewed from the top over the dog, the neck will seem to flow into the shoulders gradually, evenly and cleanly. There should be no heaviness around the shoulders, but a smooth line. Because of the importance of a strong front, the shoulder assembly needs to fit well into the oval of the ribcage rather than seeming as though tacked on to the sides, creating a bowing in the upper arm. The ribs are rounded, more oval than barrel shape. The back is not overly long and topline is level in appearance, but a slight rise over the loin area is evident.

Forequarters and Hindquarters

The best test of proper placement of the front legs is with the dog in motion. Where and how does he place his feet under himself? As the dog moves towards you he does not single-track but, to support him, his front legs move inward and under his body toward his center of gravity. He should move free at all speeds. In going away, as he increases speed, his rear feet come underneath him. Hind legs move parallel and the rear of the dog provides the thrust and drive necessary for covering ground.

Like the rest of the body, the rear must be muscular and strong. The second thigh should be well defined and curved. The distance from hock to toes should be short. Good, balanced angulation, in harmony with the rest of the dog, will make for smooth and effortless motion. A choppy gait is useless for the dog as it easily causes fatigue. He needs stamina and staying power.

Front legs should be straight, with a little turnout of the feet acceptable. Any evidence of a bowing upper arm, or at the point of the elbow, is a fault in the bone structure of the dog. This and knuckling over are major faults, as it would be difficult for the dog to do a day's work with incorrect front construction. This, however, is a fault relatively easy to hide in the showring. Judges should not only give the dog a thorough examination to feel for any abnormalities, but should also raise the front end and let it fall naturally to see the true placement of the front legs and feet.

Tail

A well-carried tail helps to create the overall appearance of a well-balanced dog. It is of medium length, set on rather high, strong at the base and tapering like a candle to the tip. It has long hair, is carried proudly like the head and held like the blade of a saber. Like the ears, the hair on the tip of the tail can give an illusion of a tail being too long. It is easy to check the actual length by taking the tip and curving it downward to the hock joint. This is the ideal length.

Coat

PBGV coat length will vary with the texture; usually, the harder the hair, the shorter it will be. A dog with an extremely hard outer coat may be lacking in undercoat. The undercoat is for warmth; the outer, harsh coat for protection. Textures vary but should never be silky or woolly, although some coats have a slight wave. It is the harsh coat that creates the overall characteristic appearance of roughness.

In summary, remember first and foremost that the Petit Basset Griffon Vendéen is a rustic hound. He is a hunter with stamina, good voice and a sound body structure capable of a full day's work. Every breeder, every judge and every owner should bear in mind these important qualities for, without them, there is no true PBGV.

CHAPTER NINE

PET PETITS —
PERSONALITY PLUS!

The misery of keeping a dog is his dying so soon;
but to be sure if he lived for fifty years, and then died,
what would become of me?
—Sir Walter Scott (1771–1832)

There is a world of difference between being enchanted by the looks of a certain breed—and PBGV puppies are particularly strong on charm—and having one to care for as a family member.

If you are thinking about buying a PBGV, find out as much as you can about the breed. Admiring a friend's PBGV or one that you have seen on television is not enough. Do as much research as you can. Start by contacting the kennel club *and* the secretary of the breed club, who will be only too willing to help and to give you a list of reputable breeders. Check for details on the Internet, read dog papers and magazines, go to dog shows, chat with breeders. In this way you will get a feel for the different "type" each one produces.

Hello!

As we have already seen, type and breed characteristics are synonymous—but the combination of distinguishing features that add up to stamping the PBGV's individuality varies from one breeder to another. So take time to find the breeder who has the particular "type," or style, of PBGV that you are looking for.

Talk to people who already own PBGVs. You will then understand exactly what these endearing little characters are like, and you will be aware of what you are taking on.

Above all, bear in mind that PBGVs are *hounds*. Hunting is the *"raison d'être"* of any hound and natural instincts such as its nose, voice, exuberance and tenacity are what make a PBGV different from other breeds of dog.

So, what exactly does this mean for you, the prospective pet owner?

The Nose

As a scenthound, the PBGV uses his nose for hunting. Beneath the happy-go-lucky exterior is a complicated personality. The PBGV possesses all the highly tuned senses and cunning guile of any expert hunting hound, and a strong streak of independence sets it apart from the usual pet or lap dog.

Since the PBGV's hunting instincts are strong, he is constantly alert to anything that moves or emits a scent. The PBGV will sit motionless for long periods, just waiting and waiting. The slightest movement and he will leap into action, nose down and off after his quarry.

The Voice

One of the ways PBGVs communicate is with their voice. PBGVs' voices are deep in comparison with their size. Apart from the usual bark, an excited PBGV giving chase or with something to tell you will give voice with a full-throated "Arrrooooo!"

While this makes for an excellent watch-dog and deters any

Bracken doing what comes naturally.

would-be intruder, there is no doubt it can be annoying for neighbors, especially if your love for the breed tempts you into owning more than one. However, if it is protection you seek, do not consider having a PBGV. As outgoing characters, who lavish affection and licks on all they meet, aggression is not a word to associate with the breed.

The Exuberance and Tenacity

A PBGV, highly intelligent, quick to learn and eager to please, will settle easily into his new home environment. However, the breed has a high activity level. They are playful and full of curiosity and mischief.

Your PBGV will probably be no respecter of flowerbeds, and fences around the back yard or garden need to be escape-proof. You may be fortunate enough to have a home-loving PBGV

Dashing through the snow.

(and they do exist), but occasionally ones are born capable of hopping or bouncing to astonishing heights or, alternatively, digging very efficiently.

Novel methods of preventing PBGVs from escaping under fencing have ranged from putting anything from dogs' feces to bowling balls down the hole that has been dug. Further tales of woe have produced other good ideas.

"I have often read about PBGVs that dig out but have never before had this problem myself—until now. It has cost me two new fences and concrete gravel boards at the bottom, which we have sunk into the ground."

"We have gone through some pretty frustrating times with our guys digging. We had 20 tons of rock put down and they even dug through that. We had to lay down chicken-wire along the bottom. They still try but have to stop when they hit that. They are just so full of energy and want to keep exploring."

"Ours got stuck between our fence and the neighbors—she could hardly turn around. I had to dig a larger hole and show her how to wriggle backwards because it was too small an area for her to even turn around."

"Ours made great excavations under the doghouses, which would end up on four corners with huge holes underneath. After a while I admitted defeat. Then one cold, rainy night she chose to whelp her first litter a week early—under the dog house."

"I spent all my time replacing earth one of our PBGVs was digging out from under the conifers—and the flower beds that were extending onto the lawn. I resorted to laying large roofing slates under the conifers and edging the flower bed with bricks."

"I've got one escape artist. I bought fairly heavy gauge mesh in rolls and wired it to the existing fence but left about

12–18 inches on the ground and stomped it down. It's worked!
Eventually the grass grows over it and the little darlings can't
dig because there's mesh fencing preventing them from
making any headway."

Is this the Breed for You?

If you:

- are looking for a laid-back, quiet breed,
- want to walk your dog off-leash in urban areas, or
- value your light-colored upholstery, carpeting or
  fragile collectibles...

think again!

However, if you accept this innocent devilment, have a great
sense of humor, patience and time; and in general, prefer a
smart dog to an obedient one—and you decide that the breed is
for you, you are now ready to embark on the exciting adventure
of finding the little character who will change your life for ever.

Finding the Right Puppy

The time has come to contact a reputable breeder. To ensure
that you get exactly what you want, be prepared to do a little
traveling and to wait until the breeder of your choice has a
litter—it will be well worth it in the long run. A good breeder
will always be willing to advise you and can pass on a wealth
of knowledge to help you rear your new puppy.

Call the breeder and explain exactly what you want. Ask
questions. If you are happy with the answers you get, make an
appointment to visit, even if there are no puppies available at
the time. A good breeder will ask *you* questions, too.

- Are you sure you are not buying on impulse?
- Have you ever owned a dog before? If so, what
  breed?
- Why did you decide on a PBGV?
- Do you have a good size garden or yard?

- Is it well fenced?
- What is your lifestyle? Do you work outside your home?
- If so, what arrangements are there to make sure your PBGV is cared for and has company?
- Do you have children? Are they old enough to treat the puppy with respect?
- Do you want a household pet or one for showing?
- Why do you want the sex you have chosen?

These are all questions *you* should ask *yourself* to be satisfied that you are doing the right thing.

When you visit the breeder's home or kennels, you will be able to see the dam and, possibly, the sire—unless it lives elsewhere, in which case the breeder may be able to show you a photo of him. Ask, too, to see any other PBGVs. Reputable breeders will be only too willing and proud to let you see them. If the dogs look fit and healthy and are in clean living conditions, you can feel confident that your own puppy will be happy and well.

Don't worry if you are asked not to handle any puppies. Until they have been inoculated, any source of infection may be fatal. So, respect the breeder's wishes.

A good breeder will always aim to produce a litter of strong, healthy, contented puppies, who will make several families very happy. Each puppy will be good in its own way but, from the litter, one may have those extra few features that make it a promising show prospect. So, by the time you see the puppies, the breeder may have already decided to keep one back for showing. If you, too, want to show, make sure you ask early, have a good choice or are prepared to wait for the right one.

The breeder will help you with any decisions you have to make, talk about any health problems you are likely to meet, discuss feeding and grooming and, most importantly, depending on its age, let you know the number of sets of vaccines and de-worming the puppy has had.

Collecting your Puppy

When the exciting day arrives, you should not only come away from the breeder carrying the precious newcomer to your family, you should also leave with a wealth of information and paperwork.

Breeders typically give you a health record showing exactly what treatment your puppy has received to ensure he is in peak condition.

You should also receive a bill of sale, pedigree form, guidance on how to transfer ownership to you and, if available, information about how to insure your puppy. Accidents or veterinary bills can be expensive.

Remember to ask for a diet sheet. Your puppy is likely to be unsettled going to his new home so continuity of diet is important, and the breeder should give you a supply of whatever food the pup has been used to. This should make the transition easier by avoiding any digestive upsets. You can introduce any changes gradually once your puppy is settled.

When collecting your pup, it is a good idea to take something such as an old towel from home, which will give him an idea of smells to come. The breeder may also give you a piece of bedding, a toy or something that the pup will associate with its previous home, making the move from the old to new home that much easier.

Carry something to clean up with, too; in case your puppy is travel sick on the way home.

Advance Preparation

Before collecting your puppy, make sure you know the name and telephone number of your local veterinarian. Better still, make sure you have everything you need at home to help your PBGV settle in well. Some items you will need immediately, others can wait until your puppy is a little older.

Basic Puppy Needs

Dog bed, basket or crate	Suitable bedding
Water bowl	Feeding bowl
Diet sheet	Canned or dry puppy food
Milk	Collar and dog tag
Light puppy leash	Comb, brush, shampoo
Safe chew products	A dog crate
First aid kit	Small dog biscuit treats/ rewards

Getting to Know Each Other

Try to bring your puppy home fairly early in the day. This allows time for the newcomer to get to know both you and the new environment. Holiday periods are far from ideal since the extra excitement and noise will frighten and confuse. Ideally, pick a routine day or the beginning of a weekend.

During the first few hours, watch your puppy as he explores and gets used to his new home. If you already have dogs, introduce them one at a time—too many at once will be overpowering and frighten your puppy. It may take a little while for the "oldies" to accept the newcomer, so be ready to separate them if there are any signs of aggression. Pay equal attention to the puppy and your older dogs, who may become jealous if ignored.

Whether or not you already have dogs, the puppy will miss his mother and littermates, so warmth at night and a draft-free spot are top priorities. Ideally the area should be quiet. However, the PBGV has a great liking for human company. Rest is important for your new puppy but, when awake, he needs lots of attention to exercise his agile mind. So don't cut him off completely from family activity since he needs to socialize.

Teething...crying at night...toilet training. Do these sound familiar? Puppies, like human babies, go through stages of growth and learning. If you aren't prepared to experience it with them, don't have one! However, most people will tell you that the short period of inconvenience is well worth the many years of joy your PBGV will bring you.

Teething

Your puppy will be teething, so wait a while before you buy that expensive dog bed. A low-sided plastic crate will do for the early days. Cheaper still is a strong cardboard box, with one side cut down for getting in and out. Or consider a wire dog crate, more expensive, but this will give many years' service. The pup will soon get used to this little house and feel secure inside it, even with the door left open. It is portable, ever so useful when traveling, and your PBGV will adapt easily to being left for a short time with the door shut.

Whatever type you decide on, make sure it is not too large and is easy to clean. As your puppy grows, you can replace this with a larger, adult-sized bed or even a bean bag once your PBGV has outgrown the chewing stage.

The PBGV is a playful breed with a mischievous mind, full of life and curiosity. You can minimize damage to bedding and your own furniture if you channel your puppy's chewing into constructive behavior by ensuring a good supply of suitably safe toys or bones.

Crying

You may, of course, be lucky enough to have a puppy that

snuggles down with the blanket, or whatever you brought back from the breeder, and sleeps straight away. However, be prepared for a few restless nights. The newcomer may cry when first left alone. This will test you! Are you strong enough to teach him where his own bed is—or are you going to give in and let him sleep with you?

Remember, once allowed into your cozy bedroom, you will find this a difficult habit to break.

Try giving the puppy a well-wrapped hot-water bottle to provide warmth and comfort in his own surroundings. If this fails, when you hear crying or barking at night, open the door and smack the floor with a rolled-up newspaper. Shout, "Quit!" and slam the door shut. This may seem harsh, but your puppy will soon associate its yapping with an unpleasant noise and the crying will stop.

Housebreaking

Training your puppy from the outset is important. This includes teaching him to be clean indoors. However, don't expect miracles at the beginning. Until about 12 or 13 weeks old, he will have little control over his bladder. If he has been kennel reared, expect learning to take slightly longer than it would for a PBGV who began life indoors.

Like many hound breeds, PBGVs are extremely sensitive so *don't* automatically punish or hit your puppy after an accident or you may end up with a nervous, frightened dog. Above all, don't rub his nose in the feces, or you will end up with a bewildered PBGV who feels rejected and afraid.

Do not give the newcomer full run of the house because, as with all puppies, accidents *will* happen—and probably on your best carpet! But a well-toned "Aargh" or "Yuk!" will work wonders. Remember it is *your* responsibility to help your PBGV puppy learn. Praise, encouragement and reward at the right time will produce far better results and give confidence.

Start house training as soon as you arrive home. Always put

your puppy outside right after every meal or as soon as he wakes up. Praise him lavishly when he does the right thing. In this way the puppy soon learns what is routine. In the evening, put your PBGV outside as late as possible to help him to manage through the night. Put layers of newspaper near the door away from your puppy's bed so he gets the idea where to go in emergencies. Once he begins to move around, the kidneys increase activity to clear the body of toxins and filter the blood, so the frequency of urination increases. During the day, when you can leave the door open, gradually move the newspaper from inside to just outside the door. Leave a small piece of soiled paper with the clean layers for smell association.

Remember routine plays an important part in successful housebreaking. Have patience. Your PBGV is keen to please. Give plenty of encouragement and understanding and you will be surprised how quickly he learns. By four months, he should be fully reliable.

Diet and Good Eating Habits

All PBGV puppies need plenty of food in the first few months so that they grow into adults with good bone and substance. Good bone cannot be made—it is inherited. However, much can be done to improve it or to encourage it to develop during these formative months.

As the proud owner, you will naturally want your PBGV puppy to grow up fit and healthy and to reach his full potential. The first few months are vital. Now is the time your highly active puppy, who is growing rapidly, will need a digestible and enjoyable diet of just the right blend of protein, carbohydrates, minerals, fats and vitamins. However, the diet must be balanced to ensure your PBGV receives the correct amount of nutrients. The diet should also be concentrated so your pup takes in all the nutrients needed before he is full.

The breeder's diet sheet will tell you how much to feed your PBGV during his first few months with you. It will be a good guide so don't be in too much of a hurry to alter this. There will be time enough to change type or brand once your puppy has settled in. There is no substitution for good common sense when deciding how much to feed.

Look at any old dog-care book and you find marvelous diet sheets that relied heavily on items such as calcium phosphate powder, raw or cooked minced meat and vegetables, brown bread, cod liver oil, raw eggs and evaporated milk.

With balanced commercial canned dog foods, dry complete feed, biscuit, milk powder and supplements of combined vitamins, minerals and nutrients, the puppy owner has a relatively easy time producing a good, strong, healthy dog.

Both the old and new methods are good in their own way. If you have an obstinate or finicky feeder and feeding by hand fails, it may be a simple case of changing diet to find something that suits. However, if your puppy is happy with what you are giving him, don't change the diet just for the sake of it.

Try to feed your puppy at the same time each day and in the same area so that good feeding habits develop alongside this daily routine. Unlike many breeds, PBGVs on the whole tend to be well-mannered eaters. They will inspect food before accepting it very gently. The adult dog has a good appetite and any favorite food will be devoured steadily. Bear in mind that your ideal is neither a thin dog nor one that is overweight. Aim to have a well-balanced hound with plenty of flesh over his ribs and the healthy appearance that goes with a well-fed animal.

Number of Meals a Day

2 months to 3 months	4 meals a day
3 months to 6 months	3 meals a day
6 months to 12 months	2 meals a day

Suggested Diet

2–3 months

Breakfast Complete puppy food, amount as recommended by the manufacturer, softened with warm water or a mixture of warm water and milk (either evaporated or goat's milk). To make the food more palatable and to give the puppy extra nutrition, mix in a small amount of canned puppy food.

If you are not feeding a complete dry food and only a biscuit mixer, you will need to add more canned food. Always ensure a good supply of water nearby.

Mid-day Repeat breakfast.

Or

Milky porridge, made with evaporated or goat's milk.

Late afternoon Repeat breakfast.

Late evening Repeat breakfast.

Some prefer to end the puppy's day with warm milk. However, be warned, your puppy is unlikely to last the night if he has had a large drink.

4–6 months

Breakfast Complete puppy food, amount as recommended by the manufacturer, dry or softened with warm water. This can be fed alone or with a small amount of canned puppy food mixed in. Always ensure a good supply of water nearby.

Or

Half a can of puppy food, with puppy mixer.

Mid-to-late afternoon Milky porridge, made with evaporated or goat's milk.

Or

Repeat breakfast.

Evening Repeat breakfast.

7–12 months

Complete puppy food twice a day, either dry or with warm water, amount as recommended by the manufacturer. Mix in small amounts of canned puppy food or feed alone. Supply of cold water nearby.

Or

Two meals a day of half a can of puppy food with puppy mixer.

As an extra, give milk, a raw (or boiled) egg, diced baked chicken or cottage cheese in small amounts. Your puppy's movements may become loose until he adjusts to this new food. The decision on whether to continue feeding milk alone or mixed with food after weaning is a personal choice. Give nutritional supplement sparingly. Good quality manufactured food contains all the nutrients your puppy needs, so you could do more harm than good by overdosing.

Children and your Puppy

PBGVs are lively hounds and any children in the family must learn how to respect the new puppy. They should not pull him around, handle him too much or over-excite him. Rather, they need to be

Innocence.

gentle and considerate.

It is your responsibility to ensure the puppy isn't squeezed, teased or hurt in any way. Avoid accidents by not leaving pup and child together without supervision. All family members can play an active part in puppy care. Your child may like the responsibility of grooming him regularly, while an adult can clean ears or trim nails.

Socialization

At this early age, from 8 to 12 weeks, the contact and love your PBGV puppy gets from you and your children is very important. All this socialization will help make him secure and will build a permanent bond between you. This relationship will stand you in good stead when expecting your puppy to accept gentle discipline.

Exercise

A puppy scampering around and playing will get all the exercise he needs. Great damage can be done by over exercising while your pup is still growing, and too much running about when under six months old is likely to harm developing limbs. So, above all, don't let your puppy go up and down steps or stairs until at least six months old as jarring the PBGV's short front legs may lead to malformed front limbs and being out at elbow.

Similarly, don't let your puppy get into the bad habit of climbing up onto your best sofa. Both the effort of pulling himself up and jarring his limbs when jumping down is likely to damage them. The associated problems of allowing him to "take over" your favorite chair and become a couch potato are self-evident.

Never pick up your puppy under the armpits or by the front legs. Support the entire body by placing one hand under the chest, between the front legs and the other hand under his bottom. This will make your puppy feel comfortable and he will be less inclined to wriggle if you are carrying him somewhere.

Leash Training

Leash training time will soon arrive but, in the early days, sessions should be frequent and brief. Attention span is short at this age and your puppy will tire quickly. Neither leash training nor socialization with unknown dogs should take place in public areas until the pup has had his full set of vaccines, which is usually at about 12 to 14 weeks of age.

Begin by getting your puppy used to wearing a light collar. It is best not to leave this on for long periods since young puppies are into everything and a collar can get hooked on low branches or caught on another dog's nails and restrict breathing. When introducing the leash itself, your pup may initially buck all over place, pull away or simply sit down and refuse to budge. If you have an older hound, linking the two together can be a great training aid since your puppy will follow. If not, be patient and firm. Don't lose your temper. It is vital that you don't frighten your puppy at this stage. Rather, lavish praise for something done well.

At four months, give your puppy a little exercise, possibly a run in an enclosed field or park. Very short spells of road walking are also excellent for tightening up his feet at this crucial time in development.

The Collar and Leash

Your PBGV has a harsh coat. A choke collar or chain around the neck can be an effective training tool, but you will soon find that it tears at your puppy's coat, resulting in short, flat hair around the neck, which is undesirable if you want to show.

Beware, too, of the body harness. Although ideal for controlling your exuberant PBGV and for preventing pulling, too much use may also wear away the coat, not only around the neck but over the shoulder blades and under the arms as well.

A rolled leather or nylon noose-type slip collar or choke chain with larger links will help reduce hair damage. However, many favor the nose halter. Like a horse's halter, it controls from the head. All a dog's pulling power is in its shoulders. Use a normal collar or chain around the neck and the power is still there. Put the harness around the dog's head and nose and you reduce your PBGV's ability to pull, with the bonus of no damage to the coat. It may take your puppy a little while to accept but, after a few outings of rubbing his nose on the ground, you will find your walks are enjoyable.

As your puppy gets older, introduce the various types of control—leather collar with leash attached, choke chain, harness, nose halter—to find out which one works best for your PBGV. Devote just a short time each day to training and your hound will accept any type of collar. This is especially useful if you need greater control when walking more than one dog. No longer will your PBGV tow you along the road like a competitor in a Husky race!

Pets Win Prizes

Own a PBGV and you will soon be owned *by* him. Countless adjectives describe the breed—unrepentant, stubborn, sweet, smart, rugged, active, curious, exuberant and, above all, happy.

Combine that deep musical voice with a rear-end that is constantly wagging; the quick, lively gait and high activity level with a busy nature—and you have the irresistible PBGV. Whether yours is a top-winning show-dog or a family pet, the greatest prize that he will ever win is your heart.

Here are a few exceptional PBGVs that illustrate just what special dogs they are.

Plain Sailing with a PBGV

Mike and Glenna Clark chose Monkhams Cadfael ("Bracken") because they were keen to ensure that he would be a seafaring type of guy. From ten weeks he wore his little life jacket around him for short periods. He even took it to bed with him. This familiarization process helped avoid any traumatic experiences when he was first introduced to their dinghy. From the small dinghy, Bracken progressed to life on board their boat, where he was allowed to wander around always under their watchful eye. He soon found his favorite spot to lie down—the hatchway. Each session on board and every stage of learning was always followed up by a reward of playing on the beach.

"Ahoy there!" Captain Bracken in sailing mood.

As Bracken grew, he ventured further afield until he was strong enough to climb up on deck and is now often seen on board in the English waters around Devon and Cornwall. He commands from the bow or, when wanting a change of scenery, goes to the back of the boat and sits with his paw on the tiller. During rougher weather he stays below, comes up occasionally to sniff the sea air both seaward and landward, takes stock of where he is and goes back below. What better life for a seadog?

Stars in His Eyes

Dudley lives with actress and film star Mary Tyler Moore, who wrote, "To my constant delight is the number of grim-faced New Yorkers who end up smiling from ear to ear on seeing Dudley and inevitably ask me what kind of dog he is.

"When I give the name 'Petit Basset Griffon Vendéen' followed by the impressive 'dating from the 16th century,' etc., background, they often back away shaking their heads, empathizing with poor

Dudley with doting owner Mary Tyler Moore.

Mary Tyler Moore, who was obviously sold a bill of goods. Dudley and I share a laugh over this."

Who Hunts Rabbits?

John and Susan Wilbur moved from Chicago to Barbados in 1996. After a round-trip spell of quarantine in England, their two PBGVs, "Emily" (Jamar 'n Fitzcap's Emily) and "Phoebe" (Monkhams Tuppence), joined them on the island. They soon acclimatized to the heat and realized that life in this British independent state wasn't too bad after all.

Emily took charge of patrolling the perimeter of the grounds to ward off monkeys who came in to eat mangoes and, between them, she and Phoebe spent much of the cooler part of the day checking for birds, frogs, mongooses and, above all, lizards. Hunters' paradise!

So—Who Does Hunt Rabbits?

PBGVs may be natural hunting dogs, with incomparable scenting ability, chasing and killing hare and rabbit by instinct if the opportunity presents itself. But when the Ritchies brought "Tracker" (Emeraude Tyto Albavultus), a ten-week-old whirling dervish, into their home in Lebanon, Indiana, they soon realized he was different.

Al Ritchie recalled,

> I don't know what we were expecting, but he would run in circles, jump on everything, drag things all round the house—he just went crazy for an hour every night and then collapsed in deep sleep. Nothing seemed to control him—nothing until his housemate Kiss-Kiss, a three-pound black bunny, decided to say who was the boss! Kiss-Kiss would chase Tracker around the house and they became great friends.
>
> As Tracker got bigger and older, the bunny was slightly out-classed in exuberance and weight, but if Tracker bugged him to play and he didn't want to, he would cer-

tainly put this PBGV in his place! Tracker could have killed him with one lunge, but he never showed an ounce of aggression towards his little buddy. When Kiss-Kiss died after seven years of companionship, Tracker's heart

One dog and his bunny.

was broken. For weeks he kept looking and wouldn't go near the room where the bunny spent his last two weeks.

An All-Star Team

For many years Ken Caminiti's life revolved around his passion—baseball. Ken started his professional career as third base with the Houston Astros. In 1995, he was traded to the Californian San Diego Padres. Top honors followed. In 1996 he was voted the National League's Most Valuable Player and he became a three-time Golden Glove winner.

Despite moving with the sport, permanent residence has always been Texas. There the family home has included a much loved Cocker Spaniel, but in 1997 Ken found a new interest—PBGVs. With friend Bruce Smith, he became co-owner of the "one-in-a-million" Ch. Pepperhill-Dehra Charmaine. Charmaine lives just one street away with Bruce and his wife Debby. When in town, Ken visits almost daily, determined to get his PBGV-fix. Charmaine soon won them over by her magnificent, typical PBGV attitude. In less than two years, she was awarded 65 Group 1s and 13 BISS, something of an achievement considering the previous BIS record was four. But, for all her achievements in the showring, Charmaine is primarily a much loved household member. Debby enthused, "She is truly one of a kind and we are blessed to call her ours."

CHAPTER TEN

YOUR PBGV's HEALTH

We all care for our dogs, but caring is not enough.
Caring without knowing means that we are often
bewildered in the face of illness...
—(Foreword by) James Herriott, The Dog Owner's
Veterinary Handbook, *Bower and Young 1989*

Many new owners are keen to learn or, in the early days, want advice on puppy care. For the novice owner there is a wealth of alternative information available on how to look after your dog, from puppy through adulthood. Therefore, in this book we only touch on dog care general to all breeds. Our main focus is to give advice on aspects specific to this breed, on what it means to own a PBGV and how to care for one.

Since we are inexpert on veterinary matters, we are very grateful to Kasmin Bittle, DVM, North Carolina, for detailing known health problems in the breed. Under the kennel name of Pathos, Kasmin has been involved with PBGVs since 1989 when she bought her first dog from Pepperhill. Like many others, Kasmin has taken an active interest in the breed and, at the PBGVCA's invitation, she established and chaired a Health Committee in 1994 in response to her request that the club look into the known problem of aseptic meningitis within the breed. All owners of the breed will, we are sure, benefit from reading her contribution.

Selecting a Healthy Puppy

The first challenge facing the prospective PBGV owner is choosing a healthy puppy. Good healthcare begins in the whelping box and continues throughout the remainder of the puppy's life.

Remember to talk with several experienced and reputable breeders before selecting your puppy. Responsible PBGV breeders are knowledgeable about health problems within the breed and should be willing to discuss these with you both before and after purchase. They select dogs to breed not only based on appearance but also on their health.

A reputable breeder should be able to deliver a well-socialized puppy that has been weaned from the mother at least two to three weeks prior to sale. The puppy is then fully prepared to "go it alone," with human assistance, in his new home. He should preferably have had at least one set of vaccines and two de-wormings or fecal analysis for parasites before leaving the breeder's premises. The puppy should also receive a thorough physical examination by a veterinarian, either just before sale or soon after. Health warranties are best discussed before sale.

Diet and Protection against Worms

Whatever feeding plan you use, make sure your dog is getting top quality. Also, to get the best out of the food, worm regularly. The two main types of worms found in dogs are roundworms (nematodes) and tapeworms (cestodes). Of these, roundworms are usually the more common. All nursing bitches and puppies tend to have roundworm. Most of the puppy's worms are acquired in the uterus or via the bitch's milk. As opinions differ, consult your veterinarian before any mating for advice on optimum time to treat the bitch. Also ask the vet about the type, dosage and frequency of worming your PBGV from the time he is a puppy through routine worming in adulthood.

Beneficial Exercising into Adulthood

Complete fitness is essential. This can be achieved by careful feeding and plenty of controlled exercise. Letting your hound run freely in the back yard is fun for the dog and fine for you but, once your PBGV is mature, road work is necessary to tighten up feet, harden the pads, shorten nails and build muscle tone. PBGVs are working hounds and, if you intend showing yours, he must be in good hard condition, well covered, neither fat nor too lean.

Grooming for Health

If the standards still hold good, surely we are right in assuming that they define a quality of coat that can be got in a natural manner, without resort to artifice?

—The Kennel

Even a century ago in England, the questionable practice of trimming certain breeds was discussed at a Kennel Club meeting! *Never* trim your PBGV—the breed is characterized by its tousled appearance. However, unless your hound is a hunter whose coat is stripped naturally by brambles and dense undergrowth, he will need attention to keep him looking his best.

Whether or not you intend showing, grooming is an important routine and should begin soon after purchase. Although your puppy will have a short coat until he is approximately four months old, thorough combing at this age will accustom him to the more essential combing of the mature coat. PBGV coats vary considerably from dog to dog and from puppy into adulthood. Generally they do not shed much. However, during seasonal shedding periods regular attention removes dead hair and particles of dirt. It encourages production of natural oils that provide protection from the weather and helps give a healthy appearance when your dog is in good condition.

Importantly, this close attention gives the opportunity to

check for parasites, small wounds or any abnormality, such as skin tumor, which may require a veterinary check. A grooming session, at least once a week from early days, will encourage your new puppy to enjoy the sensation and will probably be followed by a joyful and proud run about the yard.

Use a fairly stiff pin-brush or comb with well-spaced teeth. A wire slicker brush or hound glove is particularly useful for grooming the body. Extra care needs to be taken with facial hair as, being a bearded breed known for its inquisitive nature, all manner of things collect in this area. Using a comb, gently tease out any knots or other matter from the beard. Vigorous brushing all over the body keeps the coat tidy and in good condition. Carefully comb the legs, paying particular attention to under the armpits and the insides of elbows and thighs to remove any matted hair.

Also brush or comb the tail, remembering to check the hair under the root and around the anus, where matted hair may also form or become soiled. While scissoring is not allowed and will remove the tousled, natural look of the breed, this is a sensitive area, so you may need to cut hair out carefully. Other areas where scissoring is acceptable are under the paws and between the pads, which will give better traction on slick floors, and around the sheath of a male, where plucking the hair by hand could hurt.

Don't just rely on a brush or comb to smarten up your PBGV. A little hand-stripping will enhance appearance, especially if you intend to show. Time and experience will help you become expert at making your PBGV look his best. To hand-strip, take a few hairs between your finger and thumb and tug sharply in the direction of growth. On the head, pluck any long hair off the ears. This will remove any heavy look and make them look neater and in proportion with the length of foreface.

Profuse hair growing forward and obscuring vision should be tidied and shortened and a small amount of hair growing at the inside corners of the eyes should also be removed. Pluck until your dog's eyes can be seen when viewed from the front.

Long hair around the feet also needs attention to enhance the neat shape and to discourage matting, burrs or dirt build-up. If the hair at the tip of the tail is unduly long, pluck off the excess and your PBGV will look more balanced, with the tip of his tail just reaching his hocks when lowered. A thick ridge of hair tends to build up on either side of the neck. Removal of this enhances its length. Any overly long hair hanging from the stomach should also be removed to give a clean outline but, remember, *never* scissor! Thinning sheers or a stripping knife are useful tools, but, as they encourage regrowth, hand stripping is preferable.

The amount of tidying a PBGV needs differs between individuals, whose texture and quality of coat may differ, but remember to keep hand-stripping to a minimum. Your PBGV is distinguishable by his unrefined outline and natural appearance.

Bathing

Unlike some hound breeds, the PBGV is not known for exuding a distinctive smell. He does, however, have a reputation for rooting around in just about anything, which may persuade you that regular bathing is desirable. Bathing too often will remove the natural oils from your PBGV's coat but, if showing regularly, bath your hound a couple of days beforehand, preferably with an insecticidal shampoo that will help prevent bringing home extra passengers.

Coat texture is a product of heredity, so the softening that occurs following bathing is only temporary. Coat harshness is a result of the diameter of the hair shaft and this is not altered by bathing. An apparent increase in texture on the dirty dog is caused by dirt particles on the hair shaft, very similar to the effect created by powder some use before showing. An experienced judge can tell the difference. Frequent bathing results in clean dogs with unstained coats. For dogs that are chronically dirty, last minute baths prior to shows will not remove the evidence of neglect. If your PBGV ever shows signs of skin problems, consult a veterinary dermatologist.

Ears, Nails and Teeth

These aspects of dog care may be the ones that novice owners either worry about most or ignore completely. They are so important. PBGVs have fairly large ear flaps that fall close to the head, thus stopping air getting to the ear canal. Consequently, problems can arise. Therefore, the inside of the ears should be checked regularly for signs of mites, canker or excessive wax. Odor and discharge usually indicate the presence of either yeast or bacterial ear infections, which will need veterinary treatment.

Some PBGVs have excessive hair growing both within and around the openings of the ear canals so, to help ventilation, remove some of the hair from inside the ear. The ear is sensitive so, again, do this by tugging sharply but gently a few hairs at a time, either with your fingers or hemostats, in the direction of growth. Use of ear powder first will help dry the hairs and allow a firmer grip.

Healthy ears need only minor cleaning of the ear flap, going gently into the ear canal. *Do not go too deep.* Use cotton swabs moistened with a proprietary ear-cleaning solution. This will leave the ears clean, cool and sweet-smelling.

The long hair covering your PBGV's ears tends to trap objects like foxtails and, if you find him rubbing his ear along the ground or shaking his head, chances are a foreign body has entered the ear canal. This will need your veterinarian's attention. Neither delay, as considerable pain can result, nor try and deal with this yourself. You will do more harm than good.

An adult PBGV given the right amount of roadwork will have nice, short nails, but it is worthwhile spending a few minutes each week checking feet to ensure that long nails, burrs, grit or other foreign bodies are not causing discomfort or difficulty walking. Good habits start early.

Most PBGVs dislike nail trimming and will not hesitate to voice their concern. Don't be afraid to check your puppy's feet and trim nails. If done regularly from the beginning, it will be accepted as part of the grooming process and, most importantly, nails will be kept under control. If dewclaws have not been removed, don't neglect these or you will find a curled, sharp saber ready to catch on anything, embed itself in your dog's lower leg or, worse still, get caught and be ripped out.

Use good quality, sharp clippers and cut the nail as near as possible to the quick, without causing bleeding. If the nail is white it is easy to see how far back to cut, especially when wet. Black is more difficult, but look underneath and you will see a thinner layer which extends back to just above the area housing the quick, showing you where it is safe to cut. If in doubt, trim a little at first, then file down.

Alternately, buy a good quality nail grinder. It takes longer but may save a lot of anguish all round. If you do damage the quick, don't worry. Despite the bleeding, there will be no permanent harm, although your PBGV may be wary and reluctant the next time round. If the bleeding continues, use one of the products available to coat the end of the nail. This forms a thin film and stops blood escaping.

Large knucklebones for gnawing are a natural, ideal way to keep your adult PBGV's teeth and gums healthy. There are also many good quality, hard chews designed specifically to give your dog hours of pleasure while helping to remove tartar and provide the dental care needed. However, this is not enough. Check and brush your dog's teeth regularly.

It is important that your PBGV's teeth cleaning is a pleasant experience. Start by simply handling his mouth for several minutes daily. Then gently hold it closed with one hand, lift up the lip on one side and rub the teeth and gums with your finger. A few days later, you can add a ribbed, proprietary finger-stall that comes with canine toothpaste or use a small, medium-bristle toothbrush. Rub or brush in a circular motion. To clean the inner surface of the teeth, hold the muzzle from the top and gently pull back the head so that the mouth opens. Lack of this simple care will result in a heavy build-up of tartar, which your veterinarian will need to remove under anesthetic.

Make all these jobs part of a regular routine with your dog. It takes only a few minutes each day and your PBGV will enjoy the personal attention. As a result, he'll look his best and you will have a happy, healthy, long-living companion.

Specific PBGV Health Problems

Although overall the PBGV breed is generally robust, some health problems, have been noted. Their impact varies, and many have been noted in other breeds. In the following discussion, cosmetic problems such as soft coats and underbites are not discussed. Problems such as these may be present in pet quality puppies without affecting their suitability as pets. Likewise, some pet puppies may grow to above or below the ideal height standard. Again, as long as they are otherwise healthy, they are perfectly suitable companions.

Some of the disorders below are congenital and some are developmental. Congenital means present at birth. A congenital defect may or may not be hereditary. Developmental problems are those that develop as the animal matures.

Persistent pupillary membranes (PPMs) These are blood vessel remnants, originating from the iris of the eye and found within the anterior chamber of the eye (the fluid-filled space between the iris and the cornea). Pupillary membranes are a normal neonatal structure that should regress by the age of eight weeks. When the vascular strands persist beyond this period, they are called persistent pupillary membranes. In most instances, the presence of these strands causes no visual impairment or discomfort to the animal. If the strands are unattached, except to the iris, they may persist or regress with time without causing visual deficits. However, if the strands attach to the cornea (the clear membrane on the surface of the eye), they will cause permanent gray spots, also known as dystrophies, on the cornea. These dystrophic areas may be quite small, even pin-point, or they may be larger, causing gray patches on the cornea. Likewise, if the strands attach to the front of the lens of the eye, a cataract may be found at this location. Visual impairment results only if there is extensive corneal involvement or if a large area of the lens is affected by the attachments.

Fortunately, most PBGVs have iris-to-iris PPMs that often improve with age. PPMs are a non-progressive disorder. Dogs may be checked for the disorder as early as eight weeks of age; but importantly those examined later in life may show no evidence of the disease due to regression of the strands. However, if the strands were present at a young age, the dog is still genetically affected with the abnormality. From a genetic standpoint it is therefore useful to have puppies examined soon after weaning. The mode of inheritance in PBGVs is not known but, in the Basenji, the trait is an autosomal dominant with incomplete penetrance.

Retinal folds/Retinal dysplasia Areas of abnormal retina, the reflective layer of the eye. These folds represent areas of retinal detachment and may be straight, curved or triangular; single or multiple. Retinal folds rarely affect vision when present only as infrequent folds. However, in some breeds of dogs such as the Labrador Retriever, severe retinal dysplasia may be manifested as nearly complete retinal detachment with blindness. Retinal folds may be diagnosed at a very young age, 8–12 weeks, and do not worsen with time. Breeding animals may therefore be screened for the defect as puppies. The mode of inheritance of retinal dysplasia in PBGVs is not known.

Cataracts Opacities of the normally clear lens. In PBGVs most cataracts are found on the front capsule of the lens and are caused by PPMs. These cataracts are usually not progressive.

Glaucoma An increase in intraocular pressure. Glaucoma may be classified as either primary or secondary and as either open or narrow/closed angle. Primary glaucoma is an increase in intraocular pressure without preceding or concomitant ocular disease. It is usually an inherited disorder.

Different breeds are susceptible to different types of glaucoma. In the normal eye, fluid behind the lens circulates around the lens and through the pupillary opening and is removed from the eye via pectinate ligaments located between the angle of the iris and the cornea. If this iridocorneal angle is either narrow, closed or malformed, then drainage of aqueous fluid is impaired, resulting in glaucoma. When narrowing, malformation or closure of the angle precedes the increase in intraocular pressure, narrow angle glaucoma is diagnosed.

Some prediction as to the propensity to develop narrow or closed angle glaucoma may be made by examination of the iridocorneal angle using a technique called gonioscopy. However, in some breeds of dogs, such as the Beagle, the drainage angle remains open until very advanced stages of disease. This open angle glaucoma may not be noticed until the chronic increase in intraocular pressure causes lens luxation or subluxation or an acutely painful eye. Open angle glaucoma, often with the late development of lens luxation, is believed to be inherited as an autosomal recessive trait in the Beagle. To date, not enough PBGVs have been examined early to confirm whether relatively mild increases in intraocular pressure precede the later development of lens luxation and severe glaucoma. To minimize the spread of this disease, it is recommended that breeding stock be examined at least annually and that tonometry, the measurement of intraocular pressure, be included as part of each eye examination.

Glaucoma is usually an adult onset disease and is only rarely diagnosed in animals less than one year of age. Each eye examination reflects only a moment in time and does not, in the case of open angles, preclude the later development of glaucoma.

Because of the devastating consequences of this disease, affected or questionable animals should not be bred.

Lens luxation Partial (subluxation) or complete displacement of the lens from its normal anatomic position behind the pupil. It may result in glaucoma due to forward pressure placed upon the iris, which narrows the drainage angle between the iris and the cornea. Long-standing increases in intraocular pressure may also cause disruption of the lens attachments and result in lens luxation. Many Terriers are affected with lens luxation. The interrelationship between lens luxation and glaucoma in many breeds has not yet been clarified. Many affected animals are presented in the later stages of the disease when it can no longer be conclusively determined which event occurred first.

It is currently unclear whether lens luxation in PBGVs is preceded by glaucoma or whether, at least in some instances, the lens luxation may occur as a primary event, resulting in glaucoma. Lens luxation that is not associated with trauma to the eye is presumed to be inherited.

Hip dysplasia A malformation of the hip joints that is usually evident on radiographs by two years of age. It begins in the young animal as joint laxity. Over time this results in progressive malformation of the hip joints and degenerative joint disease, also known as arthritis. Affected animals may be lame or asymptomatic, depending on the severity of the malformation. Breeding stock may be certified between one and two years of age, depending on the requirements of the certifying agency.

Hip dysplasia is a polygenic trait, meaning that many genes are responsible for the expression of the disorder. Environmental factors also may play a role. Limiting calories and minerals during puppyhood reduces the severity of the disorder in large breeds but it is currently unknown whether caloric/mineral (e.g., calcium) restriction may decrease the severity of the disease in PBGVs.

However, the most successful way to decrease the severity of the disorder and to improve hip joint conformation is to select for improvement in structure over successive generations. Hip dysplasia is diagnosed by radiographs of the hip joints.

There are two radiographic methods for diagnosis; the standard hip extended view, as used by the Orthopedic Foundation for Animals in the United States, and the distracted view, where firm pressure to pull the femoral heads outward from the hip sockets is applied as the radiograph is taken. With the latter method hip joint laxity is actually being measured and a "distraction index" is determined. This method is used by PennHip, a privately owned certifying agency in the United States, and may be more accurate at predicting the later development of arthritis. Unfortunately the added expense incurred by this means of evaluation, coupled with the need for special equipment and training by the radiographing veterinarian, has discouraged its widespread use. However, PennHip does require that all radiographed animals, whether normal or abnormal, be submitted to their database. This avoids the bias produced in databases where only animals predicted to certify have radiographs submitted.

Patellar luxation Instability of the kneecap. The patella is normally seated into the trochlear groove of the femur and is positioned at the center of the knee joint when viewed from the front. The patella may luxate either laterally or medially, that is, either away from the body or toward it. Many dogs with patellar luxation have very upright rear limb conformation when viewed from the side. Like hip dysplasia, patellar luxation is believed to be a polygenic trait.

Instability of the patella may be detected at a young age but often worsens with age. Patellar luxation is usually diagnosed by manipulation of the limb. Radiographs may also be used to determine whether secondary rotational deformity of the limb has occurred.

Patellar luxation is graded from I to IV, with IV being most severe. Affected animals may be asymptomatic, may show a "skipping" type of gait or may be severely lame. Grade II to IV patellar luxation may require surgical correction to restore normal gait or to prevent worsening of the lameness. The true frequency of this disorder within the breed is not known since no widespread screening measures have been performed.

Seizure disorders and epilepsy Seizures or convulsions have many causes, including infections, metabolic disorders, malformations of the brain or skull, poisons or toxins, trauma and inherited disease. Epilepsy is defined as a disorder of the brain causing recurrent seizures. It may be post traumatic, that is following a head injury, or idiopathic, meaning that no underlying cause has been found. Idiopathic epilepsy is most common in pure-bred dogs and is presumed to be inherited. Most reported cases of epilepsy in PBGVs are of this type. Animals diagnosed with idiopathic epilepsy should not be bred. The mode of inheritance of idiopathic epilepsy is unknown in most breeds, but an autosomal recessive mode of inheritance is suspected in some breeds.

There have been anecdotal reports of a few PBGVs being affected with portosystemic shunts. Shunts result from abnormal anatomy of the portal vein, which drains intestinal blood to the liver. The liver then "detoxifies" this blood before it returns to the systemic circulation. With abnormal blood vessel anatomy, some of this portal blood bypasses the liver, avoiding detoxification. This allows accumulation of waste products within the bloodstream.

Portosystemic shunts usually cause seizures or abnormal behavior that is most severe following meals. Some affected animals may show poor growth rates as puppies. Shunts are presumed to be hereditary and have become quite a common problem in some breeds such as the Yorkshire Terrier. Blood evaluation of serum bile acids, measured both before and after feeding, may provide support for whether an individual animal is suspect for this anomaly. Bile acid values are expected to be normal in dogs with idiopathic epilepsy and abnormal in dogs with portosystemic shunts. Specialized radiographic procedures or exploratory surgery are required to conclusively locate the shunt. Shunts may be closed surgically, but this is both expensive and risky. Deaths may occur during or following surgery.

Hydrocephalus Literally means "water on the brain." Hydrocephalus is, in most cases, a congenital birth defect of varying severity. It is caused by an anatomic disruption to the normal flow of cerebrospinal fluid within the brain. Severely affected animals usually die before weaning. However, less badly affected animals may survive into adulthood and may show seizures or behavioral abnormalities. It is possible that some cases of seizures in PBGVs may be caused by hydrocephalus. Hydrocephalus, like epilepsy, is presumed to be inherited. If selection against seizures is practiced, then hydrocephalics should also be selected against.

Aseptic meningitis/juvenile pain syndrome Juvenile pain syndrome in PBGVs is characterized by episodes of fevers, lethargy and pain. The pain is often localized particularly, but not exclusively to, the neck region. Many affected animals will show increased white blood cell counts during episodes. The disease varies markedly in severity and often has a relapsing course.

Affected animals are usually between four months and two years, although both relapses and first episodes have been reported beyond this age. Some will have abnormal cerebrospinal fluid, indicative of meningitis. Typically, the cerebrospinal fluid will have an increase in cell count and protein and be negative on bacterial culture. Deaths and disabilities such as blindness or paralysis may result from severe episodes of this illness. Most affected animals show a beneficial response to treatment with corticosteroids such as prednisolone and dexamethasone.

Similar syndromes with varying nomenclature have been reported in other pure-bred dogs, including Beagles, German Shorthaired Pointers, Bouviers and Scottish Deerhounds. Names applied to these syndromes include vasculitis, aseptic meningitis, arteritis, steroid responsive meningitis and pain syndrome. The syndrome as it occurs in Beagles has been most clearly defined and characterized, in part because of its occurrence in colonies of research Beagles. A genetic predisposition to the disorder is strongly suspected and breeding of affected animals is discouraged. The disease has been reported in virtually every country where PBGVs are bred.

Research is needed to better characterize this disease and to develop tests that would confirm the propensity toward, or existence of, this disorder in breeding candidates. Studies in Beagles have indicated that the condition is very likely to be inherited, but the exact mode of inheritance has not been determined.

Hypothyroidism Inadequate or subnormal thyroid gland function. Hypothyroidism in most dogs is caused by immune destruction of the thyroid gland. In most animals this is progressive and thyroid function declines over months to years.

Testing periodically throughout life is required to identify the condition, as normal results at two years of age may become abnormal over time. Clinical signs of hypothyroidism include obesity, lethargy, mental sluggishness, hair loss, change in coat texture, infertility and hyperpigmentation of the skin. However, many animals may be asymptomatic, particularly in the less advanced stages of the disease.

Testing methods for hypothyroidism have improved significantly in recent years. The Orthopedic Foundation for Animals in the United States has recently begun to offer screening and certification for this disorder for breeding animals. Blood testing for hypothyroidism should include the measurement of free T–4 by equilibrium dialysis (FT4D). Prior to the development of this analysis, the most common test performed was measurement of total T–4 by radioimmunoassay. However, this test is notoriously inaccurate in diagnosing the condition and there is considerable overlap between normal and abnormal. Also, many animals with non-thyroidal illness will have falsely low values on this test. Free T–4 by equilibrium dialysis is now the "gold-standard" for the diagnosis of hypothyroidism.

Measurement of canine thyroid stimulating hormone (cTSH), produced by the pituitary gland, and measurement of antibodies to thyroglobulins (TgAA), adds support to the diagnosis. Since pure-bred dogs often have immune-mediated destruction of the thyroid gland, many animals will have measurable antibodies to the thyroglobulins produced by the thyroid gland.

Hypothyroidism is a treatable, but incurable, disease. Unfortunately, some breeders treat dogs with thyroid hormone supplements without testing first. When this is done, future testing is impaired by the presence of exogenous hormones.

Some researchers suspect a relationship between thyroid disease and the development of other immune disorders. Indeed, in many breeds, where hypothyroidism is a problem, a higher frequency of other immune mediated disease is seen. A direct cause and effect relationship between other immune disorders and hypothyroidism has not been firmly established.

Pulmonic stenosis Usually a congenital malformation of the heart. Several breeds are predisposed to this disorder, including Beagles, Bulldogs, Wire Fox Terriers and Miniature Schnauzers. It has been shown to be inherited in the Beagle. Pulmonic stenosis is an obstruction of blood flow from the right ventricle of the heart to the pulmonary, or lung, circulation. This may be caused by thickening or fusion of the pulmonic valve leaflets, constriction of the main pulmonary artery or by narrowing just below the pulmonic valve. Initial suspicion of this defect is most often obtained by the detection of a heart murmur. Affected animals may be asymptomatic, except for the presence of the murmur. If more severely affected, exercise intolerance, poor growth rate, fainting spells and fluid accumulation within the abdomen may be noted.

Confirmation of the diagnosis following detection of the murmur will require radiographs and either echocardiography (ultrasound) or angiocardiography (contrast dye studies of the heart). The murmurs of pulmonic stenosis are usually easily heard. The presence of a heart murmur in any dog, particularly if used for breeding, deserves further workup. Because this defect has been proven to be hereditary in Beagles, it is wise to eliminate affected animals from breeding consideration.

Anasarca Abnormal fluid accumulation throughout the superficial body tissues and within body cavities. Anasarca as it relates to the PBGV is a congenital defect seen in neonatal puppies. Dystocia, or difficult labor, is the typical presentation when a pregnant bitch is carrying an anasarca puppy. Delivery of anasarca puppies will usually require Cesarean section. Anasarca puppies are often born alive, but usually either die or are euthanized soon after birth. Radiography will usually reveal a normal size fetal skeleton but, because of the fluid accumulation within the tissues of the fetus, the puppy will usually be about twice normal size. The cause of anasarca is unknown. An hereditary predisposition to this disorder is suspected but has not been proven. No treatment or means of prevention is known.

Hernias Defects in the body wall, mostly congenital. The two most common congenital hernias seen in dogs are umbilical and inguinal. Both types have been seen in PBGVs. Some congenital hernias will close with maturity, while larger defects may require surgical repair. Umbilical hernias appear as protrusions at the umbilicus. Inguinal hernias appear as swellings in the groin of female dogs and swelling within the scrotal sac in male dogs. Both inguinal and umbilical hernias are presumed to be inherited.

As you can see, there are many considerations for PBGV breeders. Some problems are more common in the breed, but even those that are met infrequently have great potential for adverse impact on its health. There is a great need for further study of many of the above health problems so that breeders can make informed decisions about which dogs are the most suitable breeding candidates. The great challenge facing today's breeder is to produce healthy, attractive hounds, suited to their intended purpose, that are also good companions that thrive in a modern world.

Chapter Eleven

Mating, Whelping and Puppy Care

Whoever said you can't buy happiness, forgot about
puppies.
—Gene Hill

There is nothing more appealing than a PBGV puppy. From about five weeks the eyebrows and whiskers begin to emerge, the endearing appearance and personality come into their own and any reasonable person must admit to being drawn to these little creatures, who are independent, fun loving and charming even at this young age.

Who can Resist—and Who Should Resist?

The dictionary defines "to breed" as to bring about; to reproduce; to raise. A breeder is a source or cause. That is a serious responsibility. Or at least it should be. The decision to mate a bitch and raise a litter of puppies should not be taken lightly by either the novice or the experienced.

For the novice there are many questions to be asked and answers found before such a

decision is made. What are your motives for wanting to breed a litter? To keep something? So that the children can witness the miracle of birth? To make money? How well has the breed and pedigree been researched? Does your choice of stud dog and his bloodline complement your bitch? Has the whelping process been studied so that you know what to expect? How will you sell the litter, place the puppies? Can you support the litter both in terms of day-to-day care and financially, if necessary, for an indefinite period of time?

For the experienced, questions should also be asked but at a different level. Is the objective to keep something out of this particular breeding? Is the integrity of the breed foremost in your program? What is the objective—to produce working hounds? For show purposes? Do you have reservations for pet puppies that do not meet this criteria?

Several aspects must be considered. Any reputable breeder will make the issue of health a top priority, ensuring that only hounds in the best possible condition, mentally and physically, are used in a breeding program.

What other important factors must be considered in producing a litter of puppies? Temperament, personality and stability; instinct and soundness; and type. One aspect should not take priority over the other, as this is the combination that makes the whole, complete PBGV.

Each of these issues needs to be evaluated in your breeding stock and taken into consideration when choosing a mate. Then, and only then, is the integrity of the breed maintained.

The Right Age

Most veterinarians and experienced breeders say the optimum age for a first litter is around two years or on the second or third heat cycle. It is never in the best interest of the bitch to breed on her first heat cycle or beyond the age of eight. Typically, bitches come into their first heat around six months old and continue on a biannual cycle. However, all bitches are different. For some, nine months or even more is normal.

There is no evidence to support the view that breeding at a young age is beneficial. Pregnancy does help to mature a bitch and it can make subsequent whelping easier, although this may be purely from experience and have nothing to do with age. Alternately, an older bitch of five or six that is being bred for the first time may not be at the peak of her fertility.

Regardless of age, the critical factor is whether the bitch is a good mother. And, typically, PBGVs are naturals. A good mother is one who readily takes to her new role, cleans and feeds the puppies regularly and settles down quickly after whelping. She copes without fuss in a businesslike manner.

Easy whelpers and good mothers invariably run in lines. Jamars Class Action had her first litter on her second heat cycle at 20 months of age. She proved to be the ultimate brood bitch, handling everything quite easily on her own, settling into the role of mother to her seven puppies and not needing any help until the weaning stage. After two litters, she is the typical "earth mother," as was her dam and her litter sister. Her daughter has followed in her footsteps.

It is a great misconception to believe that mating a small male to a large bitch will produce the correct sized animal; or that by breeding a male excelling in certain points to a bitch failing the same, you will reach perfection. It is far more likely that the litter will consist of extremes such as the parents. This method of mating has little value as it intensifies undesirable traits by breeding two animals with major, yet different, faults.

Ideal mates are correct in themselves in every respect, with four correct, similar parents. In this sense, "correct" does not mean perfect, as all dogs have imperfections that the breeder is trying to eliminate. "Correct" means true to the standard, without major faults, and to the "type" the breeder is striving for.

How Close is too Close?

Out-crossing

As out-crossing suggests, it is the breeding of dogs where no common ancestors can be traced in the pedigrees for several generations. To introduce a new line and qualities into your existing bloodline can be beneficial. In fact, there comes a time in tightly line-bred pedigrees where it may become necessary to out-cross, before breeding back into your dominant line.

The value of out-crossing relies on the different characteristics being crossed. The offspring of this breeding can be of exceptional quality when the characteristics they possess are the combined good qualities of both sire and dam. It is interesting to note that many experienced breeders, with knowledge of the desirable and dominant traits of the parents and several generations back, find this first out-cross combination very successful. The danger comes when a breed is out-crossed for several generations by novices or indiscriminate breeders not truly aware of what they are producing.

Under certain circumstances out-crossing can mean the mating of two different breeds. As we have seen in years past, people would do this to try and revive or redefine a breed that had become nearly extinct. This process has also been used to strengthen qualities needed for a particular purpose. For example, over the years the PBGV has been introduced into other scenthounds, such as the Beagle, to improve hunting traits.

Line-breeding

The objective of any breeder should be to establish a consistency in type and to produce sound, healthy hounds. This is achieved through knowing the line(s) of the dogs involved and working carefully to perfect the right combination. A sound knowledge of the pedigrees as well as an overview of canine genetics is necessary.

Typically, the most successful line-breedings will involve grandmother to grandson, niece to uncle, and half-brother to half-sister. The latter should only be done if the common grandparent is sound and very true to type. Subsequently, mating back to a common ancestor also true to type (and of the same type) will set a foundation in a line-breeding program.

Establishing a line does not happen overnight and typically takes several generations. This is what most dedicated breeders strive for. There is nothing more rewarding than having hounds from your line recognized at a glance by a knowledgeable eye.

In-breeding

There is a fine line between line-breeding and in-breeding and much is left to interpretation of the individual breeder. It is generally accepted, however, that in-breeding is the mating of more closely related animals, such as mother to son or brother to sister. Only those breeders who have tremendous knowledge of the line they are working with should consider this—not only of the dogs themselves and their pedigrees, but their genetic make-up. If done without sufficient knowledge, such breedings bring out recessive genes, especially those affecting health. This can be heartbreaking. In terms of quality, these breedings tend to bring out extremes—the best, the worst and with some level of mediocrity.

The Right Mate

Once the decision is made, the first step is to find a stud dog. Hopefully, you will already be familiar with your own bitch's pedigree. It is helpful to see the sire, dam, grandparents and so on, so you know first hand their assets, faults and temperament. In other words, get your hands on the dogs in question! This, of course, is not always possible due to distance and with so many PBGVs being imported from other countries. This is where the homework comes in. Find out everything possible about the dogs named in your bitch's pedigree and look at photographs.

You will want to see color, size, type, and so on. The same process should be done with your stud dog choice so that you are fully equipped to select the best possible sire for the prospective puppies.

It is true that many people have a shaky beginning, since it can be time consuming to put such effort into the research. The easy answer is to use a male that is close, which avoids having to travel, or to ship the bitch. Another alternative is to use your own male since he is available in your own back yard. These are usually not the right choices. Even experienced breeders, who have been working on a particular "line" in a breeding program, will not always use their own stud dog because it may be necessary to go outside to make improvements and introduce a new bloodline.

Don't be tempted to use to a male simply because he is winning, as he may be totally unsuited to your bitch. And it is a well-known fact that even the top winning dogs are not necessarily top producers, hence the saying, "If you like the dog, breed to his sire." There are many top champions who will never excel in the breeding department and you may have to look behind that particular dog to get the right mate.

When the homework has been done, it is time to test your selection. With blank pedigree forms and pencil in hand, fill in the spaces. This is the best way to get a clear picture of the lineage and how it all comes together for your hoped-for litter. At this point it is clear to see how closely related the dogs in question are or if they have nothing in common.

The Contract

Having come to an arrangement with the owner of the chosen stud dog, the terms of the stud fee must be agreed. There is no standard contract, payment is usually either pick of the litter or a fee equivalent to the price of a puppy. Typically if a fee is due, a deposit is paid at the time of mating, with the balance due at some point after the puppies are born. It is also common for two puppies to constitute a "litter" and if only one pup results or no puppies at all, a repeat stud service is offered on the next heat cycle.

Ideally, you will be dealing with someone with an easy-going nature so that the stud contract is written in simple language and in friendly terms. It is not unheard of, however, to be drawn into a stud service contract that appears to have been written by an attorney in legalese. Be very careful, read thoroughly and seek advice before signing.

Typically, the stud owner may ask for the bitch to be tested for brucellosis prior to the mating. Brucellosis is an infectious venereal disease in dogs, which can be transmitted to the male through mating. The blood test is simple and inexpensive. Many stud owners will also ask for the bitch to be OFA certified and CERF cleared.

These tests are simple, precautionary measures that any responsible breeder should undertake. A thyroid test on breeding bitches, which can be achieved by a simple blood test, is also advisable.

The Moment has Arrived

The female heat cycle lasts approximately 21 days. The first sign will be swelling around the vulva, followed by a red, bloody discharge. When anticipating a bitch coming into heat (or season), keep her on light-colored bedding so that the first day of bleeding is easily noticed. This counts as day one. Gradually the color of the discharge lightens and, by around the tenth day, it should be pale pink. The vulva remains enlarged and, by this time, it is also quite soft. This is considered the right time to mate the bitch.

The dog and bitch usually flirt when they are first introduced. They will sniff each other, run and play, "talk" and otherwise be quite comical to watch. Some males are very loving towards their mate, licking her around the ears and muzzle as well as the hindquarters. This doggy foreplay should be allowed as it is natural and makes most bitches more cooperative when mounted. It is when they get down to business that the breeder has to be available to assist. Many are firm believers in letting nature take its course. There should, however, be a happy medium between the philosophy that "dogs have been doing this for thousands of years" and sometimes getting too involved when the dogs can handle the event quite well. That said, there must be a person in charge of the situation; to observe and know when to step in and when not to

Once playing has ceased, the bitch will stand firmly with her tail flipped over to one side. The male will mount her. At this time it is critical to be all eyes and ears and ready to assist. When penetration is imminent the breeder should be prepared to slowly lean in to hold onto the bitch without disrupting the dog's momentum. The maiden bitch may be frightened or it may be painful for her, so watch out, she may turn to bite the dog or try to escape him. This can be very dangerous and may injure the male. As soon as they tie, the dog will dismount the bitch and turn around by lifting one of his front legs over her. Most dogs will handle this maneuver without any help from the breeder. This is the tie. They will stand locked together until the swelling of the male's penis subsides and the bitch no longer experiences vaginal muscle spasms. In a tie, the male's bulbous swelling will be held tightly and this helps to stimulate ejaculation, but a tie is not necessary for this to happen. It is also a myth that the dog alone is responsible for the tie. It is the bitch's

The tie.

muscle spasms that hold the male and, when these subside, the hounds will separate.

Ties can last from a couple of minutes to an hour, though the average is probably 15–20 minutes. Most breeders feel more confident about the mating if a tie results, although it is a misconception that the length of the tie (or having a tie at all) affects the size of the litter. However, several matings between the bitch and dog over a period of days naturally increase likelihood of conception.

After a successful mating, the dog and bitch should be separated, the bitch being crated immediately to discourage urination for at least 30 minutes. Also remember to keep her separated from other males after all matings are finished as some bitches will accept a male well into the third week. The male should also be put somewhere quiet to rest, away from the bitch.

Beforehand, check that his penis has returned to its normal state, as occasionally the sheath will become inverted due to the hair surrounding it. With the longer PBGV coat, this is not easily visible but, if not attended to by freeing the surrounding hair and encouraging the sheath to return, swelling of the penis may result, which can be dangerous and painful for the dog.

Troubleshooting

Suffice to say things do not always go according to plan. Generally, PBGV bitches are easy breeders, but some may breed early; for example, on the seventh day, and some late, up to the 22nd day. This is not common, but it does happen. A novice bitch must be observed daily and, if at all possible, it is wise to put her with the male from the seventh day to see how they respond. Most PBGV bitches enjoy flirting and are very willing, some standing for the male from the first day of the cycle. Smears may be taken at the vet to determine the approximate stage of the reproduction cycle, indicating that the cells are cornified, or that there is a higher estrogen level.

Alternately, more accurate progesterone tests may be done from a blood sample.

Not all bitches are receptive and maiden bitches especially may need help. This is fine as long as the stud will allow it. Some experienced males do not want help of any kind. In fact, the intervention of a person may put the dog off altogether. In some extreme situations, artificial insemination (AI) may be the best way to ensure the mating. Although not as common, males too can be disinterested. Some simply don't have the drive necessary to make a good stud dog. The pedigree may be super, he may complement your bitch perfectly and may be the type you are striving for, yet in stud terms, he is a dud! Assistance in the breeding from the stud's owner or AI may be the only way to achieve a successful mating.

At the other extreme, some young males become over-excited. At the time, this is frustrating, but patience, some restraint and gentle assistance may be all that is necessary. Neither disinterested, nor over-zealous—it is strange how many dogs and bitches become *inhibited* when the moment arrives, some not wanting to perform in front of their owners, or anyone for that matter. Let nature take its course. Leaving them alone, yet watching from a distance, may be the best route to success.

The Longest Nine Weeks

Once the bitch is bred, consider it a successful mating and assume she is pregnant until proven otherwise. Her routine should remain the same through the first few weeks, with exercise and diet unaltered. From the fourth week it is wise to increase food slightly and split her meals into two a day to make digestion easier. At this time an ultrasound scan can be done to determine pregnancy. This is generally the most accurate method and the heartbeats of the pups can be seen from the 28th day.

The bitch's level of exercise will be determined by what she feels like doing but, at minimum, regular walks should be rou-

GESTATION/WHELPING CHART

Mate on
Jan: 1 2 3 4 5 6 7 8 9 10 11 12 13 14 15 16 17 18 19 20 21 22 23 24 25 26 27 28 29 30 31
Whelp on
Mar-*Apr:* 5 6 7 8 9 10 11 12 13 14 15 16 17 18 19 20 21 22 23 24 25 26 27 28 29 30 31 - *1 2 3 4*

Mate
Feb: 1 2 3 4 5 6 7 8 9 10 11 12 13 14 15 16 17 18 19 20 21 22 23 24 25 26 27 28 29
Whelp
Apr-*May:* 5 6 7 8 9 10 11 12 13 14 15 16 17 18 19 20 21 22 23 24 25 26 27 28 29 30 -*1 2 3*

Mate
Mar: 1 2 3 4 5 6 7 8 9 10 11 12 13 14 15 16 17 18 19 20 21 22 23 24 25 26 27 28 29 30 31
Whelp
May-*Jun:* 3 4 5 6 7 8 9 10 11 12 13 14 15 16 17 18 19 20 21 22 23 24 25 26 27 28 29 30 31- *1 2*

Mate
Apr: 1 2 3 4 5 6 7 8 9 10 11 12 13 14 15 16 17 18 19 20 21 22 23 24 25 26 27 28 29 30
Whelp
Jun-*Jul:* 3 4 5 6 7 8 9 10 11 12 13 14 15 16 17 18 19 20 21 22 23 24 25 26 27 28 29 30 - *1 2*

Mate
May: 1 2 3 4 5 6 7 8 9 10 11 12 13 14 15 16 17 18 19 20 21 22 23 24 25 26 27 28 29 30 31
Whelp
Jul-*Aug:* 3 4 5 6 7 8 9 10 11 12 13 14 15 16 17 18 19 20 21 22 23 24 25 26 27 28 29 30 31- *1 2*

Mate
Jun: 1 2 3 4 5 6 7 8 9 10 11 12 13 14 15 16 17 18 19 20 21 22 23 24 25 26 27 28 29 30
Whelp
Aug-*Sep:* 3 4 5 6 7 8 9 10 11 12 13 14 15 16 17 18 19 20 21 22 23 24 25 26 27 28 29 30 31- *1*

Mate
Jul: 1 2 3 4 5 6 7 8 9 10 11 12 13 14 15 16 17 18 19 20 21 22 23 24 25 26 27 28 29 30 31
Whelp
Sep-*Oct:* 3 4 5 6 7 8 9 10 11 12 13 14 15 16 17 18 19 20 21 22 23 24 25 26 27 28 29 30 31- *1 2*

Mate
Aug: 1 2 3 4 5 6 7 8 9 10 11 12 13 14 15 16 17 18 19 20 21 22 23 24 25 26 27 28 29 30 31
Whelp
Oct-*Nov:* 3 4 5 6 7 8 9 10 11 12 13 14 15 16 17 18 19 20 21 22 23 24 25 26 27 28 29 30 31- *1 2*

Mate
Sep: 1 2 3 4 5 6 7 8 9 10 11 12 13 14 15 16 17 18 19 20 21 22 23 24 25 26 27 28 29 30
Whelp
Nov-*Dec:* 3 4 5 6 7 8 9 10 11 12 13 14 15 16 17 18 19 20 21 22 23 24 25 26 27 28 29 30 - *1 2*

Mate
Oct: 1 2 3 4 5 6 7 8 9 10 11 12 13 14 15 16 17 18 19 20 21 22 23 24 25 26 27 28 29 30 31
Whelp
Dec-*Jan:* 3 4 5 6 7 8 9 10 11 12 13 14 15 16 17 18 19 20 21 22 23 24 25 26 27 28 29 30 31- *1 2*

Mate
Nov: 1 2 3 4 5 6 7 8 9 10 11 12 13 14 15 16 17 18 19 20 21 22 23 24 25 26 27 28 29 30
Whelp
Jan-*Feb:* 3 4 5 6 7 8 9 10 11 12 13 14 15 16 17 18 19 20 21 22 23 24 25 26 27 28 29 30 31- *1*

Mate
Dec: 1 2 3 4 5 6 7 8 9 10 11 12 13 14 15 16 17 18 19 20 21 22 23 24 25 26 27 28 29 30 31
Whelp
Feb-*Mar:* 2 3 4 5 6 7 8 9 10 11 12 13 14 15 16 17 18 19 20 21 22 23 24 25 26 27 28 - *1 2 3 4*

FOR LEAP YEARS:
Mate
Dec: 1 2 3 4 5 6 7 8 9 10 11 12 13 14 15 16 17 18 19 20 21 22 23 24 25 26 27 28 29 30 31
Whelp
Feb-*Mar:* 2 3 4 5 6 7 8 9 10 11 12 13 14 15 16 17 18 19 20 21 22 23 24 25 26 27 28 29 -*1 2 3*

tine to keep her fit. By the sixth week, the meat in her diet should be increased and a calcium supplement added to one of her meals. It is a good idea to feed puppy food to the expectant bitch at this stage to give her more of the needed protein and nutrients. By the eighth week, the bitch may be less enthusiastic about her food and may need to be fed smaller portions more often. She will be uncomfortable and regular activity may be awkward, so the exercise routine will change.

From the 58th day of gestation, it is wise to take the bitch's temperature in the morning and again at night. The normal body temperature is 101°F–102°F. This generally drops several degrees within 24 hours of whelping.

The whelping box should be ready for her and placed in a room that is away from most of the house traffic where she can rest in warmth and quiet. The box itself should be at least 3 feet by 3 feet with railing around each side to prevent the puppies from getting trapped between the bitch and the sides of the box and suffocating. It should be full of newspaper, as this is easiest to replace as necessary. Stacks of clean towels, a covered hot water bottle, baby (or kitchen) scales, sterilized scissors, undyed white thread, a bulb syringe, a pair of hemostats (to clamp down on any bleeding umbilical cord before tying off), and a nice clean fleece should all be ready and waiting.

The bitch may become restless up to a week before the birth

A safe whelping box.

of the litter. This is normal. Panting and even nesting or digging days before are signs of preparation, not necessarily of early stages of delivery.

When birth is imminent, these actions will intensify. The bitch will be unable to settle. She will prefer a dark corner, hidden away from any bright lights and noise. Help her find her way into the whelping area. She may be reluctant to stay but, after the first puppy is born, she should settle in the whelping box. There is not much to do at this stage except observe quietly and let her get on with the job at hand. The early stages can go on for quite some time but, once she is well and truly in labor and the contractions become more frequent, you should expect to see a puppy within, at most, two hours. PBGV bitches tend to be easy whelpers and take it all in stride. However, they do seem to have a rather low tolerance for pain and, with each contraction and first delivery, the bitch may certainly make her situation quite clear vocally!

The period between subsequent arrivals can vary between minutes and hours. Sometimes an entire litter can be whelped in less than two hours, but for others a day can pass with up to two hours between each birth. It is difficult to pinpoint a danger period, but in general for anything beyond three hours between whelps, you should seek the help of a veterinarian.

At the birth of a puppy, the bitch will usually break open the membrane (or sac) surrounding the puppy, bite the cord and clean the new arrival dry. If she does not take care of this immediately after the birth, it is up to the owner to take over the job. The fluid-filled sac should be torn open and the puppy removed swiftly from it. With a pair of sterilized scissors, cut the cord approximately two inches from the body and tie the end with plain white thread to stop any possible bleeding. This also helps guard against infection. Dry the newborn puppy with a clean towel, as gently or as roughly as necessary, until you hear a cry or a squeak indicating the lungs are clear. It may be necessary to use a bulb syringe to clear the fluid from the nostrils and mouth. If there is still no sound coming from the newborn, hold it firmly upside down in the towel and swing it from the level of your face downward, being careful to hold on tightly. This will often clear out any fluid and the puppy will begin to show signs of life. Remember the new mother will be anxious for the puppy to be returned to her.

The placenta (afterbirth) may or may not be attached to the puppy. If attached, it is normal for the bitch to eat it following delivery of the puppy. However, although the puppy may be fully delivered, situations such as the owner having to sever the cord while the afterbirth is still inside the bitch, or the bitch chewing through the cord with the same scenario, may lead to the retention of the afterbirth.

The bitch must pass this and usually does so within a short period of time. However, it is wise to have a veterinarian inject her with oxytocin or similar to clean her out following entire whelping and ensure all afterbirth has been passed. A word of warning—most bitches do not like this! It is uncomfortable and, in reality, puts them back into labor when they have finished. However, the added contractions help to clean out all the debris remaining in the uterus.

A bitch will seldom want to eat or drink during the whelping period, but offer her small amounts of water or water mixed with evaporated milk. She may also be reluctant to go outside to relieve herself, and more often than not the new mother will have to be encouraged out into the back yard on a leash for the first couple of days.

Litter size can vary tremendously from a single puppy to the largest known American-born litters to date, both of 11 PBGVs. The average number of puppies is between four and six, an easy number for the bitch to cope with. Since ovulation in the bitch can happen over a period of days, especially if several matings occur, at birth some puppies may be full term (63 days) and some premature (58 days).

It is generally thought that the dam determines the size of the litter, the sire the sex. If the other way around, all the offspring would be female as the only chromosomes the bitch can contribute are the homozygous ones. However, several factors account for the size of the individual puppies at birth, including the number of puppies in the litter, their date of conception, genetic factors, the size of the bitch and her nutritional intake throughout pregnancy.

Remember, just takes things in stride—the bitch does! Once all the worry is over and the whelps have arrived, there is nothing more fulfilling than to see a row of clean, newborn puppies nursing from their resting mother.

Possible Problems

"Fading puppy syndrome" is not a disease, but a term used to describe puppies that seem to simply fade away with no cause, usually a few days to two weeks after birth. It is survival of the fittest in the most basic terms. There are signs though that a breeder should look for and, with immediate intervention, some puppies may be saved.

Various viruses and bacteria have been associated with fading puppy syndrome and, if discovered in the early stages, there are tests that may aid in a diagnosis. Swabs of the puppy's throat and rectum, along with a vaginal swab of the dam, may determine if bacteria are considered responsible. An appropriate course of antibiotics may then be started. It is critical, however, that the affected puppies have adequate fluids and that a normal body temperature is maintained.

Uterine infection in the bitch is also thought to be a factor in fading puppy syndrome. It may induce early whelping. This can cause the puppies to be underweight, have subnormal temperatures (they may, in direct contrast, have an unusually high temperature), find it very difficult to settle or, alternately, appear lethargic. They often look wizened and will not nurse well. Soon the weakness progresses and the puppy will no longer have the strength to suckle. Breathing becomes labored and frequently the puppy does not survive.

"Flat puppy syndrome," also known as "swimmers," is most common in broad, heavy, short-legged breeds. These puppies have a flattening of the thorax, as opposed to the more serious deformity of funnel chest, where there is actually a curvature of the sternum. At about ten days puppies normally come up first on their front legs raising their chest off the ground, then a few days later on their back legs raising their rear. Swimmer puppies fail to do this and, as they grow, their rapid weight gain often makes standing impossible. The ones most at risk appear to be puppies very weak due to muscle wastage or, more typically in the PBGV, the heavier puppy is more likely to be affected.

The affected puppy will take on the look of a frog with the front and rear legs splayed sideways. It seems impossible for it to lie on its side. This throws considerable strain on the thorax, encouraging the flat chest deformity, and eventually can result in respiratory distress.

A flat chest can usually be corrected if the condition is noticed and managed early. As soon as it is detected, the puppy should be placed on a soft, padded surface, such as a pillow, to minimize further pressure on the chest. Avoid slippery surfaces like newspaper, which will give him no chance of standing unaided. Various methods have been devised to encourage any affected puppy to stand on its legs and to strengthen the leg muscles to enable it to walk. Simple actions, such as placing a hand under the puppy's abdomen to take some of the weight off or exercising his legs in a cycling motion, will all help progress.

If the puppy is still not up on his feet at four weeks, it may be necessary to splint the legs to force him to lie on his side. Soft splints can easily be made with wooden popsicle sticks, padded with gauze bandage material, bracing the front legs, and then taping the legs together in a normal position.

The Four Developmental Stages

Geneticist Malcolm Willis' statement, "Temperament and behavior overrule any physical virtues," is worth remembering. There is a general shortage of conclusive data that defines which behavioral traits are inherited and which are not. There is proof that temperament and behavior can be inherited in some form but, more importantly, that they are influenced by environmental factors. There are four (Piaget-like) stages in a dog's life:

Neonatal Period: Newborn to 14 Days

PBGVs tend to be large puppies at birth. Although it is not unusual to see a puppy weighing one pound, the average weight

Bronte—a typical PBGV puppy weighing 14 ounces at birth.

is around 10–14 ounces. It is hard to imagine a litter of five or six of that size coming out of such a petite dam. They are typically strong and sturdy puppies, full of gusto—in other words, PBGVs!

Puppies are born in a very dependent state, with their body systems in the early stages of development. The first 36 hours are the most critical for a puppy's survival. It is best to have the litter on a warm fleece, with a well-wrapped hot-water bottle placed somewhere in the box. The ideal temperature is 75°F. Regardless of climate or time of year, always have a heat lamp placed reasonably high above, ready for use since this constant temperature is vitally important.

All puppies may appear scraggy at birth, but should fill out rapidly within 24 hours. Healthy pups sleep most of the time, waking only to nurse. The occasional twitching is associated with rapid muscle development and a still puppy is likely to be

Bronte at eight days, weighing 1 pound 6 ounces.

an unhealthy one. Weigh regularly to ensure weight gain—this gives an indication that all is well. Sensitivity to touch is well developed at birth as all puppies like something warm to snuggle up to for sleep and comfort. They benefit from daily handling, which even in these early days is the foundation for socialization.

By the end of the first two weeks the puppies' ears should be open and they become sensitive to sounds. Their eyes will also begin to open at around 12–14 days, showing a pale blue, milky color. PBGV puppies grow quickly and within a week they should have easily doubled in weight.

Transitional Stage: 14–21 Days

This is a time when puppies become more aware of their environment. They respond to sounds and voices, begin to focus their eyes, canine teeth start to emerge, and the muscles should be strong enough to support standing and attempts to walk. They begin to use their paws to scratch themselves and shake. By about 18 days they will be able to excrete without being stimulated.

Mother's milk remains the only source of food. They are still dependent on nursing and need to be kept in a warm environment. From 14 days they are better able to control a body temperature of 96–98°F. Digestion creates warmth; therefore, keeping the puppies on the dam through at least the

Bronte exploring at 21 days, weighing 2 pounds 12 ounces.

fourth week is ideal.

Socialization Stage: 4–12 Weeks

At this stage PBGV puppies become great time wasters as anyone who has a chance will spend hours at the whelping box watching, enjoying and laughing at their antics. The constant change during this time is extraordinary. The coat texture starts to alter and whiskers and eyebrows begin to emerge. The fourth week finds them beginning to explore, becoming interested in objects such as toys, and the first barking sounds are heard. They may become startled by this new and unusual noise which can knock them off their feet!

Their vision continues to improve and the pups have the increasing ability to focus, although full vision is probably not attained until several months. The color of the iris starts to change and darken by four to six weeks. The hearing is very acute at this age and slowly they will learn the relevance of different sounds. This is also the time when congenital defects, not previously apparent, may start to show. Mobility becomes easy and, by the fourth week, playful interaction is obvious within the litter.

Talisman at five weeks weighing 5 pounds. Note the nice, square muzzle, showing no sign of being too long or snipey. Also the correct amount of bone the puppy carries for his age.

This is a time of rapid development during which puppies learn to adapt to independent life. Careful socialization with people and other dogs is important. They should be gradually exposed to normal household noises and activities such as the television, radio, vacuum cleaners, etc. Lack of experience at this stage could cause problems later in life.

Juvenile Stage: Week 13 to Maturity

This stage, before sexual maturity is reached, simply builds on stages two and three and is the ideal time to develop socialization and begin training.

The First Meal

Depending on the size of the litter and cooperation of the dam, the weaning process will ideally begin at the end of the fourth week. Schools of thought on weaning puppies are many and varied. Some breeders will stick with the simple, tried and tested method of introducing specially formulated milk and then nutritionally balanced canned puppy food. However, the following combination of meals has proven successful. Amounts will vary depending on the size of the litter.

Days 1–3 in the Weaning Process
Dry, powdered baby rice cereal or softened rusks.
Equal parts of evaporated milk and warm water.
Mix together and let each puppy lick the mixture off of your finger. Two feedings a day are sufficient.

Days 4–6
To the above, add moist baby food from the jar or can, such as chicken, turkey and/or vegetables. This will make a stiffer mixture than that given on days 1–3. If using food with noodles or vegetables, make sure there are no lumps or large pieces. At this stage, place a mixture equal to one tablespoon per puppy on a plate for them to lap up. Increase to three feedings a day.

Days 7–10
Replace the baby cereal with dry, kibbled complete puppy

food. Place puppy food in the blender and chop until you have the consistency of breadcrumbs. Mix with warm water (or still use equal parts evaporated milk and warm water for some of the feedings). Make sure the mixture is well blended but, at this stage, it can be rather thick. By the tenth day increase from three to four meals a day.

Once the puppies are approximately five to six weeks old and have nice sharp teeth, discontinue chopping the puppy meal. Place it in a feeding pan and soak in water until softened. If using a complete, good quality puppy food, it can be used alone. If not, add canned puppy food with cottage cheese or continue adding meat from cans of baby food.

Who's Who?

All puppies are cute. How many times have we heard that? And it's true. Though remember that during the first few weeks PBGV puppies do not necessarily look like PBGVs. It is not until they reach about four weeks that the distinct characteristics begin to emerge.

At birth their color may be misleading. For example white and lemon dogs will be born white and the lemon markings come through slowly as they grow; white and sable dogs are typically born white and black, with the black softening into the brown and beginning to blend at around four weeks. So what you see in terms of color at birth, is not necessarily what you get. Markings *are* there from birth with some tiny patches intensifying as the puppy grows. Despite many breeders and prospective owners preferring a well-marked dog, one cannot breed color or markings to order.

When evaluating PBGV puppies, there a few things to look for in each one from the time they are mobile at three to four weeks. By this age you have an impression of length of body, shape of head, markings (although not actual coloring), and conformation of the forequarters, low earset and short foreface (this will develop over the next month or so).

Clockwise from above: Much Ado About Jamar at 8 weeks...4 months...20 months.

This comparison can be made between the litter mates, with past litters and against the standard. Although no teeth are present, the shape and placement of the jaw can be seen with any apparent over or underbite. However, bites can change and nothing is 100 percent certain until the permanent teeth come at around five to six months of age.

As they become more mobile, the individual personalities start to appear. Some are more outgoing puppies and the shy ones that tend to keep to themselves are obvious. Temperament should be paramount. The more outgoing, almost fearless pup

Talisman at 12 weeks weighing 11 pounds 6 ounces. Measurements taken from sternum to buttocks: height 8 inches at withers, length 12 inches (50 percent longer than tall).

is likely to be the best prospect for the showring. However, conformation is equally important and, unfortunately, they do not always go hand in glove.

By six to eight weeks the puppies have reached an ideal age to start serious evaluation. Balance, con-struction and personality can be looked at with a crit-ical eye. It is good to get them familiar with standing on a table, stacked, from the age of four to five weeks so that they are used to it. By starting young, it certainly makes life easier if serious show training is planned.

It is important to assess the same points while the puppies are standing as well as walking, playing and generally being left on their own: proportion of head to body; length of back (rib cage and loin); shape of the head; ear placement; tail set, length and carriage; rear angulation; whether hocks are too high; layback of shoulders; construction of upper arm; front assembly; atti-tude and personality. The coat should start showing signs of becoming nice and hard, with undercoat.

In movement, even at such a young age, the placement of the feet and front-end movement is critical, as any bowing in the upper arm should be apparent by six weeks. A reasonable indi-cation of rear movement is possible though, at this stage, diffi-cult to analyze since there is little strength and drive, due to immaturity. However, it is possible to notice poor angulation or construction. A video taken at about eight weeks can be invalu-able for re-evaluating the pups at three months. This will help detect bone structure and any defects in movement, such as

Left: Gambit of Kasani at 16 weeks.
Below left: Gambit of Kasani as a fully matured adult. (photo Pearce)

side-winding, bouncing or choppy gait.

It is also a useful tool for reassessing proportion. This is an excellent time to begin measuring height and length to get an accurate idea of ratio. Even at this age a puppy should be within the correct range of 50 percent longer than tall. Between the age of 6–10 weeks, the PBGV puppy should be an adult in miniature, in terms of proportion and balance. Some puppies do hold together and never go through the growth spurts common to the breed, but for many at around three months their parts begin to grow at different rates.

The rear end may grow faster than the front, making the puppy high in the rear; the body can lengthen before the legs grow and chest develops, making the pup look too long; the coat may still be sparse, soft or lacking undercoat. In other words the pup starts to go through "the uglies!"

But fear not, by the age of 10 months or so, the puppy should be back in proportion with all body parts developing and filling out at the same rate. The PBGV youngster will grow very quickly and, at this age, should be full-grown in terms of height, length and overall size. From now on, it is simply a matter of filling out and maturing.

As you have seen, taking into account the care before conception and the decisions afterwards, the job of a conscientious breeder is not an easy one. You need the right reasons, sufficient knowledge and the correct breeding stock. Select wisely, choose the right dog for the right bitch, and aim to produce quality puppies at the ideal time. It may sound simple, but it takes many years and experience to produce the ideal. Meanwhile, remember with affection your foundation stock and, as a responsible breeder, continue to study all aspects of your chosen breed. What better way to seek and find improvement?

For those breeders, and prospective buyers, who wish to deepen their understanding and thus secure the very best, either from a mating or in what they buy, there is one other subject to consider. It is the study of heredity.

CHAPTER TWELVE

GENETICS

*My experiments came to some very unsatisfactory
results, as I might have known had I thoroughly
absorbed the teachings of Mendel.*
—Joseph B. Thomas 1927

Genetics is the study of heredity and variation in animals and plants. In dog breeding, genetics is of interest so that dogs with particular characteristics are or are not bred—preferably in the shortest time with the minimum of "wasters." The aim might be to breed the best hunting animal, the ultimate show winner, the pet with the best temperament and so on. Inevitably, the dogs produced in such breeding programs reflect a human agenda— possibly even the socioeconomic styles of breeders and owners themselves. Consider, for example, the differences in trend between hounds bred in France compared with those bred in the U.K. and U.S.A. Are the hounds bred to hunt, to show or to cohabit as pets?

Mendel's laws show us that although what you see is not necessarily what you get, there is a certain order in the apparent randomness of heredity. If two dogs mate, the puppies inherit from the sire and dam a cocktail of genetic material, some of which manifests itself physically, some of which lies dormant, perhaps to emerge in later generations. The "cocktail" is different for each puppy. We call the physical characteristics phenotype and the genetic characteristics genotype. (Note that a pedigree is a mechanism for recording ancestry, from which an attempt may be made to deduce genotype.) It is only by influencing the genotype that we can possibly obtain a hound with the physical characteristics we require. The genotype is hidden from our physical senses and so careful analysis of bloodlines over many generations is essential to detect the secrets of a hound's genotype.

Mendel carried out his work with single genes, since the permutations and combinations of inherited characteristics that can be passed on from two single genes at each breeding are both limited in time and mathematically easy to understand. Hounds are more complex because they possess 78 chromosomes— paired as 39 from the sire and 39 from the dam; and each chromosome contains thousands of pairs of genes, between 2,000 to 4,000, depending on the size of the chromosome. We don't know the total number of genes in a hound, but there are between 50,000 and 100,000. This would present an insoluble problem for the breeder if it were not for the fact that genes have unusual properties. Two of the most significant are that genes express dominant and recessive characteristics or traits, and some genes work in groups called modifiers or polygenes. With experience and some understanding of genetics, a breeder can (at best) narrow the odds of physical characteristics being manifest or not.

When sire and dam mate, they may (for example) produce a wire-coated puppy (its phenotype) but its genotype may contain the recessive "non-wire coat" characteristic. We wouldn't know this for perhaps several generations and the reason for this can be illustrated by referring to an example from the PBGVCA magazine *Saber Tails* (March 1998) "Introduction to Canine Genetics" by Martin Vuille. (The dominant genetic instruction "grow wire coat" is notated as *Wh* and the recessive "non-wire" as *wh*.) In a mating where the sire's genetic make-up is *Whwh* and the dam's is also *Whwh*, the breeder cannot guarantee that all puppies will be wire-coated phenotype (only a 75 percent chance). Although there is a 75 percent chance of the puppies being wire-coated, there is also a 75 percent chance of the non-wire, *wh*, gene being retained in the genotype of the progeny. Equally important, a wire-coated puppy from this breeding has a 67 percent chance of carrying the undesirable non-wire coated gene.

To see how this works over subsequent generations, let us ignore phenotype showing the *wh* (non-wiry) characteristic (undesirable) as it would not be bred from (although in reality this may not be the case). This eliminates *whwh* from the breeding program. The phenotype of sire/dam is observed as wiry coat (*Wh*). As this is a dominant characteristic, this could be from either a *Whwh* genotype or a *WhWh* genotype. If from a *Whwh* genotype, then the breeding will produce the same pattern as before, i.e. 75 percent chance of *Wh* (wiry) and 25 percent of non-wire. If from a *WhWh* genotype, then the odds are narrowed.

Mathematically, we would expect that, by the second generation, the breeder would be guaranteed (100 percent chance) of a wiry coat in the progeny, with a 50 percent chance that the recessive *wh* characteristic will be passed on. However, the genetic argument is different because (as stated above) there is a 67 percent chance that the first generation progeny is *Whwh* and only a 33 percent chance that it is *WhWh*—the breeder does not know whether a *WhWh* or a *Whwh* hound has been used in the breeding. The chance of being guaranteed a wiry coat breeding from two *Whwh* genotypes is shown in the following "genetically weighted" mathematical argument:

1st generation = 75 percent
2nd generation, there are 2 possibilities:

(a) 67 percent chance of 1st generation progeny are*Whwh* (giving a 2nd generation of 25 percent *WhWh*, 50 percent *Whwh*, 25 percent *whwh*)
(b) 33 percent chance of 1st generation progeny are *WhWh* (giving a 2nd generation of 50 percent *WhWh*, 50 percent *Whwh*)

The net result of these two genetic sums is (a) + (b) as follows (rounded to the nearest whole number):

WhWh = (a) 67% x 25% + (b) 33% x 50%
= 17% + 16%
= 33%
Whwh = (a) 67% x 50% + (b) 33% x 50%
= 33% + 17%
= 50%
whwh = (a) 67% x 25% + (b) 0
= 17%

Third generation, assuming that *whwh* is eliminated, similarly produces 35 percent *WhWh*, 50 percent *Whwh,* and 15 percent *whwh*.

This highlights two interesting points that can be applied to any simple dominant-recessive trait:

1. The breeder will always be guaranteed of wire-coated puppies if sire and dam have Wh phenotype, assuming that one is from the litter in our example.
2. Look what has happened to the chance of perpetuating the recessive gene expression *whwh* across three generations:

1st generation	= 25 percent chance
2nd generation	= 17 percent chance
3rd generation	= 15 percent chance
(4th generation	= 14.75 percent chance)

In other words, the breeder's selection of hounds for "first generation" breeding is by far the most critical, and there will always be a chance (less than 15 percent, or greater than 1 in 8) that progeny of subsequent generations will carry the recessive *wh* gene. This equates to at least one puppy in every litter of eight with the recessive gene.

Applying the above to two terms that breeders often use,

"out-crossing" and "line-breeding," we can see why these techniques can be beneficial to a kennel and, conversely, why inexpert use of these techniques can be disastrous. Out-crossing involves introducing a new line that has no apparent connection with your particular pedigree. Breeders do this to add a desirable phenotype to their line (another "first generation"). However, unless a breeder has explored the phenotype of the out-cross in detail for at least four generations, there is a significant chance that unwanted genotype will be introduced unwittingly into the pedigree. It is advisable for a prospective buyer to ask about the reason for the out-cross, and particular caution should be exercised if the breeder quotes the introduction of a number of desirable characteristics. In *The Theory and Practice of Breeding to Type,* C. J. Davies asserts that the wise breeder will be cautious and out-cross for a single trait or characteristic at a time. In so doing, the breeder minimizes the chances of introducing a number of unknowns into their line's genotype. However C. Battaglia, quoted in the *AKC Gazette*, appears not to agree with this view and reminds us to avoid tunnel vision and to "keep in mind that you are breeding a whole dog, not body parts."

Line-breeding involves breeding within a bloodline, usually between generations that are either in line two generations apart, or once removed at least one generation apart. It is a kind of "double or quits" approach to breeding that can speed up the reinforcement of desirable traits in a pedigree—or, conversely, accentuate undesirable traits in the hands of the inexperienced breeder.

There is a great deal of data on dominant and recessive traits, most of which has been derived from crossbreeding experiments and studies. The results are widely available (e.g., as summarized in *Understanding the Petit Basset Griffon Vendéen,* Steidel), much of it derived from studies such as that of Little (1934), who crossbred short and long-tailed Belgian Griffons showing that the short-tail characteristic was dominant. Many other studies have also been carried out by, for example, Chulishvilyi, Marchlewski, Wellmann, Whitney and Winge.

The behavior of genes in groups, modifiers or polygenes, is far more complex. We can think of a modifier group as maximizing a trait or minimizing a trait—turning the volume up or down. The phenotype will show the net, or sum, effect of a modifying or polygenetic group. However, the genotype of a modifier group is not transmitted to the next generation as a net effect since each individual polygene is inherited individually and may act with a different combination of polygenes in the next generation. In these circumstances, the concept of dominant and recessive is not useful. Instead, geneticists use the concept of heritability. Although understanding how heritability is calculated requires a good comprehension of statistics and statistical analysis, understanding the concept of heritability is relatively straightforward.

Heritability is based on statistical data of phenotype and, strictly speaking, only holds true for the population being studied. For example, litter size (a heritable trait) was studied by Lyngset in 1973 with a statistical population of 159 sires across 14 different breeds producing 2,304 litters. Lyngset's data applied only to the 2,304 litters being studied. There is no such data for PBGVs but it is reasonable to apply such statistically valid conclusions with caution across species and between breeds.

In calculating heritability, it is important to think about three concepts:

1. Variance: This relates the number of hounds displaying a difference in trait to the most common result. For example, if there is a group of 100 hounds, 70 of which have a wither height of 13–14 inches, then 30 hounds deviate from the norm. These 30 hounds represent the variance.

2. Additive variance: By additive, we mean that part of the variance (1. above) which is more easily passed on to the next generation (the most transmissible polygenetic components of genotype). Willis describes this as "the breeding value." Its opposite is the non-additive variance, which represents a trait that is not easily inherited by the subsequent generation.

3. Phenotypic variance: This is actually what we see in a hound and is what we have referred to earlier as (and what most people mean by) phenotype. It is made up of different portions of polygenetic trait that are phenotypic, genotypic, dominant, additive and those that result from other influences (such as environmental).

Using these ideas, geneticists define heritability as being the ratio of additive variance to phenotypic variance. In real terms, this provides a measure of whether polygenetic traits are likely to be passed from one generation to another. The greater the heritability (nearer to 100 percent), the greater the likelihood that a trait can be modified from one generation to another; and the smaller the heritability (nearer to 0 percent), the harder it is to modify a trait between generations. A trait with a heritability of 50 percent or more is said to be highly heritable.

The concept of heritability epitomizes the natural tension between the science of genetics and the art of dog breeding. Heritability is, on the one hand, an indispensable part of dog breeding and its definition depends on the careful collection and analysis of data. On the other hand, how many breeders religiously collect and analyze the data of their kennels?

There are some important general points to be drawn from the above:

- Low heritability does not equate to less genetic control. It means that the additive variance is low.
- Selection in a breeding program for traits with a low heritability value will mean that prepotence may

never be achieved, or will certainly take many years. The prospective owner should therefore be on the lookout for "breeding shortcuts" (e.g., too frequent out-crossing).

It is self-evident that phenotypic traits such as weight can be strongly influenced by other, non-genetic (environmental) factors. The significance of environmental variance in the calculation of heritability is usually very small and would relate to a particular study, rather than being significant for a breed as a whole. However it appears that those polygenetic traits that are more easily affected by environmental factors have low heritability, whereas those traits with high heritability are less affected by environmental factors.

TRAIT	HERITABILITY	SOURCE
Litter size	<15%	Willis
Diestrus periods	38%	Smith & Reese
Age at 1st estrus	8%	Smith & Reese
Gestation length	40%	Preston & Willis
Body weight (at 60 days)	34–45%	Reuterwell & Ryman
Body length	40%	AKC Gazette
Body depth	50%	"
Body width	80%	"
Head width	35%	"
Muzzle length	50%	"
Height at withers	40–65%	"
Hunting instincts	10–30%	"
Temperament	30–50%	"

Hunting behavior is an interesting and relevant heritable trait, totally absent in some breeds and overpowering in others. Within a breed, hunting behavior can range from "complete apathy to a passionate hunting zeal" (Winge). Pointing, backing (copying another dog's pointing attitude) and hunting (or scenting) are all held to be heritable traits.

Color is genetically complex because of its many possible

combinations and the number of genes involved. The coat hair carries color pigmentation granules and this pigmentation is genetically controlled. Russell (1946) showed that seven factors (but many more than seven genes) affect pigmentation. In addition, the pigment in most mammalian coats exists in two color types: brown/black and yellow/red. Coat color ultimately depends on the degree to which these pigments are present or absent and on the combined effect of Russell's seven factors. Also, some colors take time to develop, so a newborn PBGV, for example, only has his undercoat and black/brown and/or yellow/red colors showing. His outercoat will not grow until he is six to eight weeks old. Only when he has grown sufficiently will the "primary" colors develop into the intermediary combinations of sable, grizzle, etc.

Coat hair affects the appearance of color. It is of two types: short undercoat and outercoat with long, thick guard hairs. The PBGV has both kinds, and the long hair reflects color differently from the short hair partially due to the effect of light. Hence, colors registered at birth may be somewhat different from those of the full-grown hound. With the French PBGV standard being somewhat more complex to interpret in genetic terms, it is simplest to consider the colors as stated in the U.K. and U.S.A. breed standards: "White with any combination of lemon, orange, black, tri-color or grizzle markings."

A summary of the main color genes at work in hounds goes some way towards explaining expected or unexpected results of breeding, and might help planning for those breeders to whom color is important in their breeding program. Our list does not take account of color genes whose existence or effects are not yet proven, and it uses the genetic shorthand for each color.

A - *ay* (dominant yellow), dominant to *ag* (wolf gray), dominant to *at* (black or liver saddle with tan markings)

S - *sp* (piebald spotting), dominant to *sw* (extreme white piebald)

C - allows pigment to be formed, dominant to ***cch*** (chin-
chilla), dominant to ***cd*** (white coat, with black nose
and dark eyes)

D - pigment intensity, dominant to *d* (pigment dilution)

E - extension without black mask, dominant to *e* (restriction)

G - causes progressive graying of coat, dominant to *g* (no
graying)

T - causes ticking, dominant to *t* (does not cause ticking)

This brief list is by no means exhaustive. For further information about the complex subject of color in dogs, the works of
Burns and Fraser, Little, Warren and Winge are useful. There is
no comparable work yet available on the PBGV.

Black and tan is a color combination worthy of mention in
the context of genetics, for two reasons. The first is that it has
aroused some controversy in the breed—not conforming to the
letter of the U.K. and U.S.A. standards (although it is included
in the 1909 and 1999 French standards). The second is that it
illustrates the importance of always considering the genotype
and genetic argument in a breeding program. French breeder
René Tixier is recorded (Dupuis 1997) as having bred PBGVs
without any white over a number of years. Apparently, the black
and tan first appeared spontaneously in the bitch Unica (1969,
confirmed by Abel Desamy, RCGV 2737). Earlier RCGV and
LOF records which are available make no mention of *"noir et
feu"* in any hounds. For example, the RI and LOF of the 1930s
and 1940s only show "traditional" colors—white and orange,
white and gray, and tri-color. So where did the back and tan
color combination come from?

The 1909 standard recognized it as acceptable, so it must
have been in evidence at that time. It was many years later
before the first black and tan champion was achieved—René
Tixier's Goldorak de Fin Renard (1994)—but this hound was
originally registered as tri-color. He reportedly had a small

white patch on his chest as a puppy, which subsequently grew out. Perhaps Goldorak's initial registration shows us how the traditional *"tri-colore"* description in the older records may possibly have concealed other color combinations. In addition, it is said that some French breeders culled (*"la sélection"*) black and tan puppies in the earlier years. (Was this a matter of fashion or was it for functionality in the chase?) It is therefore possible that black and tan PBGVs had not been allowed to come to the fore until Hubert Desamy encouraged M. Tixier to register Unica.

PEDIGREE OF UNICA DE FIN RENARD BC, BORN 1969
Jalon de Coeur Joie
Oslo Bolo de la Tour César
Ninon de le Brèche des Charmes
Soprano des Vaillants Limiers
Emir des Vaillants Limiers
Princesse II des Vaillants Limiers BC
Fanfare du Createur
Unica de Fin Renard BC
Pirate des Vaillants Limiers BC
Quitos II de Fin Renard
Miss Foxy de Fin Renard BC
Schippie
Oscarol de la Vrignaie
Quina du Pays de Retz
Islande du Pays de Retz

Tixier stated that his experience shows that the black and tan combination is recessive and this is supported by the findings of various geneticists (see *at* in the foregoing summary table) together with the mathematical argument showing that recessive genetic combinations are virtually impossible to remove completely. Looking at the summary of the main genetic series at work in the PBGV, we would expect black and tan to appear only if one parent was **atat** and the other parent also had **at** present. (Similarly, we would expect expressions of the **S**, **G** and **T** series to be suppressed or at least expressed in their most recessive form in either one or both parents.) M. Tixier's experience is that it is impossible to obtain black and tan coloring without at least one parent (preferably the dam) being black and tan. His experience is summarized as follows:

Sire/Dam	Progeny
(1) B&T/B&T	B&T and/or Tri-color
(2) Tricolor/B&T	B&T and/or Tri-color

Mating only tri-color progeny from breedings (1) and (2) above will not produce B&T progeny.

From a genetic point of view, M. Tixier's experience over a period of 30 years is no great surprise. However, results from breeding black and tans appear to be unpredictable; presumably resulting from the imbalance created by the presence of too many recessive genetic expressions. For example, a grandson of Unica is registered as *fauve* and gray (Leo de la Bougrière, RCGV 3239), and even the undesirable solid *fauve* has been reported to have occurred.

Size is another aspect of PBGV phenotype to be considered. All aspects of size are quantitative traits controlled by polygenes, and it is appropriate to introduce a further aspect of genetics here, namely correlation. Correlation is where polygenic groups or genetic series appear to act together. There is remarkably little data on correlation but it has been commented on by a number of researchers in relation to size and color.

For example, the size of color patches is known to be correlated to intensity of color—darker/larger and lighter/smaller. The same is true of size, weight, angulation, litter size, etc. Willis advises that to select animals for breeding down in size is therefore likely to be a harder task, as smaller hounds tend to produce smaller litters. This correlation may have played a part in the length of time taken for the PBGV to become established as a breed in its own right during the 20th century.

The end of the 20th century sees the beginning of a new era in canine genetics that will have implications for all dog breeders. The link between genotype and health disorders has long been established. The European dog map consortium published the first publication of an incomplete linkage map of the dog. This was followed by a larger, but still incomplete, linkage by a Canine Health Foundation project in the U.S. This has been followed by a number of projects working on the canine genome, a "DNA map," both in the U.S. (funded by the Canine Health Foundation/AKC) and the U.K. (funded by Guide Dogs for the Blind/the Animal Health Trust/Kennel Club). Once defined, the canine genome will indicate the answers to many unanswered questions about health disorders and heredity. This information, together with the Canine Health Foundation project on the development of a reference resource on canine genetics for breeders, will help PBGV breeders and owners study the phenotype thoroughly and complete as much detective work as possible to discover the hidden mysteries of the genotype before breeding or buying.

Also, honesty among breeders must be the best policy, as stated by Willis and expanded upon by Martin Vuille (*Saber Tails* 1998, "PBGV Genetics: Inherited Problems"). The clues are to be found in the phenotype of all branches of a puppy's ancestry. But should the day arrive when geneticists control hound breeding, then the love of our breed will have been extinguished and breeders will be doing the same work as pig farmers.

Chapter Thirteen

A Versatile Happy Breed

If I have any beliefs about immortality, it is that the dogs I have known will go to heaven, and very, very few persons.
—James Thurber

The PBGV may be a hound strong in hunting instinct but this friendly, comical, mischievous, energetic, bold and intelligent dog who is "independent, yet willing to please" is a busy, active hound with a plethora of capabilities. In this final, lighthearted chapter, we hope to give you a snapshot of the many talents our beloved Happy Breed possesses.

Tracking

Valerie Link has been involved in all aspects of dogs, bred over 30 champions and won at several national specialties. But nothing compares to when Hannah found a gardening glove in the middle of a field!

A day I'll never forget. The tracking test was on a cold, cloudy March morning in Northern California. I was nervous—but she was great. In fact, I nearly made her fail at the start by not allowing enough distance between us as she set off. She made all the right moves, every turn, without hesitation. Nine minutes later she stopped and looked at me. Not being a retriever, she would not pick up the items; but I knew that look. She had done it.

Tracking is a sport that uses the dog's superb olfactory skills to follow where a stranger has walked and locates an article that has been dropped at the end of the trail. To mark the starting point, a stake is left in the ground where the track-layer begins. A second stake, several yards forward, shows the handler the initial direction. The track must be between 30 minutes and two hours old.

In a Tracking Dog (TD) test there are several turns, but the track, on grassed area or pasture land only, will never intentionally cross a conflicting track. While the length varies, the total distance is about 500 yards. An article bearing the scent of the track-layer is placed at the end of the track. The dog's objective is to "Find it!" (In contrast a Tracking Dog Excellent (TDX) track takes the dog over at least 1,000 yards, crossing a road, perhaps water, with several articles and confusing cross-tracks along the way.)

For years, tracking dogs have served many purposes. The initial training and testing are the beginning stages of scent work. There is no competition with other dogs or handlers, simply owner and dog working as a team, bonding through learning and trust. Tracking dogs have gone on to work in Search and Rescue, identification of narcotics, searching for bombs and weapon detection. Many have careers in termite detection or working in airport baggage areas, trained to search for items as diverse as meat, fruit, currency or drugs.

Training starts slowly. The track-layer stands in front of the dog and feeds treats from a glove. Then he turns and walks away, not more than 15 yards to start, and places the glove on the ground (usually with hot dogs sitting on top). Using the words "Find it!" dog and handler set off to find the hot dogs. Sometimes the track-layer even rubs hot dog on the soles of his shoes for initial scent training. As training progresses, the tracks are aged, become longer and turns are introduced. The dog's enthusiasm dictates the time taken to complete successful training.

All dogs can track, but scenthounds are naturals. Unfortunately, this unique ability to use their highly developed sense of smell is not coupled with natural retrieving instincts and, while the dog must follow the man-laid track, the objective is to retrieve the article at the end. This sometimes creates a problem. A minor detail!

> I quickly learned to read Hannah. Any slight hesitation and she would look at the ground. She was so keen to keep tracking, it was up to me to recognize that sign. I would call out, "Good girl," make a fuss of her and she would stop. Her overall technique was quite methodical—sometimes quick, sometimes slow, but always straight ahead on the track. On a turn she would stop, maybe circle and then take off quite confidently in the right direction. Turns never gave her a problem.

To date only five PBGVs in America have obtained tracking titles. Hannah was the first in 1990. Two of Hannah's daughters also joined this elite group: JoJo (Jamars True Value CD) owned by Wendy Jeffries passed in 1992 and, in 1994, Elizabeth Wagner's Elinor (Jamars Equal Lender). In 1994, Barbara Wicklund's Ch. Axmo's Inca De La Garonne CD earned his title and, in April 1995, Lena Wray's and Barbara Galbraith's Lacebark's Lucille took the award.

Search and Rescue

If you are lost or hurt, what would be more wonderful than being found by a PBGV? Wendy Jeffries has worked with many different breeds in both tracking and Search and Rescue (SAR). She has also trained many breeds, but none so enthusiastic as her PBGV, JoJo. Certified by CARDA (California Rescue Dog Association, Inc.), they work with police agencies, the Office of Emergency Services, Civil Air Patrol and county sheriffs' departments.

Working similar to tracking, SAR takes the task one step further—a matter of trailing versus tracking. Trailing involves tracks and cross-tracks since a dog may be thrown into an area full of different and confusing scents in real situations.

He must learn to distinguish these and retain the scent of whatever is being sought. The handler too must acquire a range of skills, such as radio communication, map and compass, crime-scene preservation, survival training.

"Studies are endless—drug labs, human bone ID, child abuse, Incident Command System (for

JoJo.

planning a search). Usually the dog is ready before the handler has all the requirements," Wendy explained. When working with old trails, style changes. The head is at chest height or halfway instead of nose glued to the ground, and the speed of travel changes. Off the trail itself, the dog may smell eye-level bits of weed or brush before moving on again. SAR training includes working in water, across traffic, in city streets, following old and fresh tracks (sometimes with scents mingled), matching a person to a scent article and being lowered from helicopters. Teams are called out to search for missing persons, criminals, cadavers—everything imaginable.

Wendy described JoJo's style:

Some think a small dog has to work much harder to cover the same amount of ground, but human marathon runners are often much shorter than sprinters, with a more economical method of travel. JoJo doesn't tire any more than a big dog and often finishes the trails much faster than her taller team-mates. She can be lifted easily over fences, into canoes, out of helicopters and my male colleagues are quite happy to sling her across their shoulders to get through the cactus fields. She can't jump as high but can be lifted much higher.

SAR is intense training for both dog and owner. Working with a team, sessions and demonstrations are a routine way of life, as is being called out for actual searches at any time.

JoJo did exceptionally well in AKC tracking events, passing first time out, but there are some differences, as Wendy explained.

In SAR, tracking differs slightly; therefore, so too does training method. JoJo's first SAR training was a wandering trail around a grass and cement park. A mission-ready Beagle ran it first as JoJo watched. This is typical in SAR and probably one of the reasons our dogs ignore cross-tracks so well. In addition to cross-tracks from people walking in the park, there were also the scents of the other handler and the Beagle all over the track. She smelled the scent article and instinctively knew what to do. The only thing that threw her was finding a man face down in a ditch and not a glove!

For JoJo's first attempt at water training, a diver laid a trail around a pond, then almost totally submerged into the water to wait. We followed his trail and she eventually found him—underwater hidden in the reeds. Treat rewards for JoJo! Next came her first boat ride. In the middle of the pond, the same diver began swimming back to the docks underwater on a path close enough to our canoe for JoJo to get a whiff of him. Excitedly, she jumped into the water to find him. Fortunately, she was wearing her harness, so I lifted her 36 dripping pounds into the canoe. Everyone was impressed at her impromptu find.

Two years' training and four on the team gave JoJo experience to pick a person out of a line-up after scenting on an article, to locate the backyard burial place of a baby and to track anyone who had traveled in a car. "She checks tire prints and goes off the road, sniffing. When she finds the car, she creates havoc until the doors are opened, then jumps inside. More barking indicates this is it. Then she carries on working to find the person."

JoJo's greatest experience was before she was mission ready. There was no certified dog available that night. An estranged husband, with a history of abusive behavior, had apparently murdered his wife, then set the mountain cabin on fire, where the daughter was hiding in the attic. The police could only find an abandoned, damaged car down a nearby dirt track. Had he gotten away on foot?

JoJo was called out two-and-a-half days later. By then the car had been towed away, resulting in confusing scents from various sources. The only scent article available was a swab of blood from the car. Much to Wendy's surprise, this was barely needed. She could hardly control JoJo near the abandoned car.

She couldn't have been more excited had she seen the biggest bunny of her life hopping off in the distance! She had never smelled adrenaline before, but she knew exactly what she wanted to do! All day JoJo followed scent, keen to enter homes and garages, but we pulled back for the police dogs to check them out. They found blood on one garage and evidence of an attempted break-in. Occasionally JoJo lost scent and cast around looking, but later border patrol men arrived to look at what I thought was blood. A few feet away they found more on a locked car and JoJo was on him again.

Down a steep ravine of pine and fallen trees, JoJo's unique tracking style covered the full length of the crevasse. Instead of going straight, she quartered first up and then downwind. After half-a-mile of crawling through undergrowth that JoJo tackled easily, we found some cabins and watched while the police, guns drawn, cleared each building. Despite police deliberations that the fugitive had gone toward a town to the right, JoJo insisted on going left, leading us to an Indian reservation well outside the mountain community area. At this, the police felt that the man was no longer in the area and confidently called off the search.

Three months later hikers found a body in the middle of the reservation. He had made a campsite, sat for a few days and apparently shot himself in the head. It's probably just as well they called off the search as JoJo was only about two hours behind him. I would have found myself walking into a well-hidden camp to be greeted by a madman with a gun.

Agility

Throughout the U.S., PBGVs are making their presence known in performance events—and Phoebe is no exception. With Charlotte Allmann she has become well known at agility events in the Midwest, earning many agility and obedience titles. In fact, Phoebe has more letters after her name than the most highly accomplished scholar. She is Fitzcap's Sonya Silhouette, CD, AX, OAC, EJC, AD. No need to know what this means, it is impressive! "Phoebe is my first agility dog and, even though it has been a long road to success, we never gave

Phoebe in competition.

up. Now I can't imagine a better way to play with a dog."

Agility involves a course set out with obstacles such as jumps, tunnels, "up and down" ramps and weaving through poles. The dog and handler run in a team, with owner prompting the dog at various stages. This can be done simply for training, enjoyment or in timed competition. It encompasses all of the fun and positives of pet ownership but also involves hard work, training (based on positive motivation) and a bonding of owner and dog that exceeds all others. From picking the right puppy (with the temperament suited to this sport), to the thrills of a clean run, agility has increased in popularity in recent years and the PBGV is now a breed to be reckoned with.

What characteristics make a good agility PBGV? Boldness, busyness, intelligence, confidence, willingness to please, vigor and energy—all natural to this breed. Since a dog sport is affected by many things out of human control, the most important consideration is temperament.

Charlotte explained agility training with her two PBGVs Phoebe and Clue.

> Petits are well-suited for agility. The sport is dominated by herding dogs bred to work with a handler—and work until they drop; but the PBGV's strong prey, play and pack instinct are an extra advantage for motivation. Since the work ethic for the breed is not as strong (some would say non-existent) as in others, extra patience and careful, creative, individualized training techniques are necessary for effectiveness. Success equals fun, and fun equals success, so your relationship with the dog is key. The foundation for teamwork is to build slowly, day by day, with you as the benevolent leader, in charge but not domineering. You should enjoy spending time together.

Training starts young, done in stages. A four-month old is unable to do any kind of jumping or climbing and, typically, training with the weave poles begins once the dog is a year old. Relationship building, basic obedience skills and directional commands start as soon as possible, the younger the better.

The PBGV mind works differently from working dogs, so a crucial element is the relationship and bonding between hound and owner. The most important part of the bonding experience is coming when called.

Having had hounds all my life, I know only too well the pitfalls of living with a hunting fool with four swift legs and a one-track mind! From initial training, the rewards for coming quickly are great. Treats and toys are always involved and, when playing, they soon learn that coming when called does not mean the fun stops. I never call the dogs to come for any reason that is negative, such as nail trimming or bathing—only positive.

Reinforcement must follow through in all training. PBGVs are 'up' dogs and agility is an 'up' sport. The attitude must be THIS IS FUN! The mistake is made by owners wanting success, expecting the dog to work ever harder. What sensible PBGV is willing to run through a tunnel, walk over a teeter-totter or carefully weave himself through poles if his owner is too demanding and anxious?

Toys and treats are a must for all training sessions. These should be short and filled with praise, play and happy voices—always a positive attitude. PBGVs have tremendous confidence, so they are easy to train using

Up and over the teeter-totter in the semi-finals at the USDAA Grand Prix of Dog Agility National Championships, July 1998.

agility course equipment. The pack drive is just as strong. In particularly independent dogs, building this up will get results—much closer teamwork. Develop this on walks and around the house. Obedience is a great pack-drive enhancer, if done with play in brief sessions without too much repetition. When the dog gets it right, give lots of praise and immediately go on to something else. End all training sessions with something that is easy and fun, to quit on a high note. If you and the dog have a problem with something, take a break and play. Your PBGV should look forward to agility practice sessions.

Conditioning is important, as well as general fitness. A dog on the lean side will last longer in the sport and is less likely to be injured. I take my two PBGVs out 'hunting' in the fields once or twice a week in addition to training sessions and let them cover more ground by calling them to come more frequently.

Training a PBGV for agility is a challenge but worth every moment. When asked, Charlotte said, "I always keep up my enthusiasm and energy level when working with the PBGVs. It's sometimes frustrating since they can simply decide not to do something! But bearing in mind an agility course has 20 obstacles and Phoebe completes it in less than 30 seconds, seeing her having fun and full of confidence is the ultimate reward."

Obedience

There is a common misconception that hounds are disobedient and stupid but, as Sue Polley of Essex, England knows, this is not true. Sue shares her experiences and expertise with us, explaining that, by understanding our breed and what motivates it, it is possible to have a well-trained PBGV.

Hounds are unlike other breeds. They have been selectively bred over centuries to hunt on their own initiative and to integrate with a pack. The PBGV has a very strong hunting instinct, having been brought only relatively recently into the domestic environment. This urge to hunt is one of the great treasures of the breed. To lose this ability, whether by neglect or design, would be to destroy the PBGV character. It is therefore important to work *with* the dog's natural instincts, rather than suppress them. Whether training your hound for obedience, or just to be a well-behaved pet, similar principles apply.

Sue recommends motivational training methods that are fun for the dog. She sees no joy in browbeating a dog into obedience. If your PBGV doesn't enjoy learning, it's no fun for either of you. The motivations used are your voice, toys, food treats and the dog's respect for you as pack leader.

*Sue Polley with Harriet
(Kasani Zephyre L'Artiste).*

Obedience training, agility, flyball and other canine activities are only enjoyable if you have a strong bond with your PBGV. To develop this you must understand how your dog thinks and perceives the world. He does not think like humans. He learns largely by trial and error, repetition and reward. If he chases a rabbit and it brings a reward, such as a good meal, he will repeat the action hoping for further reward. However, snapping at a wasp and getting stung soon teaches him not to repeat *this* action! This is the principle behind Sue's training methods— rewarding pleasurable actions she wants her PBGV to repeat and ignoring undesirable ones.

Basic Training

Before teaching anything, you must hold your hound's attention, making yourself the most interesting thing in his world. This can be difficult with a hunting breed, but PBGVs are very people oriented, an asset you can build on. Whether your dog is a puppy or an adult, spend as much time as possible playing with him. Choose toys he likes. Knotted ropes are favorites, although furry and squeaky toys are exciting for hunting breeds. Get down on the floor and play tug, or hide the toy on you and encourage him to find it. Don't be tempted to throw the toy for your dog to fetch, unless *you* are going to get it first. The object of playing is to ensure that your hound has fun *with you* and enjoys being close. By throwing it, he is likely to pick it up and run off to play. This only teaches him that he can have fun on his own, without you, thank you very much!

Not all dogs like toys so, alternatively, instigate a game by using food treats. Show the treat, hide it in your closed hand and let your PBGV chase your hand around the floor. In a while give him the treat, then play again. He will soon learn that being *with* you is best because you play fun games and reward him with treats.

Once your PBGV is focused on you, you can begin to teach him. The following exercises give a good basis for either "pet" or "competition" obedience. Beware though, like many other canine activities, once you get started, obedience can become addictive.

Take care and advice when choosing a training club. Most use the kind, reward-based methods that are both successful and suitable for our Happy Breed. Some, however, are still in the dark ages of "compulsion" training, dragging the dogs around a hall on a choke chain, and yelling "Heel" at them. On your initial visit, ask if they use toys or food treats. If the answer is no, this is not the one for you.

Equipment

Little equipment is needed for teaching obedience. Your voice and hands are the most important tools. Your PBGV should regard them only as a source of kindness and praise. *Talk* to him. Unlike toys and treats, you can't forget to take your voice with you when you go out together. Use an excited tone when calling him and a calm, bold tone to give confidence when teaching "stays."

Avoid hitting him, especially around the head, as it will destroy confidence in you and make him nervous and shy. If you catch him in the act, a tap on the rump combined with a sharp "No" gets the message across.

Keep commands consistent, especially in a household where more than one person looks after your PBGV. Write a list of command words and actions. For example:

Command Word	Action
Sit!	Sits
Down!	Lies down
Get off!	Gets off (e.g., sofa, flower bed or visitor's lap)

Remember to differentiate between the last two. Don't shout, "Get down" when you mean "Get off." If your hound is lying on the sofa, he is already "down" as far as he is concerned.

Training is best done with the dog wearing a plain, flat, buckle collar with soft, rope leash. Choke chains and expensive, chewable leather leashes are unnecessary. A comfortable fit for the collar should allow room for three fingers between the collar and dog's neck, ensuring it won't slip over his head. Leash length should measure from the floor to just above your waist.

Invest in fun toys for training, which can be easily held in your PBGV's mouth. Balls are unsuitable since they may become stuck at the back of the mouth. For food treats, try cubed cheese, sausage or liver brownies or complete dog or cat food.

Recall

This is probably the most important exercise you will ever teach. Within the breed, there are two schools of thought about letting hounds off the leash. Some say they never have problems getting PBGVs back when called. Others recount terrifying stories of theirs missing for hours, even days, having run off in pursuit of game. PBGVs are independent creatures when it comes to the great outdoors. Hunting urge is overwhelming so, to get yours to return when called, you have to work extra hard to make yourself more attractive than the local wildlife! Circumstances will dictate whether or not you can let your hound run free. In an urban area, it is safer to exercise your hound on an extending leash. Those lucky to be near woodland, fields or seashore, away from roads, can exercise their hounds freely in relative safety. Being able to recall your PBGV in an emergency could save his life.

Begin training indoors where there are less distractions. Armed with irresistible treats, sit on the floor, legs stretched into a "V." Call your PBGV excitedly, continuing until he reaches you. As he nears, show the treat in your hand. Once his nose is on it, guide him toward you by bringing your hands up to your chest. Reward him with the treat and much praise. Practice often, rewarding *every* time, reinforcing that being close to you is great.

Once reliable indoors, repeat the exercise in your backyard. Here there are more distractions, requiring extra work to keep his attention. Next, repeat the exercise sitting on a chair. Perch on the edge, leaving room between your knees for your dog to fit in. Call as before, guiding him in with a treat. Adjust the position of the treat according to your PBGV's size, getting him looking up at you and sitting as close and straight as possible. The final stage is to stand up, finishing with your hound sitting straight between your feet.

This is the basis of the competition recall—your dog will come close enough for you to slip his leash onto his collar. However, neither grab his collar nor fuss about if he doesn't sit straight. Thoughts of being pulled about may deter him from coming within arms' reach. Rewarding him quickly will encourage his desire to come to you.

Fun Recall

This is a fun exercise, quickening up your "recall" and encouraging your PBGV to listen to you. Practice often, using an extending leash or "tracking line." When your dog is distracted, sniffing at a smell, crouch down and call enthusiastically. He should come running at high speed. Greet him with outstretched arms, lots of fuss and a treat. If he ignores you, tug the leash sharply, call and help him in with the leash if necessary. Alternately, stand with legs apart and, as he comes towards you, throw a toy between your legs behind you, encouraging him to follow through and pick it up.

The Sit and the Down

These are two of the easiest commands to teach as your PBGV will naturally do both without even asking. Initially, don't give the "Sit" or "Down" command. He will understand neither. Words alone mean nothing to dogs. Your PBGV must learn to associate each position with the relevant word before expecting him to obey on command. Wait until he sits or lies down of his own accord, then praise with "Good sit" or "Clever down," stroke him and give a treat. This method, called *shaping,* is also used to train dolphins.

Stroking your hound gives positive reinforcement. If he gets up in his excitement at doing something well, stroking also allows you to gently restrain him in the desired position, until *you* decide that he can move.

Sit

With your dog standing close, hold a treat a little way from his nose and let him sniff it. Once he is interested, raise your hand over his head so he has to lift his head up and back to reach the treat. As he does so, his rear is inclined to sit. Be patient. Wait until he sits, then praise him with "Clever sit" and give the treat. Your PBGV will quickly learn to sit in anticipation of reward. You can now tell him "Sit" as he sits, and soon he will do so on command alone, but still reward him with a treat and praise.

Down

With your hound standing beside you and a treat in your right hand, slip your left hand into his collar. Hold the treat by his nose, then move your right hand down to the floor, to a point between your dog's front legs. Simultaneously exert gentle pressure down and back on his collar, giving the command "Down." When achieved, praise him with "Clever down" and reward him. Introducing a "release" command at this point (e.g., "Finished," "Okay" or "All done,"), tells your PBGV that the exercise is over and he is free to move.

Practicing these exercises regularly will build a strong bond between you, and your PBGV will soon understand what is expected of him.

Walking to Heel

There is often confusion between "competitive" heelwork and a dog walking nicely on the leash. Competition heelwork is highly stylized, designed to show the absolute peak of canine/handler teamwork skills. Most PBGV owners would settle for being able to walk their hound without a struggle.

Begin this exercise indoors and only practice when you can devote time to allow your dog to learn at his own pace. Five minutes twice a day is enough for both of you. Do not practice when you are in a hurry to take your dog for a walk.

Using a collar and clipped-on leash, hold the leash with your right hand through the looped end, and stand still. Praise your PBGV while the leash is slack. If he puts tension on the leash by pulling away, say his name, "Steady," and give a sharp check on the leash. The *moment* the leash goes slack and he is looking at you, praise him with "Good (name of dog). That's steady," and give him a treat.

The next stage is to take *one* pace, in any direction. This gives your PBGV a different area of ground to sniff and thus the stimulation to move away to explore a fresh area. If he tightens the leash, repeat the exercise as before. Once he understands, increase to two steps, then three and so on. Your PBGV will soon learn that "Steady" means walking on a slack leash beside you, and then you can both enjoy walks together.

Sue has found these methods effective and fun for her dogs. She believes that, with the right motivation, kind handling and training, PBGVs can succeed in any sphere of canine competition. The late animal-trainer, writer and TV personality, Barbara Woodhouse, although now considered outdated in her training methods, did much to encourage well-behaved dogs, and Sue's expanded quote from her works encapsulates the principles of obedience.

Be firm. Give your dog defined boundaries to help him understand what is and what is not allowed. A simple "Yes" or "No"—PBGVs do not understand "Maybe."

Be fair. Have realistic expectations of your hound's abilities. Good training comes with patience and practice—don't expect him to learn all the exercises overnight.

Be fun. Ours is the "Happy Breed." They are happiest when having fun with their pack and in the domestic environment, which is us. Spend whatever time you can with your dog each day, make it fun and enjoy each other's company. After all, isn't that what owning a PBGV is all about?

Lure Coursing

We know that PBGVs are scenthounds but they also have very keen eyesight and do, to a degree, hunt by sight. With noses to the ground they set off following by scent but, once they sight on their prey, their heads are lifted to somewhere between the ground and full upward position and, the fact is, they *do* follow by sight. If the quarry is lost, the nose returns to the ground to once again follow scent.

Coursing: To hunt with hounds of the chase. Although somewhat simplified, this definition of "coursing" is perhaps the easiest and most comprehensive for the novice to understand. Of the subcategories of coursing—open field, park and lure—the American Midwest Heartland Petit Basset Griffon Vendéen Club put lure coursing to the test.

This desire, coupled with a group of people out to have fun with their hounds, resulted in a PBGV Lure Coursing Fun Run in 1997, which attracted 19 hounds and owners from several states. They had a fully fenced pasture, experienced lure operator, and a very enthusiastic crowd.

In typical hare coursing, the hare has two speeds—steady/methodical and high gear. In contrast, the lure has one speed and can run all day without exhaustion. The hare is replaced by a shredded plastic bag, which only thinks in one gear. This is not as farfetched as it sounds. In competitive lure coursing the maximum distance is 880 yards (805 meters) and a hare can sprint at full speed for the duration, which is a rather short sprint.

The lure never tires and is controlled by an operator rather than relying on nature and the hound. When the "hare" approaches a turn, it slows down. The hound will key in on the change and act accordingly. The hound learns to follow and not overshoot at every turn. It is an art!

For the lure operator to make use of this valid information, he must maintain a distance of 10–30 yards (9–27 meters) between the lure and the hound. He must also be certain that the lure goes through the turn well ahead of the dog. He strives for, and judges look for, the effort a hound expends on:

- maintaining, or attempting to achieve the position;
- forcing, or attempting to force the turns; and
- attempting to complete the distance.

Hounds are judged on endurance, follow and speed but must, however, hold the speed down to where turns can be made effectively (not a problem with the slower, methodical scenthound).

At the Start of a Run

The hounds stand with owners/handlers behind. Slip leads, or any leash used as a slip lead, are used for easy release. The lure is close, several feet in front of the hounds. The operator moves the lure slightly to tease and get their attention. As the hunt master shouts "Tally Ho," the lure operator releases the lure (run by a generator on a pulley) and the hounds are off. The typical length of a run is 300 yards (274 meters), with three to four turns. The hounds will follow the lure by sight to the finish, which is back to the handler.

Points for Judging

Follow Ability to stay with the quarry (the lure). This is not

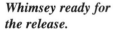

Whimsey ready for the release.

merely speed and agility, but also includes visual contact while negotiating turns, obstacles and difficult terrain, if any. Also persistence in attempting to re-sight after the quarry has broken visual contact.

Speed The rate at which the hound is capable of pursuing the quarry, in relation to the terrain on which the course is being run, and any type and number of obstacles encountered during the chase. Also the dog's acceleration capability (ability to regain maximum speed once it is reduced due to a turn or meeting an obstacle).

Endurance Related to the hound's top physical condition and his capabilities within that condition.

Enthusiasm The eagerness and determination a hound displays while in pursuit. Not to be confused with endurance, which is purely physical. Enthusiasm is entirely mental.

The 19 assembled PBGVs all had different ideas. Some were keen to run and amazed everyone by their aptitude, brilliance and sighting abilities. Others decided they were *only* scenthounds and took no interest in a plastic bag whatsoever as the smell of the many horses and rabbits that had been in the pasture was much more interesting. The initial enthusiasm of the remainder soon waned and their promising start turned into a look of disinterest as they wandered off half way through.

Conclusion? Scenthounds by design, sighthounds by choice!

The long walk home.

Therapy Dogs

Special dogs deserve special attention and Lauren Kovaleff was looking for an activity that would use Lucy's talents to the fullest. By chance she found out about the SPCA's animal therapy programs.

Studies in many countries have linked pet ownership to better health and subsequent research in the U.S. found that pet owners were less prone to heart disease and lived longer. Lucy was soon enrolled as a therapy dog volunteer in the San Francisco Bay Area visiting the sick, elderly, children, people with mental or physical challenges—anyone who would benefit from interacting with a pet and welcome the therapeutic effects that seeing, stroking or patting a lovable PBGV brings!

Lucy's ID to happiness.

Most therapy organizations have animal health and training standards, and programs vary, from fairly informal with little or no requirements to stiff entry and renewal standards. Requirements range from a temperament test to evaluation of the dog by an animal behaviorist. Others expect the handler to have a TB skin test annually and declare absence of exposure to any communicable disease before each visit. But this is just the beginning.

Group visits, or just Lauren and Lucy? See many people at once or just one? Group living situations, retirement communities, senior centers, AIDS/other specialized centers, hospitals, convalescent and rehab units? The scope is endless. Whatever the choice, the rewards of seeing the smiling faces and hearing laughter and clapping at the sight of Lucy modeling one of her fancy hats are immense.

With the PBGV's fairly short attention span and natural interest in a variety of odors, it takes skill to cope with the varied situations. However, Lucy takes an interest in everyone, regardless of health, age or appearance and, on group visits especially, Lauren finds it fun to watch the different animals interacting with people and each other.

Lucy does find it tough, though, being in the same room for an hour without being allowed to sniff around. So visits where she can go from room to room are usually her favorite, with five to ten minutes per room, new environments and new people keeping her on her toes. This is sometimes hard on Lauren because she may frequently have to lift all 36 pounds of wriggling, happy PBGV up to bed height—though it has been known for Lucy to attain a higher level by riding in a wheelchair.

Patients learning to deal with the physical and emotional effects of severe injuries, burns or chronic illness relax knowing that Lucy accepts them as they are. On one first visit to a children's hospital a nine-year-old girl, who was totally paralyzed and unable to feel sensations except on her face, squealed with laughter after requesting and receiving lots of kisses from Lucy. Residents who have few visitors are eternally grateful for the unconditional love and affection Lucy gives, without regard for how they look or move. Lauren says it is touching when Lucy

The Happiness Breed.

brings memories of a past pet, and the look that comes over the patient's face when this happens is indescribable. Sometimes sad, sometimes happy, wistful, relaxed and animated all at the same time. And how wonderful to experience a patient, who is normally silent, talking animatedly to Lucy.

One group visit to mentally ill children found a small boy hanging back as he was afraid of two "big, powerful dogs." Standing next to Lucy, his hand gradually crept onto her head and he began stroking her. Everyone held their breath as Lucy licked his fingers. When he asked to walk her on her leash, proof that she had won him over was complete. Lauren has been told that the smiles she sees from the minute she arrives are there long after she and Lucy leave, so, if you have a curious, friendly, loving PBGV and an hour or two to spare each month, consider animal-assisted therapy. You and your PBGV will provide immeasurable happiness without even trying.

As we have seen, the PBGV is infinitely versatile—first and foremost a hunter, splendid in the showring and a superb, adaptable family pet. What more could we ask of our faithful companion?

In sharing our research with you, we hope that you have enjoyed reading about the Petit Basset Griffon Vendéen, learned a little and now have a greater appreciation of this fascinating French hound. We end by quoting Jim Scharnberg MBH of the Skycastle, "These hounds are all heart—and they certainly lift mine!"

What greater tribute to our favorite breed?

APPENDIX

Pedigrees

Patachou des Barbus d'Entre Lac
Pacha des Barbus d'Entre Lac

Gambit of Kasani

Eng. Ch. Jomil Zadok

Int. Am. Can. Mex. Ch. Lacebarks Lydia

Am. Can. Ch. Jacobin At Dehra
Am. Ch. Fredwell Birribi At Dehra

Am. Chs. Elan-Vogue d'Mont Jois
Elan Cartouche de Qubic,
& Elan Christmas Surprise

Am. Can. Ch. Charlen's For Your Eyes Only

Am. Can. Ch. Charlen's Paradox

Patachou des Barbus d'Entre Lac
Pacha des Barbus d'Entre Lac

	Parents	Grand Parents	GG Parents
			Travailleur des Petites Brosses (P)
		Idalgo de la Bougrière (P)	
			Silène de la Bougrière (P)
	World Dutch Lux. Ch. Loy du Val d'Orbieu (P)		
		Isabelle du Val d'Orbieu (BGV)	Fr. Ch. Ulysse I de Fin Renard BC (P)
PATACHOU DES BARBUS D'ENTRE LAC PACHA DES BARBUS D'ENTRE LAC			Voxi du Val d'Orbieu (G)
May 17, 1979		Ch. Wiedoc von Schloss Isabella (P)	Fr. Int. Ch. Titus de la Réote (BGV)
			Fr. Ch. Salée de la Bougrière (BGV)
	Mireille de Kweb (P)		
			Vic des Genêts Roux (P)
		Iris von Lilienwappen (P)	
			Victoire I (P)

P = PBGV   G = GBGV   BGV = Not classified

Patachou des Barbus d'Entre Lac
Pacha des Barbus d'Entre Lac

GG Parents	GGG Parents	GGGG Parents
	Sallo (P)	not known
Travailleur des Petites Brosses		not known
(P)	Rachel des Petites Brosses (P)	Quecho de la Bougrière (G)
		Olleda de la Levraudière (G)
	Pirame de l'Echo de Cere (P)	Marko du Relais de Richemond (BGV)
Silène de la Bougrière (P)		Laika d'Echo de Cere (BGV)
	Querelle de la Bougrière (P)	Odéon de la Bougrière (G)
		Maya de la Bougrière (G)
	Soprano des Vaillants Limiers (P)	Oslo Bolo de la Tour César (P)
Fr. Ch. Ulysse I de Fin Renard		Princesse II des Vaillants Limiers BC(P)
BC (P)	Sirène de Fin Renard (P)	Ranfort de Fin Renard (P)
		Quebelle de Fin Renard (P)
	Rialto de la Vrignaie	Pillou
Voxi du Val d'Orbieu (G)		Noisette de la Vrignaie
	Suzy de Fin Renard	Quidam de la Tour César (P)
		O'Croa de la Lipaudière
	Orlon de Coeur Joie (BGV)	Gino du Avel Mor (G)
Fr. Int. Ch. Titus de la Réote		Lady II de Coeur Joie (BGV)
(BGV)	Olida de la Lipaudière (BGV)	Gamin des Landes d'Argevillère (BGV)
		Ignace de la Lipaudière (BGV)
	Pirame de l'Echo de Cere (P)	Marko du Relais de Richemond (BGV)
Fr. Ch. Salée de la Bougrière		Laika d'Echo de Cere (BGV)
(BGV)	Querelle de la Bougrière (P)	Odéon de la Bougrière (G)
		Maya de la Bougrière (G)
	Ut de la Brèche des Charmes (BGV)	Ostrogoth de la Brèche des Charmes (BGV)
Vic des Genêts Roux (P)		Polka (BGV)
	Roquepine du Marais de Riez	Lutino
		Kadie
	Tango de Fin Renard (P)	Rodeo de Fin Renard (P)
Victoire I (P)		Querida de Fin Renard (P)
	Unique (BGV)	Syrus de la Vrignaie (P)
		Surprise (BGV)

P = PBGV   G = GBGV   BGV = Not classified

Gambit of Kasani

Parents	Grand Parents	GG Parents
		Marquis de la Plaine des Gravettes
	Rabio des Rives de la Garonne	
		Sibelle de Rodabertny
Dan. Ch. Ursins des Rives de la Garonne		
		Ma Pomme de la Volette
	Perine du Clos Garnachois	
		Lausanne du Clos Garnachois
GAMBIT OF KASANI		
November 20, 1984		Ilot de la Roimelière
	Noiro de l'Égalité	
		Java du Pays de Retz
Ristourne de Crislaure		
		Lassac de la Belle Musique
	Nanouche de Crislaure	
		Laisse de Fin Renard

Gambit of Kasani

GG Parents	GGG Parents	GGGG Parents
	Ugo de la Bougrière	Tapette de la Levraudière
Marquis de la Plaine des		Maya de la Bougrière
Gravettes	Janou du Grangeot de Callou	Virus de Fin Renard
		Vodka du Grangeot de Callou
	Quidam de la Tour César	Portos
Sibelle de Rodabertny		Miss
	Oliene de la Lipaudière	not known
		not known
	Petit Prince de la Levraudière	Jacobin de la Levraudière
Ma Pomme de la Volette		Levraudière de Coeur Joie
	Ines	Ubu
		Urielle
	Vasco de la Jaranne	Sanspeur des Grands de Hurlevent
Lausanne du Clos Garnachois		Tapette de la Jaranne
	Iselle du Clos Garnachois	Syrus de la Bougrière
		Touchlac des Petites Brosses
	Syrus de la Bougrière	Ocelot de Vauluard
Ilot de la Roimelière		O'Belle de la Bougrière
	Unité des Petites Brosses BC	Quecho de la Bougrière
		Olleda de la Levraudière
	Ultra de la Roimelière	Syrus de la Bougrière
Java du Pays de Retz		Saturne des Petites Brosses
	Urette de l'Égalité	Silou du Pays de Retz
		Rite de l'Égalité
	Japy de Fin Renard	Fr Ch Ulysse I de Fin Renard BC
Lassac de la Belle Musique		Vendée de la Bougrière
	Javotte	not known
		not known
	Tambour de la Bougrière	not known
Laisse de Fin Renard		not known
	Urlette de Fin Renard	Soprano des Vaillants Limiers
		Sirène des Vaillants Limiers

Eng. Ch. Jomil Zadok

Parents	Grand Parents	GG Parents
		Ilot de la Roimelière
	Noiro de l'Égalité	
		Java du Pays de Retz
Eng. Dan. Lux. Ch. Salto de Crislaure of Morebess		
		Vasco de la Jaranne
	Musette de Crislaure	
		Tulipe du Pays de Retz
ENG. CH. JOMIL ZADOK		
January 16, 1987		Arilica Otello of Jomil
	Varon Zorro	
		Jeannemart of Varon
Jomil Reverie		
		Armand of Jomil
	Jomil Leda	
		T'Annetta

Eng. Ch. Jomil Zadok

GG Parents	GGG Parents	GGGG Parents
	Syrus de la Bougrière	Ocelot de Vauluard
Ilot de la Roimelière		O'Belle de la Bougrière
	Unité des Petites Brosses BC	Quecho de la Bougrière
		Olleda de la Levraudière
	Ultra de la Roimelière	Syrus de la Bougrière
Java du Pays de Retz		Saturne des Petites Brosses
	Urette de l'Égalité	Silou du Pays de Retz
		Rite de l'Égalité
	Sanspeur des Grands de Hurlevent	not known
Vasco de la Jaranne		not known
	Tapette de la Jaranne	Oural de la Vrignaie
		Oona
	Requin de la Vrignaie	not known
Tulipe du Pays de Retz		not known
	Rincette	Oka
		Islande du Pays de Retz
	World Int. Italian Ch. Untel de la	Tapette
Arilica Otello of Jomil	Bougrière	Maya de la Bougrière
	Junon de Fin Renard	Iléande
		Sirène
	Windsor von Schloss Isabella	Fr. Int. Ch. Titus de la Réote
Jeannemart of Varon		Nina de la Réote
	Jomil Gitane	Rigolo de la Vrignaie
		T'Annetta
	Windsor von Schloss Isabella	Fr. Int. Ch. Titus de la Réote
Armand of Jomil		Nina de la Réote
	Jomil Farandole	Rigolo de la Vrignaie
		T'Annetta
	Petit Prince de la Levraudière	Jacobin de la Levraudière
T'Annetta		Levraudière de Coeur Joie
	Orée	Jalon de Coeur Joie
		Ninon de la Brèche des Charmes

Int. Am. Can. Mex. Ch. Lacebarks Lydia

Parents	Grand Parents	GG Parents
		Echo
	Gourou of Wakelyns	
		Calina del Doppo Réal
Am. Ch. Wakelyns Noblesse		
		Jomil Flambard
	Eng. Ch. Twinrivers Duchesse of Wakelyns	
		Twinrivers Alouette
INT. AM. CAN. MEX. CH. LACEBARKS LYDIA		
		Twinrivers Herspereus at Dehra
July 6, 1988		
	Twinrivers Ivor of Wakelyns	
		Twinrivers Babette
Am. Ch. Wakelyns Javelot		
		Gourou of Wakelyns
	Huntswold Trefle of Wakelyns	
		Fixed Asset of Huntswold

Int. Am. Can. Mex. Ch. Lacebarks Lydia

GG Parents	GGG Parents	GGGG Parents
	Brigand	Igor de la Brèche des Charmes
Echo		Vitrex des Petites Brosses
	Ninon de la Brèche des Charmes	Iram de la Bougrière
		Urleuse de la Brèche des Charmes
	Ico de la Réote	Orlon de Coeur Joie BC
Calina del Doppo Réal		Ulida de la Réote
	Ixia	Ulric
		Utah
	Rigolo de la Vrignaie	Pillou
Jomil Flambard		Noisette de la Vrignaie
	T'Annetta	Petit Prince de la Levraudière
		Orée
	Windsor von Schloss Isabella	Fr. Int. Ch Titus de la Réote
Twinrivers Alouette		Nina de la Réote
	Jomil Farandole	Rigolo de la Vrignaie
		T'Annetta
	Varon Zorro	Arilica Otello of Jomil
Twinrivers Herspereus at Dehra		Jeannemart of Varon
	Twinrivers Alouette	Windsor von Schloss Isabella
		Jomil Farandole
	Jomil Flambard	Rigolo de la Vrignaie
Twinrivers Babette		T'Annetta
	Huntersbrook Mystery	Windsor von Schloss Isabella
		Jomil Danielle of Huntersbrook
	Echo	Brigand
Gourou of Wakelyns		Ninon de la Brèche des Charmes
	Calina del Doppo Réal	Ico de la Réote
		Ixia
	Jomil Flambard	Rigolo de la Vrignaie
Fixed Asset of Huntswold		T'Annetta
	Wakelyns Adele	Pacha des Barbus d'Entre Lac
		Eng. Ch. Twinrivers Duchesse of Wakelyns

Am. Can. Ch. Jacobin At Dehra
Am. Ch. Fredwell Birribi At Dehra

Parents	Grand Parents	GG Parents
		Tonus des Rives de la Garonne
	Morebess Élégant de la Baule	
		Dan. Ch. Urfa des Rives de la Garonne
Eng. Ch. Morebess Haveloc at Dehra		
		Eng. Dan. Lux. Ch. Salto de Crislaure of Morebess
AM. CAN. CH. JACOBIN AT DEHRA July 27, 1988		Dan. Fin. Ch. Oleine de Biars
		Dan. Fin. Swe. Nordic Ch. Morebess Thérèse la Tranqueuse
AM. CH. FREDWELL BIRRIBI AT DEHRA August 27, 1989		Arilica Otello of Jomil
	Varon Zorro	
		Jeannemart of Varon
Jomil Reverie		
		Armand of Jomil
	Jomil Leda	
		T'Annetta

Am. Can. Ch. Jacobin At Dehra
Am. Ch. Fredwell Birribi At Dehra

GG Parents	GGG Parents	GGGG Parents
	Poly des Rives de la Garonne	Niko
Tonus des Rives de la		Ostie
Garonne	Ch. Noisette des Rives de la	Luron de Val d'Orbieu
	Garonne	Jenny du Grangeot de Callou
	Rabio des Rives de la Garonne	Marquis de la Plaine des Gravettes
Dan. Ch. Urfa des Rives de la		Sibelle de Rodabertny
Garonne	Perine du Clos Garnachois	Ma Pomme de la Volette
		Lausanne du Clos Garnachois
	Noiro de lÉgalité	Ilot de la Roimelière
Eng. Dan. Lux. Ch. Salto de		Java du Pays de Retz
Crislaure of Morebess	Musette de Crislaure	Vasco de la Jaranne
		Tulipe de Pays de Retz
	Dan. German Dutch Ch. Morebess	Dan. Ch. Jomil Hotspur
Dan. Fin. Swe. Nordic Ch.		Raymond le Rebelle Dan. Ch.
Mignonnette de la Belle Musique		
Morebess Thérèse la	Dan. Ch.Mignonnette de la	Uron
Tranqueuse	Belle Musique	Jira
	World Int. Italian Ch. Untel de	Tapette
Arilica Otello of Jomil	la Bougrière	Maya de la Bougrière
	Junon de Fin Renard	Iléande
		Sirène
	Windsor von Schloss Isabella	Fr. Int. Ch. Titus de la Réote
Jeannemart of Varon		Nina de la Réote
	Jomil Gitane	Rigolo de la Vrignaie
		T'Annetta
	Windsor von Schloss Isabella	Fr. Int. Ch. Titus de la Réote
Armand of Jomil		Nina de la Réote
	Jomil Farandole	Rigolo de la Vrignaie
		T'Annetta
	Petit Prince de la Levraudière	Jacobin de la Levraudière
T'Annetta		Levraudière de Coeur Joie
	Orée	Jalon de Coeur Joie
		Ninon de la Brèche des Charmes

Am. Chs. Elan Vogue d' Mont Jois
Elan Cartouche de Qubic, & Elan Christmas Surprise

Parents	Grand Parents	GG Parents
		Eng. Dan. Lux. Ch. Salto de Crislaure of Morebess
	Eng. Ch. Jomil Zadok	
		Jomil Reverie
Am. Ch. Dehra Requin		
		Jomil Larbi of Varon
	Dehra Astre Brumeuse at Bareve	
AM. CHS. ELAN-VOGUE D'MONT JOIS September 11, 1991		Mistinguet at Dehra
CARTOUCHE D'QUBIC & CHRISTMAS SURPRISE September 15, 1992		Morebess Moustache de St. Foy
	Edeängs Fridolf	
		Idolens Ésire
Am. Ch. Balmar's Mignonnette		
		Dan. Ch. Ursins des Rives de la Garonne
	Morebess Charlotte de St. Florent	
		Dan. Fin. Ch. Morebess Oleine de Biars

Am. Chs. Elan Vogue d' Mont Jois
Elan Cartouche de Qubic, & Elan Christmas Surprise

GG Parents	GGG Parents	GGGG Parents
	Noiro de l'Égalité	Ilot de la Roimelière
Eng. Dan. Lux. Ch. Salto de		Java du Pays de Retz
Crislaure of Morebess	Musette de Crislaure	Vasco de la Jaranne
		Tulipe du Pays de Retz
	Varon Zorro	Arilica Otello of Jomil
Jomil Reverie		Jeannemart of Varon
	Jomil Leda	Armand of Jomil
		T'Annetta
	Armand of Jomil	Windsor von Schloss Isabella
Jomil Larbi of Varon		Jomil Farandole
	T'Annetta	Petit Prince de la Levraudière
		Orèe
	Jomil Mistral	Aricila Otello
Mistinguet at Dehra		Jomil Fauvette
	Mondalis Zeta	Arilica Otello of Jomil
		Jomil Hebe
	Dan. German Dutch Ch. Morebess	Dan. Ch. Jomil Hotspur
Morebess Moustache	Raymond le Rebelle	Dan. Ch. Mignonnette de la Belle Musique
de St. Foy	Ristourne de Crislaure	Noiro de l'Égalité
		Nanouche de Crislaure
	Nordic Dutch Int. Ch. Ixia of Jomil	Windsor von Schloss Isabella
Idolens Ésire		Jomil Farandole
	Jomil Kasmira	Armand of Jomil
		Jomil Fauvette
	Rabio des Rives de la Garonne	Marquis de la Plaine des Gravettes
Dan. Ch. Ursins des		Sibelle de Rodabertny
Rives de la Garonne	Perine du Clos Garnachois	Ma Pomme de la Volette
		Lausanne du Clos Garnachois
	Eng. Dan. Lux. Ch. Salto de	Noiro de l'Égalité
Dan. Fin. Ch. Morebess	Crislaure of Morebess	Musette de Crislaure
Oleine de Biars	Dan. Swe. Fin. Nordic Ch.	Dan. German Dutch Ch. Morebess
		Raymond le Rebelle
	Morebess Thérèse la Tranqueuse	Dan. Ch. Mignonnette de la Belle Musique

Am. Can. Ch. Charlen's For Your Eyes Only

Parents	Grand Parents	GG Parents
		Dan. Ch. Jomil Hotspur
	Dan. Ch. Morebess Uron Comme Grand-Père	
		Dan. Ch. Mignonnette de la Belle Musique
Dan. Ger. VDH Dutch Can. Ber. Am. Ch. Chouan Gimlet		
		Eng. Dan. Lux. Ch. Salto de Crislaure of Morebess
	Dan. Ch. Morebess Nadia de Cahors	
		Morebess Rosamonde la Reine
AM. CAN. CH. CHARLEN'S FOR YOUR EYES ONLY		
		Varon Zorro
December 26, 1993	Am. Ch. Dehra Nuance	
		Morebess Helga at Dehra
Am. Ch. Charlen's Isis of Chouan		
		Blake de la Baracine
	Dan. Am. Ch. Chouan Pretty Flamingo	
		Rosette de la Baracine

Am. Can. Ch. Charlen's For Your Eyes Only

GG Parents	GGG Parents	GGGG Parents
	Rigolo de la Vrignaie	Pillou
Dan. Ch. Jomil Hotspur		Noisette de la Vrignaie
	Jomil Fauvette	Rigolo de la Vrignaie
		T'Annetta
	Uron de la Belle Musique	Said de Vainqueur Hallier
Dan. Ch. Mignonnette		Q'Rita
de la Belle Musique	Jira de la Belle Musique	Turlot de Fin Renard
		Urlette de Fin Renard
	Noiro de l'Égalité	Ilot de la Roimelière
Eng. Dan. Lux. Ch. Salto		Java du Pays de Retz
de Crislaure of	Musette de Crislaure	Vasco de la Jaranne
Morebess		Tulipe du Pays de Retz
	Dan. Ch. Jomil Hotspur	Rigolo de la Vrignaie
Morebess Rosamonde		Jomil Fauvette
la Reine	Dan. Ch. Mignonnette de la Belle	Uron de la Belle Musique
	Musique	Jira de la Belle Musique
	Arilica Otello of Jomil	World Int. Italian Ch. Untel de la
		Bougrière
Varon Zorro		Junon de Fin Renard
	Jeannemart of Varon	Windsor von Schloss Isabella
		Jomil Gitane
	Morebess Élégant de la Baule	Tonus des Rives de la Garonne
Morebess Helga at Dehra		Dan. Ch. Urfa des Rives de la Garonne
	Dan. Fin. Ch. Morebess Oleine de	Eng. Dan. Lux. Ch. Salto de Crislaure of
	Biars	Morebess
		Dan. Swe. Fin. Nordic Ch. Morebess
		Thérèse la Tranqueuse
	Untel de la Baracine	Pauli des Rives de la Garonne
Blake de la Baracine		Saika du Mazel Valentine
	Saika du Mazel Valentine	Negus du Rocher de la Mer
		Nutsy de l'Égalité
	Negus du Rocher de la Mer	Vidocq
Rosette de la Baracine		Ira
	Nigelle	Jericho
		Idole de la Vrignaie

Am. Can. Ch. Charlen's Paradox

Parents	Grand Parents	GG Parents
		Sifleur du Lite
	Urio des Rives de la Garonne	
		Rousette des Rives de la Garonne
Dan. Fin. Am. Can. Ch. Morebess Sur-Moi de Fontenay		Morebess Élégant de la Baule
	Morebess Jezabel d'Evreux	
		Dan. Ch. Urfa des Rives de la Garonne
AM. CAN. CH. CHARLEN'S PARADOX		Varon Zorro
May 17, 1994	Am. Ch. Dehra Nuance	
		Morebess Helga at Dehra
Charlen's Balkhr Hollywood		Eng. Ch. Morebess Haveloc at Dehra
	Dehra Ondine	
		Dehra Astre Brumeuse at Bareve

Am. Can. Ch. Charlen's Paradox

GG Parents	GGG Parents	GGGG Parents
	Ronflot du Pays de Retz	not known
Sifleur du Lite		not known
	Orca de l'Égalité	not known
		not known
	Marquis de la Plaine des Gravettes	Ugo de la Bougrière
Rousette des Rives de		Janou du Grangeot de Callou
la Garonne	Natia des Rives de la Garonne	not known
		not known
	Tonus des Rives de la Garonne	Poly des Rives de la Garonne
Morebess Élégant de		Ch. Noisette des Rives de la Garonne
la Baule	Dan. Ch. Urfa des Rives de la	Rabio des Rives de la Garonne
	Garonne	Perine du Clos Garnachois
	Rabio des Rives de la Garonne	Marquis de la Plaine des Gravettes
Dan. Ch. Urfa des		Sibelle de Rodabertny
Rives de la Garonne	Perine du Clos Garnachois	Ma Pomme de la Volette
		Lausanne du Clos Garnachois
	Arilica Otello of Jomil	World Int. Italian Ch. Untel de la Bougrière
Varon Zorro		Junon de Fin Renard
	Jeannemart of Varon	Windsor von Schloss Isabella
		Jomil Gitane
	Morebess Élégant de la Baule	Tonus des Rives de la Garonne
Morebess Helga at Dehra		Dan. Ch. Urfa des Rives de la Garonne
	Dan. Fin. Ch. Oleine de Biars	Eng. Dan. Lux. Ch. Salto de Crislaure of Morebess
		Dan. Fin. Swe. Nordic Ch Morebess Thérèse la Tranqueuse
	Morebess Élégant de la Baule	Tonus des Rives de la Garonne
Eng. Ch. Morebess		Dan. Ch. Urfa des Rives de la Garonne
Haveloc at Dehra	Dan. Fin. Ch. Oleine de Biars	Eng. Dan. Lux. Ch. Salto de Crislaure of Morebess
		Dan. Fin. Swe. Nordic Ch. Morebess
Thérèse la Tranqueuse		
	Jomil Larbi of Varon	Armand of Jomil
Dehra Astre Brumeuse at		T'Annetta
Bareve	Mistinguet at Dehra	Jomil Mistral
		Mondalis Zeta

GLOSSARY OF TERMS

a jambes droites (Fr)   Straight front legs.

a jambes demi-torses (Fr)   Front legs with half-crook.

a jambes torses (Fr)   Front legs with full crook.

a poil dur (Fr)   Rough coated.

a poil ras (Fr)   Short/smooth coated.

affix   Word(s) attached to the dog's registered name to identify it with a particular kennel. If they come before the dog's name, it is called a prefix; if they come after, it is called a suffix.

AKC   The American Kennel Club, the governing body of the canine world in America.

all-rounder   A dog show judge qualified to assess many breeds in different Groups (e.g. hound, terrier).

amateur (Fr)   A lover of; dog fancier.

angulation   Angles formed by the joints, particularly the forehand and quarters.

asymptomatic   Producing or showing no symptoms.

autosome   Any chromosome that is not a sex chromosome.

babbler   A hound that disrupts the pack by crying when not on a scent and misleading the others.

back   The part of the dog's body between withers and set-on of tail along the vertebrae.

Balai Directive   Commercially Traded Dogs Act 1992 where, under certain conditions, dogs may be imported into the U.K. from another European country without going into quarantine.

balance   Every part of the body in proportion throughout.

basset (Fr)   A descriptive term for any of the hound group that are shorter-legged than their full-size counterparts. A *basset* breed must be longer than its height.

basset   The group of short-legged, low-set breeds, including Basset Hounds, smooth-coated bassets, rough-coated bassets, etc.

Basset   Referring to the Basset Hound, a smooth coated basset.

basset courant (Fr)   A term for, literally, a hunting/running hound with a body set low to the ground.

basset fauve (Fr)   The general term for any tawny-colored, low-set hound.

Basset Fauve   Abbreviation for the Basset Fauve de Bretagne, a popular French hound breed.

basset français (Fr)   General term for the mid-19th century, French low-set hound of both rough and smooth coat.

Basset Français   A low-set French hound that became a definitive breed in its own right from 1896 onwards.

basset griffon (Fr)   The general term used for any rough-coated hound with body low to the ground. Literally, "short-legged, rough-coated."

Basset Griffon   An abbreviation of Basset Griffon Vendéen, both the *petit* and *grand* varieties.

Basset Griffon Vendéen   The particular (pre-division into Grand and Petit) breed of rough-coated, low-set hound from the Vendée region of France.

BIS   Best in Show.

BISS   Best in Specialty Show.

bite   The position of the lower and upper teeth when the mouth is shut.

BOB   Best of Breed.

bocage (Fr)   Hedged farmland, coppice.

bone   Substance of limbs.

BOS   Best Opposite Sex.

BPIS   Best Puppy in Show.

brevet de chasse (Fr)   Certificate of hunting.

Briquet   Abbreviated term for Briquet Griffon Vendéen. The medium, more compact hound, and second-largest of the four Griffon Vendéen varieties.

brucellosis   An infectious disease of dogs, usually transmitted through mating or exposure to infected reproductive secretions.

CAC   Certificat d'Aptitude au titre de Champion; an award given at FCI-supported national shows.

CACIB   Certificat d'Aptitude au titre de Champion International de Beauté; an award given at FCI-supported international shows.

canid   Any animal belonging to the genus *canis*, which includes dogs, jackals and wolves.

CC *See* Challenge Certificate.

CD Companion Dog.

CDX Companion Dog Excellent.

CERF Canine Eye Registration Foundation. This registry records thorough eye test results performed by veterinarians.

Ch *See* champion.

Challenge Certificate (CC) The British Kennel Club award for best of sex in a breed at a championship show (where Challenge Certificates are on offer for the breed), which comes under their rules and regulations.

champion (Ch) In the U.K., a dog that has won three Challenge Certificates under three different judges. In North America, Canada and Australia, a dog that has won the required number of points, under their rules and regulations.

character The make-up of a dog combining all the essential points of appearance, disposition and behavior.

chasse-à-courre (Fr) Hunting by scent and pursuing the quarry to the death.

chasse-à-tir (Fr) Hunting by using hounds to drive game to waiting guns.

Chien Basset A low-set, short-legged hound, used for hunting hare, rabbit, fox.

Chien Briquet A medium-sized hound, used for hunting game such as hare or roe deer.

chien courant (Fr) Term for a hunting hound.

Chien d'Ordre A full-sized hound, used for running down quarry such as stag, boar and wolf, without a gun.

choke chain A chain collar that tightens or loosens depending on the dog's or handler's actions.

chest Above the brisket and between the shoulder blades.

chromosome Cell nucleus of all multi-cell organisms that contain DNA (deoxy-ribonucleic acid). Comprising the genes of that species, the building blocks of life.

confirmateur (Fr) Person who evaluates the adult dog to determine it conforms to the standard.

conformation The form and general structural makeup of a dog to fit a standard.

cornified cells   Very mature cells lining the vagina, angular in outline, which often lack a nucleus, indicating the presence or absence of estrogen, i.e., cornification increases the estrogen levels.

country   *See* registered country.

couple   Two hounds.

courant (Fr)   Running (literal).

coursing   Hounds hunting their quarry by sight.

cow-hocked   A dog's hocks bending inwards and his stifles and feet turning out. A serious fault.

crabbing   *See* side-winding.

crossbreeding   A mating between two dogs of different breeds.

croup   The back immediately before the root of the tail.

Crufts   British championship show for which all dogs must qualify to enter; founded in 1886 by entrepreneur Charles Cruft, who originally worked for Spratt's Patent Ltd., manufacturers of meat biscuits for dogs.

cryptorchid   A male animal that does not have his testicles descended into the scrotum. Unilateral cryptorchid is when only one testicle is affected; bilateral cryptorchid is when both testicles are affected.

Dam   The mother of a dog.

débourrage (Fr)   First lessons given to an animal.

dew claw   Extra claw on the inside of the lower part of the forelegs and occasionally the hindlegs. May be removed a few days after birth.

distracted   Pulled in different directions.

dominant   Color or characteristic that covers up all others that are recessive to it.

double coat   Comprised of a weather-resistant outercoat and a finer undercoat that grows near to the skin and gives warmth.

down on pasterns   Front feet coming forward at an angle instead of coming down in a fairly straight line from the forearm.

écoutez (Fr)   Meaning "listen," it is the word hunters use to teach their dogs to listen to the hound on the scent.

elbow   The joint at the top of the forearm.

elbow (out at)   Elbows that turn out from the body.

expression   A combination of the position, color and size of the eye, which gives the head an appealing, correct appearance.

estrus Period of a bitch's heat cycle during which she may be mated.

exogenous Growing or originating from outside.

fauve (Fr) Fawn-colored, tawny.

FCI Fédération Cynologique Internationale, European organization whose aims are to promote and protect the pure-bred dog.

flags (on the) (Abbreviation for "flag-stones"). Hounds exhibited loose on a hard/concrete surface.

flat-sided A dog with very little spring of ribs.

flews Fleshy hanging upper lips of breeds such as bassets, Bloodhounds, Mastiffs, etc.

forearm The long bone of the front leg between elbow and pasterns.

forechest The pad of muscle at the front of the chest.

foreface Muzzle.

forehand The front of the dog excluding the head.

front The forehand of the body—forelegs, chest, brisket and shoulders.

gait Leg action of the dog when moving.

gay tail A tail carried higher than the standard demands, usually curled over the back.

gene The smallest unit of hereditary information.

genotype Unseen genetic makeup.

gestation Period of organic development of a puppy within the uterus.

glaucoma Elevation of intraocular pressure which, when sustained, causes intraocular damage resulting in blindness.

gonioscopy Specialized procedure that uses a contact lens to examine the iridocorneal angle.

grand basset (Fr) General descriptive term for the taller of the low-set hounds.

Grand Basset Abbreviated term for the Grand Basset Griffon Vendéen.

Grande Taille The larger basset, standing around 16" (40cm).

grande vénerie (Fr) Hunting of large game with a pack of full-sized hounds.

grizzle A mixture of gray hair with another color or colors.

harsh coat A stiff, wiry coat.

haw The inner surface of the lower eyelid.

heat The term used to describe a bitch in season.

height The measurement of a dog from withers to the ground.

hemostats Blunt surgical/veterinary instruments that stop bleeding by compression of a blood vessel.

heredity The sum of what is inherited from previous generations.

hock The joint in the hindleg between pastern and stifle.

hocks well let down Hocks that are close to the ground.

homozygous Dominant for a trait or color. Carries no recessive for that characteristic.

idiopathic Disease or medical condition of unknown cause that arises spontaneously.

in-breeding Generally the mating of close relatives, such as mother to son, father to daughter, or brother to sister.

Int. International.

irido Denoting the iris of the eye.

jaws The upper and lower part of the foreface where the teeth are placed.

Junior Warrant U.K. award for a dog under 18 months of age who gains the required number of points in breed classes.

knuckling over Caused by the front legs bulging over at the knees, an occasional problem in some bassets.

lay back The placement of the shoulder, that is the scapula, in relation to the withers.

leash Three of the same kind of hounds.

leathers Flaps of the ears.

leggy Legs that are too long for the body, which put the dog out of balance.

level bite Teeth of the upper and lower incisors meeting edge to edge.

line-breeding Mating of two dogs with similar, immediately related strains.

Livre d'Origines Français The Société Centrale Canine's studbook.

loins The part of the body between the last rib and hindquarters.

LOF *See* Livre d'Origines Français.

low set ears Ears set below the level of the eyeline.

low set tail Tail set lower than or below the level of the topline.

lower thigh The part of the hindquarters from stifle to hock.

luxated lens Partial (subluxated) or complete displacement of the lens from the normal anatomic site behind the pupil.

MBH Master of Basset Hounds.

Mendel, Gregor 19th century Czechoslovakian monk who discovered the mathematical formulas for inheritance of color and size in sweet peas, leading to the science of genetics.

meute (Fr) Small pack (of hounds).

milk teeth Puppy's first set of teeth.

molar One of the rear teeth used for grinding.

monorchid A male animal with only one testicle in the scrotum.

music Melodious sound of a hound in full cry.

muzzle The foreface in front of the eyes, i.e. nasal bone, nostril and jaws, including mouth.

neck The seven vertebrae of the spine from head to withers.

nose A hound's scenting ability.

occiput The upper back point of the skull.

OFA Orthopedic Foundation for Animals in America. Acts as a hip dysplasia control registry.

olfactory Pertaining to the sense of smell.

Open class For all dogs of the breed for which the class is provided and eligible for entry at the show.

Open Show A U.K. dog show, where Challenge Certificates are not on offer, that is open to all exhibitors who must be entered before the day.

out-crossing Mating of two unrelated dogs.

overshot Upper incisors projecting over and beyond the bottom ones.

oxytocin A veterinary drug, generally injected under the skin, that is given to a bitch to stimulate contractions.

pace Gait in which the legs move in lateral pairs, i.e. both legs on one side being moved before those on the other.

pack Several hounds kept together for the purpose of hunting as a team.

pad Sole of a dog's foot.

paddling A dog throwing his front feet out sideways in a loose, uncontrolled manner, making it look wide in front on the move.

pasterns The lowest part of the front leg between knee and foot.

PBGV Petit Basset Griffon Vendéen (phonetically—puh-tee bah-say gree-fohn von-day-uhn).

PBGVCA Petit Basset Griffon Vendéen Club of America.

pectinate ligaments Ligaments that drain fluid from the eye.

pedigree A genealogical record giving the ancestry of a dog.

penetrance The percentage frequency with which a gene exhibits its effects.

petit basset (Fr) A general descriptive term for the shorter of the small, low-set hound.

Petit Basset Abbreviation for Petit Basset Griffon Vendeen

Petite Taille The smaller basset, standing under 15" (38 cm).

petite vénerie (Fr) Using small or medium sized hounds to hunt smaller game.

phenotype The actual outward appearance that can be seen—opposite of genotype.

Piaget, Jean (1896-1980) Swiss psychologist, known for his pioneering work on the four developmental stages of mental growth in children and on cognitive abilities.

pied A term used for a coat that is a mixture of two or three colors.

polygenic Trait controlled by multiple genes.

progesterone A steroid hormone secreted by the ovary before implantation of the fertilized ovum.

prognathism Having a projecting lower jaw (*see* undershot).

puppy A dog not exceeding 12 months.

quality An overall general excellence of character, expression and conformation, standing and moving.

quarantine Period of isolation for an animal to ensure no communicable diseases.

quarters Hindquarters.

recessive Color or trait that is not dominant and must link up with another recessive for expression.

registered country Area of countryside in U.K. where a pack has hunting rights.

réquerant (Fr)   A hound's ability to cast and work persistently, to fresh-find the line or scent of the quarry.

ribbed up   A compact dog with well sprung ribs.

saber tail   Tail carried in a curve.

sable   A blend or integration of black/brown hair.

sac   The membrane housing the puppy within the uterus.

scent   The odor given off by a quarry.

scenthound   A hound that hunts by nose and scent rather than by sight.

scissor bite   The incisors of the upper jaw just overlapping the ones of the bottom jaw.

scrotum   The bag of skin that holds the testicles.

season   Term used for a bitch during the period of her estrus.

second thigh   *See* lower thigh.

set-on   Where the root of the tail meets the body.

short-coupled   Short and strong in the loins.

shoulder   Area created by the shoulder blade and muscles that support it.

side-winding   A dog moving sideways to the point of direction.

sire   The father of a dog.

sloping shoulders   Shoulders well laid back and capable of allowing the dog to move easily.

snipey   Pointed, narrow and limited width in shape of muzzle.

Société Centrale Canine   French Kennel Club.

specialty   An AKC-approved show for members of single breed club, which generally attracts points towards champion status.

standard   FCI or national Kennel Club official description of the breed to which dogs should be judged.

stern   A hound's tail.

sternum   The breastbone.

stifle   Joint in the hind leg between the thigh and second thigh.

stop   The depression between the eyes, dividing the forehead and muzzle.

straight shoulders   Insufficient angulation between shoulder blade and upper arm.

substance   Having good bone, body weight and demonstrating power throughout.

TD Tracking Dog.

tongue (give) The cry of a hound when following a scent.

tonometry Measurement of intraocular eye pressure.

topline Upper profile from withers to croup.

torse (Fr) Crooked.

trochlea The groove at the lower end of the humerus.

type Distinguishable breed characteristics as given in the breed standard.

UD Utility Dog.

undercoat Soft, short hair concealed by longer coat.

undershot The lower incisors projecting beyond the upper ones.

upper arm The humerus, which is the bone of the foreleg between shoulder blade and forearm.

upright shoulders Insufficient angulation of the shoulder blade.

vairon **(eyes)** (Fr) Eyes of different colors.

VDH Champion title from the Verein Deutscher Hundeweses (German Kennel Club).

venery Hunting with dogs and running down an animal by scent.

weaving Front legs crossing when moving.

well let down Correct degree of angulation of stifle and hock joint.

whelp A newborn puppy.

whipper-in Person who helps the huntsman to control the hounds.

withers Highest part of the body just behind the neck, where the top of the shoulder blades may be felt.

workup Exploratory medical tests to investigate the cause of symptoms.

worldwinner Title awarded by organizing country at annual World Dog Show held in an FCI-affiliated country.

youthwinner Award at FCI supported show for a dog under 15 months old which may not be awarded CACIB.

BIBLIOGRAPHY

Books about Basset Breeds

Auger, Dr. Jean. *Les Chiens Courants de Vendée*. Vigot Frères, Paris, 1942.

Bourbon, Alain. *Nos Bassets Français*. A Goupil, Laval, 1911.

Dupuis, Claire. *Les Bassets Griffons Vendéens*. Editions de Vecchi SA, Paris, 1996.

Foy, Marcia A. and Anna Nicholas. *The Basset Hound*. THF Publications, Inc., Ltd., New Jersey, 1985.

Johnston, George. *The Basset Hound*. Popular Dogs Publishing Company, Ltd., 1968.

Johnston, George and Maria Ericson. *Hounds of France*. Spur Publications, Saiga, 1979.

Miller, John and Maurice Leblanc. *Les Bassets Courants*. Gerfaut Club, France, 1987.

Rowett-Johns, Jeanne. *All About the Basset Hound*. Pelham Books, 1973.

Steidel, Kitty. *Understanding the Petit Basset Griffon Vendéen—Rustic French Hound*. Orient Publications, 1987.

Books about Hunting

Buchanan-Jardine, Sir John. *Hounds of the World*. Methuen & Co Ltd., London, 1937.

Copold, Steve. *Hounds, Hares and Other Creatures*. Hoflin Publishing, Arvada, Colorado, 1977.

Daubingé, Paul. *Épreuves de Meutes*. 1951.

de Vezins, Comte Elie. *Les Chiens Courants Français pour la Chasse du Lièvre dans le Midi de la France*. Montauban, France, 1882.

Johnson, Glen R. *Tracking Dogs*. Arner Publications Ltd., 1977.

Larcher, Dr. Gérard-Philippe. *Chiens de Grande Vénerie: Le Poitevin*. Imp. Bosc Frères, Lyon, 1973.

Le Couteulx de Canteleu. *Le Manuel de Vénerie Française*. Librairie de Mme Bouchard-Huzard, 1858.

Thomas, Joseph B. *Hounds and Hunting Through the Ages*. Garden City Publishing Co., Inc., New York, 1937.

Walker, David and others. *Harehunters All*. Burrow's Press Ltd., Cheltenham, England, 1951.

Canine Books

Battaglia, Dr. Carmelo L. *How to Breed Better Dogs—Dog Genetics*. THF Publishing, 1984.

Bloomfield, Betty. *Nursing and Hand Rearing Newborn Puppies*. Able Publishing, 1994.

Cayzer, Beatrice. *The Royal World of Animals*. Sidgwick & Jackson Ltd., London, 1989.

Compton, Herbert (editor). *The Twentieth Century Dog*. Grant Richards, London, 1904.

Croxton, Smith A. *Dogs Since 1900*. Andrew Dakers Ltd., London, 1951.

Dalziel, Hugh. *British Dogs*. L. Upcott Gill, London, 1881.

Davis, C. J. *The Theory and Practice of Breeding to Type*. Our Dogs Publishing, Manchester, England.

Drury and others. *British Dogs, Third Edition*. L. Upcott Gill, London, and Charles Scribner's Sons, New York, 1903.

Gover, Linda. *The Irish Wolfhound*. THF Kingdon Books, 1998.

Hutt, Frederick. *Genetics for Dog Breeders*. Cornell University/WH Freeman and Co., 1979.

Lane, Charles Henry. *All About Dogs*. London and New York, 1900.
—*Dog Shows and Doggy-People*. Hutchinson & Co., 1902.

Leighton, Robert. *The New Book of the Dog*. Cassell, London, 1910.

Little, Clarence C. *The Inheritance of Coat Color in Dogs*. Comstock Publishing Assoc, New York, 1957.

Mery, Fernand. *The Life, History and Magic of the Dog*. Madison Square Press, New York, 1968.

Nicholas, Anna Katherine. *The Nicholas Guide to Dog Judging*. Howell Book House, New York, 1970.

Serane, Anne. *The Joy of Breeding Your Own Show Dog*. Howell Publishing, 1985.

Shaw, Vero. *The Book of the Dog*. London, Paris & New York, 1881.

Spira, Harold R. *Canine Terminology*. David and Charles, 1986.

Sutton, Catherine G. *Dog Shows and Show Dogs*. K & R Books Ltd., Edlington, Horncastle, Lincs, England, 1980.

Van Bylandt, Count Henry. *Dogs of All Nations*. Kerberos-Neerijnen-Netherlands, 1904.

Willis, Malcolm B. *Genetics of the Dog*. H F & G Publishing Ltd., London, 1989.

Winge, Ojvind (translated from Danish by Catherine Roberts, PHD). *Inheritance in Dogs*. Comstock Publishing, 1950.

General and Historical Books

Heritage of Britain. Reader's Digest Association Ltd., 1975.

The Last Two Million Years. Reader's Digest Association Ltd., 1973.

Watson, Maj. John N. P. *Millais—Three Generations in Nature, Art and Sport*. The Sportsman's Press, London, 1988.

PBGV/Canine Periodicals and Articles

Dean, Steve, MRCVS. (Various veterinary articles). *Dog World*, Ashford, Kent, England, 1998.

Frost, Nicholas G. "The Development of the Petit Basset Griffon Vendéen in Britain." *Dog World*, Ashford, Kent, England, Nov. 1988.

Grayson, Peggy. "The Great Breeders—Joan Wells-Meacham." *Dog World*, Ashford, Kent, England, June 1997.

Hancock, David and Uloth Rupert. "A Dog's Best Friend Is His Horse." *Country Life*, Feb. 1997.

Masson, Sophie. "Remembering the Vendée." Quadrant Publications, Australia, Dec. 1996.

Roland, Mark. "Estimating Heritability." *AKC Gazette*, Aug. 1995.

Smyth, Dan. "Judging the Veteran Dog." *Saber Tails*, the Voice of the Petit Basset Griffon Vendéen Club of America, Sept. 1997.

Steidel, Kitty. "Will it be Recognition and Beyond, or Beyond Recognition?" *Show Sight Magazine*, 1994.

Vuille, Martin. "PBGV Genetics—Introduction to Canine Genetics." *Saber Tails*, the Voice of the Petit Basset Griffon Vendéen Club of America, 1998.

Walton-Haddon, John. *Petit Basset Griffon Vendéen Book of British Champions*. The Basset Griffon Vendéen Club, 1994.

Watson, Maj. John N. P. "Where English Bassets Evolved—The Westerby." *Country Life*, Feb. 1979.

—"Speeding Up the Basset." *Country Life*, May 1988.

Wells-Meacham. "The British Revival." *Dog World*, Ashford, Kent, England, Apr. 1983.

—British Basset Griffon Vendéen Club Newsletters. 1978–98.

—Crufts Catalogues. The Kennel Club, 1891–1892.

—*Kennel Club Calendar and Stud Book*. The Kennel Club, 1875–1921.

—*Le Griffon Vendéen*. Magazine of the Club du Griffon Vendéen, France, 1996–98.

—*LOF, Volume 4 BGV*. Société Centrale Canine.

—"Our Dogs." *Our Dogs*, Manchester, England, early 1900s.

—*Petit Basset Griffon Vendéen—Judges Guide*. The American Kennel Club.

—*RCGV 1947, RCGV 1976–77*. Club du Basset Griffon Vendéen.

—*Saber Tails*, The Voice of the Petit Basset Griffon Vendéen Club of America, 1987–1998.

—*Standards des Races de Chiens*. Société Centrale Canine.

—*The Basset Griffon Vendéen Handbooks*. The Basset Griffon Vendéen Club, 1984–1996.

—*The Kennel*, early 1900s.
—*The Kennel Gazette*, 1880s.
—*The Ladies' Kennel Journal*, 1890s.

INDEX

A

à jambes droites, 23, 62, 74, 227
à jambes torses, 23, 31
à poil ras, 23, 55, 97
afterbirth, 294
agility, 94, 153, 197, 327, 328, 329, 330, 331, 340
agility, 327, 328, 329
AKC, 89, 91, 93, 144, 146, 151, 156, 158, 159, 161, 165, 166, 167, 173, 177, 181, 235, 238, 311, 314, 319, 325
Akerwood, 120, 135, 184, 201
Alabeth, 82, 121, 122, 123, 130, 131, 136
Alabeth Ballivernes of Ilsham 136
Albany Kennel Club, 171
Alexandra, Queen (of England) 74, 105, 106, 107, 110
Alexander, *See* Belray Alexander Gebeba
Ambaud, 34, 35
America, 79, 113, 123, 127, 133, 134, 136, 138, 144, 145, 149, 150, 153, 154, 158, 159, 160, 161, 163, 168, 170, 175, 177, 178, 179, 180, 181, 182, 186, 187, 188, 189, 191, 193, 194, 207, 224, 323
anasarca, 279
Arilica Otello of Jomil, 114
Arrian, 18, 19, 21
Artésiens-Normands, 76, 77, 195
arthritis, 273, 274
artificial insemination, 96, 290
Artois, 21, 30, 31, 97
Artois-Normand, 30
aseptic meningitis, *see* meningitis
Auger, Dr. Jean 9, 218
Axmo's, 148, 149, 155, 167, 185, 186, 187, 192, 202, 323
Axmo's Babette de la Garonne, 148, 149
Axmo's Don Ranudo de la Garonne, 155

B

back, 86, 156, 198, 209, 225, 227, 229, 230, 232, 234, 236, 237, 240, 245, 247, 248, 252, 260, 265, 269, 270, 284, 285, 286, 294, 296, 303, 304, 316, 325, 326, 333, 334, 336, 339, 343
bacteria, 295
balance, 25, 208, 209, 210, 236, 239, 286, 303, 304
Balmar's Mignonnette, 152, 169, 170
Baker, Chris, 121, 122, 141, 158
Baker, Jan, 81, 82, 127, 158
Baker, Peter, 115, 116, 120, 121, 198
Barth, Betty, 143, 144, 145, 150
Barton, William, 6, 145, 155
basset courant, 33, 36, 37
basset fauve, 36, 64, 71, 83, 120
Basset Fauve de Bretagne, 29, 30, 32, 43, 64, 71, 83, 120, 183
basset français, 35, 54, 55, 56, 58, 97, 99, 225
basset griffon, 9, 10, 18, 23, 30, 34, 36, 53, 54, 55, 56, 57, 58, 59, 60, 66, 75, 79, 87, 97, 99, 110, 117, 118, 143, 184, 211, 213, 222, 223, 226, 233
Basset Griffon Vendéen, 9, 10, 18, 23, 30, 34, 54, 55, 56, 57, 58, 59, 60, 66, 75, 79, 110, 117, 143, 184, 201, 211, 213, 222, 223, 226, 233. *See* Petit Basset Griffon Vendéen
Basset Hound Club, 74, 81, 104

Basset Hounds, 43, 74, 96, 97, 104, 105, 124, 187

Bassets Allemands, 50, 53

Bassets Courants, 50

Bassets Français, 50, 52, 53

Bassets Griffons, 15, 23, 32, 34, 36, 37, 38, 53, 54, 74, 83, 84, 105, 110, 213, 214

Bassets GriffonsVendéens, 55

Baudry d'Asson, 34

BC, *see* Brevet de Chasse

Beacontree Monet, 151, 153, 166

Beagle, 39, 43, 71, 74, 76, 77, 78, 79, 81, 83, 84, 85, 96, 150, 183, 188, 272, 277, 278, 279, 284, 325

beard, 213, 233, 235, 236, 238, 266

Beasley, Noreen, 85, 127, 144, 157

Beckford, Peter, 29, 218

Belgium, 43, 100, 104, 127, 200, 207

Belray, 85, 144, 147, 152, 166, 169, 171

Belray Alexander Gebeba, 143, 144

Belray Sirhan Braconnier, 152, 159, 166

Bett, Carolyne, 114, 128

BGV, 54, 55, 56, 57, 59, 60, 61, 62, 71, 113, 115, 116, 117, 120, 121, 122, 123, 124, 125, 126, 128, 129, 130, 131, 141, 147, 179, 180, 182, 195, 198, 214, 216, 222, 228, 346, 347

birth, 52, 58, 61, 64, 270, 276, 279, 282, 292, 293, 294, 295, 297, 301, 315

bite, 69, 136, 155, 231, 233, 234, 236

black, 41, 52, 66, 84, 128, 175, 218, 219, 220, 222, 229, 230, 231, 232, 233, 234, 236, 238, 261, 269, 301, 315, 316, 317, 318

Bleu de Gascogne, 29, 30, 65, 75, 84, 183

blood, 64, 70, 71, 73, 75, 77, 79, 81, 93, 95, 103, 104, 110, 124, 183, 205, 253, 269, 270, 275, 276, 278, 287, 290, 326

bloodline, 96, 160, 161, 282, 284, 286, 311

boar, 16, 20, 22, 40, 41, 116, 212, 232

Bocquet, Charles, 50, 52, 100

body, 27, 29, 41, 74, 156, 173, 174, 207, 208, 209, 216, 222, 228, 225, 227, 229, 230, 231, 233, 234, 236, 237, 238, 239, 240, 241, 253, 257, 266, 268, 274, 279, 292, 293, 295, 297, 298, 301, 303, 304, 311, 314, 327

bone, 26, 28, 69, 103, 114, 215, 225, 228, 231, 233, 237, 238, 240, 253, 299, 303, 324

Bradley Vale, 77, 80

brain, 28, 275, 276

breakfast, 255, 256

breed standard, 56, 116, 118, 146, 207, 209

breeder, 41, 56, 70, 99, 100, 101, 103, 106, 115, 118, 123, 126, 143, 147, 149, 151, 152, 158, 164, 168, 174, 185, 189, 193, 196, 203, 205, 209, 241, 244, 247, 248, 249, 252, 253, 264, 280, 281, 282, 283, 284, 285, 287, 288, 295, 305, 308, 309, 310, 311, 316

breeders, 10, 12, 16, 34, 37, 38, 41, 44, 51, 54, 55, 57, 65, 70, 84, 90, 99, 103, 104, 107, 108, 109, 110, 116, 118, 125, 130, 135, 144, 145, 148, 162, 169, 173, 174, 183, 185, 186, 189, 194, 203, 205, 207, 215, 222, 243, 248, 264, 278, 280, 282, 284, 285, 286, 289, 300, 301, 305, 307, 310, 313, 315, 317, 319

breeding, 18, 25, 26, 30, 32, 34, 35, 37, 38, 41, 44, 50, 52, 53, 54, 55, 62, 64, 65, 68, 69, 70, 71, 74, 81, 83, 87, 91, 92, 95, 103, 104, 105, 106, 107, 108, 113, 114, 117, 118, 120, 123, 124, 131, 138, 139, 145, 150, 152, 153, 157, 160, 161, 162, 163, 165, 169, 171, 172, 173, 175, 177, 185, 186, 187, 188, 189, 192, 193, 194, 196, 197, 198, 199, 200, 201, 215, 222, 272, 277, 279, 280, 282, 283, 284, 285, 286, 287, 290, 305,

307, 308, 309, 310, 311, 313, 315, 316, 318, 319
Brevet d'Aptitude à Chasser, 58
Brevet de Chasse, 41, 44, 58, 63, 174, 175, 197, 198, 200, 317, 346, 347, 349, 351, 353
Brevets de Chasse, 46
briquet, 23, 31, 33, 35, 37
Briquet, 23, 41, 61, 62, 63, 64, 211, 212, 213, 214, 216
Briquet Griffon Vendéen, 23
Briquets Griffons, 35, 63, 216
Britain, 9, 10, 13, 73, 74, 75, 95, 110, 112, 118, 120, 134, 135, 181, 207
Brittany, 18, 19, 36
Bronte, 297, 298
brown, 315
brucellosis, 287
Brucker, Ruth, 113, 115, 123, 127, 141, 152
Bryn Mawr, 90, 93
Buchanan-Jardine, Sir John, 73, 78
Buchanan-Jardine, Sir Rupert, 6, 9, 75, 77, 78, 79
Buche, Renaud, 6, 12, 66, 69, 70, 71, 140, 179, 181
Busk, Holger, 6, 130, 163, 169, 178, 190, 191, 192
Buttifant, Susan, 6, 84, 85, 87, 88

C

Caldbeck Fell Bloater, 76, 77, 78
Caminiti, Ken, 262
Canada, 84, 89, 124, 127, 129, 134, 144, 147, 153, 156, 157, 158, 178
Canadian Kennel Club, 85, 156
Canine Health Foundation, 319
Canis, 16
Cape Cod Kennel Club, 167
carbohydrates, 253
Casewick, 79
Castle Milk, 9, 75, 76, 78, 81, 91, 110
Castle Milk Blazer, 76
cataracts, 271
CBGV, see Club du Basset Griffon

Vendéen
Celtic, 16, 17, 18, 19, 209
Celts, 16
cereal, 300
CGV, 55, 61, 65, 66, 68, 70
Chantalle, 130, 134, 136, 159
Chaparral, 84, 87
Charlen, 162, 163, 164, 165, 175, 194
Charlen's For Your Eyes Only, 154, 163, 164, 165, 172, 345
Charlen's Paradox, 163, 164, 165, 345
Charles II, 17
Charles IX, 19, 21
chasse-à-tir, 22, 29, 30, 33, 35, 58
chest, 46, 74, 215, 216, 217, 225, 227, 229, 231, 234, 237, 257, 296, 304, 317, 324, 334
Chien Blanc du Roi, 19, 21
Chien d'Ordre, 29
Chien de St. Hubert, 19, 20
Chien Fauve de Bretagne, 19
Chien Gris de St. Louis, 19, 20
Chiens Bassets, 22
Chiens Briquets, 22
chiens courants, 9, 21, 50, 51, 52, 53
Chiens d'Ordre, 22
Chiquita des Barbus d'Entre Lac, 197, 198
choke chain, 258, 259, 332
Chouan, 130, 163, 165, 167, 168, 178, 185, 186, 187, 190, 191, 192, 193, 194, 198, 359
Chouan Gimlet, 163, 165, 168, 169, 178, 185, 191, 193, 194, 359
Chouan Hen's Dream, 130, 167, 187, 192
Chouan Kentucky Woman, 193
Chouan Xcept When I Laugh, 168
chromosomes, 295, 308
Churchill, Charles, 183
Club du Basset Français, 222
Club du Basset Griffon, 223
Club du Griffon Vendéen, 11, 12, 39, 43, 55, 58, 59, 61, 66, 91, 116, 140, 200, 231
Club du Griffon Vendéen des Pays-Bas,

199
Club du Griffon Vendéen Exposition Nationale, 164
coat, 18, 20, 32, 33, 34, 50, 52, 53, 69, 89, 97, 98, 103, 107, 156, 163, 173, 211, 213, 214, 215, 217, 218, 220, 225, 226, 230, 231, 232, 233, 234, 237, 239, 241, 258, 259, 265, 266, 267, 269, 277, 289, 299, 303, 304, 308, 309, 315, 316
collar, 258, 259, 333, 335, 336, 337
color, 98, 218, 226, 227, 230, 232, 235, 238, 314
comb, 266
condition, 69, 208, 210, 249, 265, 266, 277, 278, 282, 296, 340
confirmateur, 66, 69
conformation, 25, 26, 39, 42, 44, 58, 74, 82, 89, 93, 156, 166, 183, 203, 205, 216, 217, 274, 301, 303
congenital, 270, 276, 278, 279, 299
convulsions, 275
Copin, 202, 203
Country Girl, 107
coursing, 85, 175, 338
Couteulx Hounds, 98
crook, 38, 56, 224, 234, 237
crossbred, 49, 54, 79, 91, 94, 103, 311
crossbreeding, 64, 68, 70, 91, 95, 101, 103, 106, 108, 124, 215, 311
Croup, 225, 227, 229, 232, 234, 237
Crufts, 50, 99, 100, 101, 102, 104, 106, 109, 110, 118, 121, 126, 128, 131, 133, 135, 136, 139, 140, 156, 160, 162, 180
crying, 251, 252
cryptorchid, 69
Crystal Palace, 97, 100, 109
Cynba, 122, 130, 131

D

d'Andigné, Comte Henry, 58, 59, 61.
d'Elva, Comte Christian d'Alincy, 34, 35, 36, 37, 55, 56
Dachshund, 97

Dalby Hall pack, 90
Danish Kennel Club, 190
Daubigné, Paul, 59, 63
Dawbak, 118, 120, 121, 122, 152
de Canteleu, Comte le Couteulx 31, 32, 104
de Chambord, Hubert Devaulx, 60
de Coeur Joie kennels, 9
de Fin Renard, 40, 70, 83, 93, 128, 164, 174, 175, 192, 197, 198, 316, 317, 346, 347, 348, 349, 351, 356, 360, 362
de l'Angle, Marquis, 52
de Metz, Comte d'Incourt, 50
de Tournon, Comte, 96
de Vezins, Comte Élie, 25, 79
de Villebois-Mareuil, Vicomte 33, 35, 36
Dean, Yvonne, 127, 128, 141
Deanound, 127, 128
Debucher, 138, 139, 213
Debucher Le Barbu, 213
deer, 85, 86, 91, 116, 122, 205
Defoe, Daniel, 95
Dehra, 113, 114, 120, 125, 128, 129, 131, 132, 133, 134, 135, 136, 137, 138, 139, 151, 152, 159, 160, 161, 162, 163, 168, 169, 171, 176, 177, 180, 181, 187, 262, 352, 353, 355, 357, 358, 359, 360, 361, 362
Dehra Armand Brumeux, 114, 128, 132, 152
Dehra Celestine, 138, 168, 182
Dehra Eminent, 176
Dehra Urio, 136, 138, 162
Dehra Xato, 131, 134, 137,
Dehra Xenephon at Ekoz, 131
Dekker, Jannie, 43, 200
demi-torses, 23, 60, 62, 226, 227, 228
Denmark, 113, 120, 136, 140, 148, 149, 163, 178, 183, 184, 185, 186, 187, 188, 189, 192, 194, 198, 202
Desamy, Abel, 61, 62, 63, 64, 316
Desamy, Hubert, 6, 46, 65, 66, 90, 111, 114, 116, 147, 185, 198, 317
Deux Amies Astre, 171

developmental, 270
dewclaws, 237, 269
Dézamy, Paul 54, 55, 56, 58, 59, 61,
    63, 71, 223, 224
Dickens, Charles, 25
diet, 249, 253, 254, 290, 292
dig, 246, 247
digging, 245, 246, 293
DNA, 319
dog show, 36, 44, 49, 99, 149, 190, 195
Dogs of All Nations, 223
dominant, 175, 213, 222, 271, 284, 308,
    309, 310, 311, 312, 313, 315, 316
Dryden, John, 15
Du Fouilloux, Jacques 20, 22
Dunarden, 122, 131, 153, 169, 180, 217
Dunarden Clairon of Kasani, 131, 153,
    169, 180, 217
Dunbar, Barbara and David, 116, 125,
    126, 139, 140, 141
Dupuis, Claire, 10
Dutch Kennel Club, 199
dysplasia, 271, 273, 274

E

ears, 16, 38, 69, 96, 98, 151, 152, 211,
    213, 215, 225, 226, 228,229, 230,
    231, 233, 234, 236, 237, 239, 241,
    257, 266, 268, 287, 288, 298
Édition Limité du Greffier du Roi, 138,
    139
Edward VII, 74, 105, 108
Edwards, Sally, 115, 128, 141
Ekoz, 131
Elan, 152, 154, 168, 169, 170, 345
Elan Cartouche de Qubic, 170, 356
Elan Christmas Surprise, 345, 356
Elan Vogue d'Mont Jois, 168, 170, 345,
    356
elbow, 225, 227, 229, 232, 234, 236,
    240, 257
Elle-Belle des Barbus d'Entre Lac, 198
England, 6, 17, 32, 50, 53, 73, 80, 89,
    90, 95, 96, 97, 98, 99, 101, 103,
    111, 113, 114, 117, 121, 122, 130,

134, 144, 145, 147, 149, 151, 153,
    159, 160, 173, 176, 177, 179, 180,
    181, 182, 183, 187, 188, 192, 195,
    198, 201, 202, 213, 224, 261, 265,
    330
English Basset, 73, 78, 83
epilepsy, 82, 275, 276
Europe, 9, 16, 17, 19, 117, 135, 146,
    161, 175, 194
Evans, Bunty, 127, 141
exercise, 78, 251, 257, 258, 265, 279,
    290, 292, 334, 335, 336, 337
expression, 231, 234, 236
eye, 16, 26, 87, 160, 208, 209, 211,
    229, 231, 233, 234, 239, 260, 270,
    271, 272, 273, 285, 303, 324
eyebrows, 213, 234, 235, 236, 237,
    281, 299
eyes, 125, 154, 155, 163, 164, 165,
    172, 173, 211, 213, 214, 225, 226,
    228, 229, 230, 231, 233, 234, 236,
    237, 260, 266, 288, 298, 316, 345

F

fading puppy syndrome, 295
fanciers, 39, 52, 53, 95, 100, 104, 133,
    145, 158, 185
fanfare, 46
Farino, 56, 57
fats, 253
fault, 70, 207, 226, 232, 233, 235, 240
faults, 58, 69, 77, 81, 83, 133, 193, 194,
    207, 220, 226, 228, 230, 232, 233,
    235, 238, 240, 283, 285
fauve, 32, 34, 36, 220, 222, 230, 318
Fauve de Bretagne, 29, 30, 43, 64, 71,
    83, 120, 183
Fédération Cynologique Internationale
    (FCI), 6, 9, 66, 146, 207, 208, 224
feet, 225, 227, 229, 232, 234, 237
Fellman-Gellerman, Patricia, 145, 148,
    168, 170, 187
Festoon Around Bryony, 158
Feuille de Déclaration pour
    l'Enregistrement au Registre Initial,

61

Finland, 123, 188, 189

Fixed Asset of Huntswold, 146, 352, 353

flank, 225, 227, 229

flat puppy syndrome, 296

flirting, 287, 289

Folly Acre Buttercup at Piplaurie, 82, 130

food, 16, 38, 62, 200, 249, 250, 253, 254, 255, 256, 264, 290, 292, 298, 300, 301, 331, 332, 333

forearm, 225, 227, 229, 231, 234, 236

foreface, 228, 231, 233, 236

forelegs, 225, 227, 229, 234

forequarters, 234, 236, 240

fox, 22, 29, 41, 43, 83, 205

Foxhound, 77, 84

Foxmead's La Belle Sauterelle, 168

France, 6, 9, 11, 12, 13, 15, 16, 17, 18, 19, 21, 25, 30, 37, 38, 41, 43, 46, 49, 54, 56, 58, 65, 66, 68, 71, 75, 76, 79, 90, 91, 93, 95, 99, 104, 108, 111, 112, 114, 116, 117, 123, 128, 135, 161, 164, 174, 175, 183, 184, 185, 186, 187, 188, 191, 192, 195, 197, 198, 200, 202, 205, 211, 212, 215, 216, 218, 221, 222, 307

Fredwell Birribi At Dehra, 345

French Kennel Club, 222

French Revolution, 19, 21, 30

Fritou de Fin Renard, 174

Frost, Ellen, 182, 189

Frost, Nicholas "Nick," 93, 113, 131, 133, 134, 136, 137, 159, 160, 171, 176, 179, 180, 181, 182, 187, 188

G

Gadsby, Mike, 138

gait, 226, 228, 230, 232, 234, 237

Galbraith, Barbara, 145, 149, 153, 156, 159, 323

Gambade, 60

Gambit of Kasani, 122, 140, 153, 304,

345

game, 22, 29, 30, 31, 40, 41, 50, 62, 183, 203, 205, 212, 213, 221, 222, 235, 332, 334

Gascogne, 21, 31

Gaul, 16, 17, 18, 19

Gauls, 17, 18

GBGV, 66, 120, 183, 213, 214, 215, 346, 347

genes, 21, 215, 273, 285, 308, 312, 315

genetic, 54, 271, 277, 285, 295, 307, 308, 309, 310, 313, 314, 315, 316, 317, 318

genetics, 6, 13, 284, 307, 308, 313, 316, 318, 319

genome, 319

genotype, 307, 308, 309, 311, 312, 313, 316, 319

Germany, 140, 189, 192

gestation, 292

Gestation/Whelping Chart, 291

Gilbert, Richard and Carol, 116, 124, 125, 129, 147, 156

Gilbert-Jackson, Rebecca, 124, 125

Gimlet, *see* Chouan Gimlet

glaucoma, 272, 273

Goldorak de Fin Renard, 175, 316

Gourou of Wakelyns, 126, 146, 149, 152, 352, 353

Grand Basset, 23, 41, 50, 63, 64, 71, 146, 184, 211, 213

Grand Griffon, 23, 29, 41, 62, 211, 213, 214

Grand Griffon Vendéen, 23, 29, 211, 212, 214

grande taille, 23, 50 ,73, 215

grande vénerie 29, 31

gray, 20, 53, 98, 99, 106, 108, 152, 213, 220, 230, 271, 315, 316, 318

Greeks, 16

Griffon Vendéen, 9, 11, 19, 20, 32, 54, 55, 56, 65, 70, 73, 74, 75, 76, 78, 79, 84, 91, 95, 99, 107, 110, 173, 199, 211, 214, 224, 239

grizzle, 99, 114, 213, 220, 235, 238, 315

grooming, 173, 174, 190, 248, 257, 265, 266, 269
gums, 269

H

hair, 66, 90, 213, 214, 218, 219, 228, 229, 230, 231, 233, 234, 236, 237, 238, 239, 241, 258, 265, 266, 267, 268, 277, 289, 315
handler, 138, 154, 157, 162, 168, 170, 172, 176, 322, 324, 325, 328, 336, 339, 341
Hansen, Mogens, 148, 185, 186
Happy Breed, 13, 16, 321, 332, 337
hare, 16, 22, 27, 31, 35, 37, 39, 41, 55, 59, 73, 76, 77, 78, 80, 83, 88, 98, 103, 116, 127, 199, 213, 220, 221, 230, 232, 261, 338
Harehound, 73
Harriers, 74, 75, 78
head, 75, 86, 98, 102, 103, 107, 114, 135, 175, 194, 209, 211, 213, 214, 215, 225, 226, 228, 230, 231, 232, 234, 235, 236, 239, 240, 241, 259, 266, 268, 270, 275, 301, 303, 314, 324, 327, 333, 336, 343
health, 74, 130, 164, 203, 248, 249, 263, 264, 270, 280, 282, 285, 319, 341, 342
heart, 63, 144, 259, 262, 278, 279, 341, 343
heat, "in heat" 38, 261, 282, 283, 287, 297
height, 29, 33, 34, 37, 50, 52, 53, 59, 64, 69, 117, 146, 174, 209, 211, 213, 215, 216, 217, 224, 226, 228, 230, 232, 233, 235, 238, 239, 270, 303, 304, 312, 314, 324, 342
height index, 216, 217
Helensfield Osprey, 130, 138, 220
hereditary, 270, 275, 279
heredity, 25, 267, 305, 307, 319
heritability, 312, 313, 314
hernias, 279, 280
Hervé Tenailleau, 38, 39

Heseltine, Christopher, 74, 75, 109
Heseltine, Captain Godfrey, 74, 75
hind legs, 225, 227, 229, 240
hindquarters, 225, 227, 229, 232, 234, 237, 240
hip dysplasia *see* dysplasia
hocks, 225, 227, 229, 232, 234, 237
Holland, 43, 113, 133, 153, 161, 189, 193, 199
horn, 39, 40, 46, 86, 88
hound, 10, 15, 18, 20, 21, 22, 23, 25, 26, 27, 29, 30, 32, 36, 39, 42, 43, 44, 57, 61, 62, 65, 68, 69, 70, 71, 73, 75, 77, 78, 81, 82, 84, 86, 87, 88, 89, 91, 92, 93, 98, 99, 103, 105, 107, 109, 110, 112, 116, 122, 145, 155, 170, 172, 173, 175, 177, 184, 193, 196, 201, 213, 214, 217, 218, 222, 224, 225, 226, 233, 235, 237, 239, 241, 244, 252, 255, 258, 259, 265, 266, 267, 308, 309, 313, 315, 316, 319, 321, 329, 331, 332, 333, 334, 335, 336, 337, 338, 339, 340, 343
Hound Group, 131, 139, 157, 166, 167, 168, 170, 178, 179, 180
hounds, 6, 7, 9, 10, 15, 16, 17, 18, 19, 20, 21, 22, 25, 26, 27, 29, 30, 32, 33, 34, 35, 37, 38, 39, 40, 41, 42, 43, 44, 47, 51, 53, 54, 58, 59, 60, 61, 64, 65, 69, 70, 71, 73, 74, 75, 76, 77, 78, 80, 81, 82, 83, 84, 86, 87, 88, 89, 90, 91, 92, 93, 94, 96, 97, 104, 105, 109, 114, 115, 116, 117, 118, 121, 122, 124, 138, 153, 155, 157, 164, 168, 173, 174, 175, 176, 183, 185, 191, 193, 195, 196, 197, 200, 211, 214, 216, 221, 222, 239, 244, 256, 265, 280, 282, 284, 285, 289, 307, 310, 312, 315, 316, 318, 329, 330, 334, 338, 339, 343
Hounds and Hunting through the Ages, 25
Hounds of Britain, 74
housebreaking, 252, 253
Hubbestad Harrods, 184, 201, 202

Hubert, Saint, 20, 21
Huest, 12, 43, 44, 197, 200
hunt, 12, 25, 29, 30, 32, 34, 35, 38, 39,
    42, 44, 45, 46, 51, 52, 58, 59, 60,
    62, 69, 81, 84, 85, 86, 87, 88, 89,
    91, 92, 130, 184, 199, 200, 205,
    212, 213, 221, 235, 307, 330, 338,
    339
Hunt, Nickie, 115, 118, 130, 134
hunter, 15, 23, 27, 31, 37, 40, 94, 116,
    133, 173, 180, 213, 214, 235, 239,
    241, 265, 343
Huntersbrook, 112, 118, 134, 353
hunting, 9, 10, 12, 13, 15, 16, 17, 18,
    19, 20, 21, 22, 25, 27, 29, 30, 31,
    32, 34, 35, 37, 38, 39, 40, 41, 42,
    43, 44, 46, 49, 51, 52, 54, 55, 56,
    58, 59, 60, 62, 63, 64, 65, 70, 71,
    73, 74, 75, 79, 80, 81, 82, 83, 84,
    85, 86, 87, 88, 89, 90, 91, 92, 93,
    94, 96, 110, 116, 124, 145, 150,
    151, 173, 175, 185, 197, 199, 200,
    201, 203, 205, 210, 211, 213, 218,
    221, 222, 231, 233, 237, 239, 244,
    261, 284, 307, 314, 321, 329, 330,
    331, 332, 334
hunting trial, 43
huntsman, 22, 27, 30, 37, 40, 43, 44,
    92, 94, 184, 199, 200, 214, 222
huntsmen, 10, 18, 23, 25, 29, 30, 39,
    42, 44, 51, 52, 58, 59, 62, 73, 90,
    116, 200, 205
Huntswold Javott, 146
Hurling, Edith, 112, 113
hydrocephalus, 276
hypothyroidism, 277, 278

I

Idée des Genêts Roux, 196
Idolens, 187, 202, 203, 357, 358
in-breeding, 285
infection, 248, 293, 295
Ingher, Charles and Helen, 153, 162,
    163, 164, 165, 167, 169, 175, 178,
    193

Initial Register, 61, 62, 316
intraocular, 272, 273
Iowa du Sentier d'Aimeron, 212
Ipie du Grangeot de Callou, 196
Italy, 113, 123

J

Jaclin, 131, 132, 133, 134, 138, 152,
    153, 160
Jacobin at Dehra, 160
Jacobin At Dehra, 345
Jamar, 153, 154, 155, 157, 165, 166,
    169, 219, 220, 261, 283, 302, 323
Jamar's Kindred Spirit, 154
Jamar's Likely Lad, 166
Jamars As You Like It, 219
Japan, 161, 164
Japanese Kennel Club, 164
Jardin d'Acclimation, 34, 35, 49, 51,
    52, 96, 97
Jardin Kennels, 36
jaw, 231, 233, 236
Jeannemart of Varon, 132, 133, 350,
    351, 353, 355, 356, 358, 360, 362
Jeffries, Wendy, 6, 323, 324, 325, 326
Jernberg, Kerstin, 202, 203
Johnson, Dr. Samuel, 143
Johnston, George, 6, 10, 75, 116, 117,
    134
JoJo (Jamars True Value CD), 323, 324,
    325, 326, 327
Jomil, 81, 82, 85, 90, 112, 113, 114,
    116, 118, 120, 121, 123, 125, 128,
    129, 130, 131, 132, 133, 134, 135,
    138, 139, 140, 144, 147, 149, 151,
    152, 153, 158, 160, 161, 162, 169,
    172, 184, 187, 190, 195, 201, 202,
    350, 351, 352, 353, 355, 356, 357,
    358, 359, 360, 362
Jomil Fauvette, 113, 120, 202, 358, 360
Jomil Gallant, 90
Jomil Hotspur, 113, 184, 187, 190, 356,
    358, 359, 360
Jomil Pascal, 85, 144, 152, 162, 172
Jomil Reverie, 131, 138, 160

Jomil Rigolo, 112, 116, 120, 125, 137, 152, 162
Jomil Rolande à Cochise 139
Jomil Sirène of Monkhams, 114, 153
Jomil Ultra, 168, 179
Jomil Zadok, 125, 139, 345
judges, 10, 42, 44, 50, 51, 52, 58, 59, 71, 99, 110, 117, 124, 144, 164, 201, 241, 339
Junon de Fin Renard, 114
juvenile pain syndrome, 276

K

Kallista Christian Dior, 168
Kasani, 122, 129, 130, 140, 147, 153, 155, 158, 166, 169, 180, 220, 304, 331
Kasani Honette, 153, 155, 166
Kasani Nectaire, 153, 169
Kasani Ravissant, 153, 220
Kasmin Bittle, 6, 263
kennel club, 207, 243
Kennel Club, 6, 74, 97, 99, 100, 105, 108, 109, 110, 115, 116, 118, 128, 233, 265, 319
Knipe, Shirley, 149, 152, 159, 166
Knudsen, Per, 6, 113, 135, 136, 140, 161, 183, 184, 187, 189, 190, 202
Kovaleff, Lauren, 6, 341, 342, 343

L

La Chasse Illustrée, 36, 52
La Chasse Royale, 19, 21
La Chasseur Français, 59
La Vénerie, 20, 23
Lacebarks Lydia, 149, 150, 345
Lacey-Ames, Juli, 171
Lane Hounds, 98
Le Chasseur, 31
Le Comte d'Elva, 32, 33
Le Couteulx, 32, 34, 51, 96
Le Journal des Chasseurs, 31
Le Manuel de Vénerie Française, 31
leash, 97, 247, 250, 258, 259, 294, 333, 334, 335, 336, 337, 339, 343
leash training, 258
lemon, 77, 81, 98, 100, 108, 219, 212, 213, 235, 238, 301, 315
length, 22, 74, 174, 209, 213, 216, 217, 218, 222, 225, 233, 234, 236, 237, 238, 239, 241, 266, 267, 289, 301, 303, 304, 314, 318, 322, 326, 333, 339
lens, 271, 272, 273
lens luxation, 272, 273
Les Chiens Courants de Vendée, 9, 218
Les Chiens Courants Français pour la Chasse du Liévre dans le Midi de la France, 25
Les Chiens de Chasse, 31
Les Races de Chiens Courants Français au XIXe Siècle, 31
Leighton, Robert, 108
Lesèble, Louis, 35, 36, 53, 54
Lewis, Linda, 132
limbs, 225, 227, 229, 233
line-bred, 136, 163, 180, 284
line-breeding, 284, 285, 311
Link, Valerie, 7, 10, 123, 130, 153, 154, 157, 158, 166, 169, 180, 321
Lino du Rallye des Combrailles, 212
Lionne d'Equipage d'Ancien Pays, 198, 199
lips, 213, 215, 226, 229, 231, 233, 236, 238
litter, 37, 66, 68, 76, 78, 80, 81, 83, 85, 90, 91, 93, 100, 101, 102, 103, 106, 112, 113, 118, 120, 121, 122, 123, 124, 125, 126, 127, 128, 129, 131, 132, 134, 135, 136, 138, 147, 148, 149, 150, 152, 153, 154, 156, 157, 161, 162, 163, 169, 170, 171, 172, 175, 180, 184, 186, 187, 188, 189, 190, 191, 192, 193, 194, 195, 197, 198, 199, 201, 202, 215, 246, 247, 248, 281, 282, 283, 286, 289, 293, 295, 297, 299, 300, 302, 310, 312, 318
liver, 254, 275, 315, 334
Livingston, Clint, 162

Livre d'Origines Français (LOF), 57,
61, 64, 68, 69, 71, 222, 316
loins, 225, 227, 229, 232, 234, 237
Louis IX (Saint Louis), 20
Louis XVI, 19
Loy du Val d'Orbieu, 121, 196, 197,
198, 201
Lucy, 341, 342, 343
lure, 85, 175, 338, 339
lure coursing, 338
Lutin de Fin Renard, 219

M

Machart, Jules, 36
Mackenzie, Anne, 81, 126, 141
Mackenzie, Sandy, 81, 126, 141
Magic des Rives de la Garonne, 133,
189
Mair, Cynthia, 129, 130
Maquisard, 82, 125, 126, 139, 151
markings, 212, 213, 232, 235, 238, 301,
315
meal, 59, 255, 256, 275, 290, 292, 300,
301
Mediterranean, 17
meningitis, 263, 276, 277
meute, 11, 41, 42, 44, 50, 195, 197, 200
meutes, 43, 52, 200
milk, 254, 255, 256, 264, 294, 298,
300, 301
Millais, Everett, 6, 96, 97, 98, 99, 104,
105, 107, 110, 209
Millais, Sir John Everett, 96
Miller, John, 6, 128, 182, 205, 216, 217
minerals, 253, 254, 273
Mirliton, 60
Monkhams Hannah, 153, 157, 158, 166
Monkhams Tegan Jamars, 220
monorchid, 69
Moore, Mary Tyler, 260, 261
Morebess Charlotte de St Florent, 152,
155
Morebess Haveloc at Dehra, 128, 160,
202
Morebess Obelix de Nîmes, 161, 188,
194
Morebess Raymond le Rebelle, 187,
190, 194, 355, 357
Morebess Sur-Moi de Fontenay, 163,
177, 189
Morebess Thérèse la Tranqueuse, 187,
219, 358, 362
Morebess Uron Comme Grand-Père,
190
Morrison, Lieutenant-Colonel Eric, 75,
78
moustache, 213, 229, 230, 231, 233,
235, 236, 238
mouth, 231, 233, 236
Much Ado About Jamar, 154, 302
Musée de la Vénerie, 47
Museé Internationale de la Chasse, 47
Muséum d'Histoire Naturelle, 49
muzzle, 16, 28, 174, 213, 225, 226,
230, 233, 236, 239, 270, 287, 299,
314
My Lu's Amérique, 150

N

nails, 229, 232, 237, 257, 258, 265,
268, 329
Napoleon I, 32
Napoléon III, 49
National Specialty, 154, 159, 161, 164,
168, 170, 171, 172, 176, 179, 180,
181, 182, 194
Nationale d'Élevage, 39, 65, 70, 197,
201
neck, 40, 173, 209, 225, 227, 229, 231,
234, 236, 240, 258, 259, 267, 276,
333
Netherlands, 112, 121, 140, 161, 180,
192, 195, 196, 197, 199, 215
New Book of the Dog, 108
newborn, 293, 295, 297, 315
Nicholas, Anna Katherine, 208, 209
Nicholas Guide to Dog Judging, 208
Nichols, Diana, 134, 136, 159, 205
Normand, 30, 78, 183, 193
Normandy, 9, 12, 37, 43, 97

North America, 9, 84, 92, 124, 153, 161, 177
North American, 10, 146, 169, 185, 218
Northeastern Indiana Kennel Club, 170
nose, 20, 26, 27, 28, 77, 79, 158, 201, 213, 225, 226, 229, 230, 231, 233, 234, 236, 244, 252, 258, 259, 316, 324, 334, 336, 338
Nymann, Gunnar, 6, 130, 163, 169, 178, 190, 191, 193, 198

O

Oaktrees Hercule at Tecknique, 157, 158
Oaktrees Taiaut, 162, 163
obedience, 113, 121, 159, 162, 166, 183, 187, 197, 327, 328, 330, 331, 332, 333, 337
oils, 265, 267
orange, 33, 36, 53, 113, 121, 133, 135, 172, 212, 213, 219, 220, 227, 230, 231, 232, 235, 238, 315, 316
Orée, 111, 112, 117, 147, 351, 353, 356
Otterhound, 98, 102, 108
out-cross, 77, 114, 284, 311
out-crossing, 71, 76, 83, 96, 200, 284, 311, 314
outercoat, 315
overshot, 69
overweight, 254
Owens, Lynne, 141, 152

P

Pacha des Barbus d'Entre Lac, 82, 120, 121, 124, 127, 345, 353
pack, 12, 20, 22, 25, 27, 29, 32, 34, 35, 40, 41, 43, 44, 46, 51, 55, 58, 65, 73, 74, 75, 77, 78, 79, 80, 81, 82, 83, 84, 87, 89, 90, 91, 92, 94, 96, 110, 113, 124, 130, 150, 200, 201, 213, 221, 222, 328, 330, 331, 337
Paris, 31, 32, 33, 34, 36, 49, 50, 55, 96,

99, 105, 106, 111, 172
pasterns, 225, 227, 229, 231, 234, 236
Patachou Des Barbus D'entre Lac, 345
patella, 274
patellar luxation, 274, 275
paws, 266, 298
PBGV, 6, 10, 13, 17, 23, 26, 39, 40, 41, 44, 54, 60, 62, 63, 64, 66, 68, 71, 80, 82, 83, 85, 86, 87, 90, 91, 92, 95, 116, 117, 118, 121, 122, 123, 124, 125, 128, 130, 131, 133, 134, 135, 136, 138, 140, 143, 144, 145, 146, 148, 151, 152, 156, 157, 158, 159, 161, 162, 163, 164, 165, 167, 168, 170, 172, 173, 174, 177, 178, 179, 181, 183, 185, 187, 190, 191, 195, 197, 198, 199, 200, 201, 203, 205, 207, 210, 211, 214, 215, 217, 218, 219, 220, 222, 224, 225, 235, 238, 239, 241, 243, 244, 245, 247, 248, 250, 251, 252, 253, 257, 258, 259, 262, 263, 264, 265, 266, 267, 268, 269, 270, 279, 280, 281, 282, 284, 289, 293, 296, 297, 298, 299, 301, 304, 315, 316, 317, 318, 319, 321, 323, 328, 329, 330, 331, 332, 333, 334, 335, 336, 337, 338, 341, 342, 343, 346, 347
PBGVCA, 126, 127, 132, 144, 145, 146, 148, 149, 153, 154, 159, 165, 166, 168, 171, 172, 176, 179, 180, 181, 182, 194, 263, 308
PBGVs, 16, 39, 40, 43, 44, 45, 65, 68, 71, 83, 85, 88, 89, 90, 91, 94, 111, 113, 117, 118, 126, 129, 130, 132, 134, 135, 136, 138, 139, 143, 146, 147, 148, 149, 150, 152, 153, 154, 156, 157, 159, 160, 162, 164, 166, 168, 169, 171, 173, 174, 176, 177, 179, 184, 185, 187, 188, 192, 193, 195, 197, 200, 202, 205, 215, 221, 222, 244, 245, 246, 248, 252, 254, 256, 259, 261, 262, 263, 265, 268, 269, 271, 272, 273, 275, 276, 277, 279, 283, 285, 294, 297, 301, 312, 316, 317, 323, 327, 328, 329, 330,

332, 334, 337, 338, 340
pedigree, 70, 77, 106, 198, 249, 282, 284, 285, 286, 290, 307, 311
pedigrees, 5, 57, 103, 114, 131, 151, 164, 198, 202, 284, 285
Pène, Gilbert, 70, 150, 186, 188
Pepper, Jeffrey and Barbara 10, 147, 160, 161, 179, 180
Pepperhill-Dehra Charmaine, 162, 168, 177, 180, 181, 262
Perraudeau, Maurice, 70
Perrott, Debbie, 149, 150, 152, 159, 175
persistent pupillary membranes, 270, 271
personality, 40, 211, 244, 281, 282, 303, 337
Pervenche, 100, 101, 102, 103, 109
petit, 11, 41, 60, 65, 112, 114, 173, 174, 195, 196
Petit Basset, 5, 9, 10, 11, 12, 15, 23, 41, 64, 110, 144, 211, 214, 223, 241, 260, 311, 338, 343
Petit Basset Griffon Vendéen, 5, 9, 10, 11, 12, 15, 23, 110, 144, 211, 214, 223, 241, 260, 311, 338, 343
Petit Bleu de Gascogne, Artois-Normand, 30
petite taille 23, 37, 215
petite vénerie, 29, 31, 39
petits bassets, 50, 53
phenotype, 307, 308, 309, 310, 311, 312, 313, 318, 319
Phillips, Vivien, 135, 137, 138, 139, 160, 213
Pichot, Pierre, 49, 51, 97
pigmentation, 69, 187, 218, 219, 232, 233, 315
Point Values, 223
points, 27, 41, 44, 69, 86, 103, 146, 162, 166, 197, 200, 207, 209, 223, 235, 239, 283, 303, 310, 313
Polley, Sue, 6, 330, 331
porridge, 255, 256
Poulet, 52
Powell-Williams, Jack, 81

PPMs, *see* persistent pupillary membranes
pregnancy, 290, 295
Prince and Princess of Wales, 98, 99, 100, 105
Prince Zero, 106, 107
Probert, Sylvia, 6, 123, 125, 126, 127, 129, 131, 153, 156, 157, 169, 180, 187, 192
progesterone, 176, 290
proportion, 232, 235, 238, 239
protein, 253, 276, 292
Puissant, M. 101
pupillary membranes, 270
puppies, 37, 39, 41, 53, 66, 69, 79, 83, 90, 92, 93, 111, 112, 131, 143, 148, 156, 161, 171, 172, 186, 190, 199, 243, 247, 248, 251, 252, 253, 258, 264, 270, 271, 275, 279, 281, 282, 283, 286, 287, 292, 294, 295, 296, 297, 298, 299, 300, 301, 302, 303, 304, 305, 307, 308, 310, 317
puppy, 13, 21, 53, 64, 66, 112, 116, 126, 134, 144, 154, 170, 172, 180, 187, 188, 190, 192, 194, 196, 247, 248, 249, 250, 251, 252, 253, 254, 255, 256, 257, 258, 259, 263, 264, 265, 266, 269, 279, 281, 286, 292, 293, 294, 295, 296, 297, 299, 300, 301, 304, 307, 308, 310, 317, 319, 328, 332

Q

Queen Alexandra *see* Alexandra, Queen (of England)

R

rabbit, 22, 29, 31, 37, 39, 41, 42, 43, 54, 58, 59, 60, 62, 83, 85, 86, 88, 91, 116, 122, 130, 200, 205, 221, 261, 331
Rainstone Jubiler, 203, 204, 205
Rallye Bocage, 55, 65
Ranåker-Månsson, Marianne, 184, 201,

202
RareGems, 157, 169, 174
Raymond le Rebelle, *see* Morebess
Raymond le Rebelle
RCGV, 57, 63, 64, 66, 68, 316, 318
recall, 46, 334, 335
recessive, 272, 275, 285, 308, 309, 310, 311, 312, 317, 318
Relative Height Index, 215
retinal dysplasia, 271
retinal folds, 271
RI, *see* Initial Register
ribs, 225, 227, 229, 232, 233, 234, 237, 240, 255
Rigolo, 81, 90, 95, 111, 112, 115, 116, 120, 125, 137, 147, 152, 201, 351, 353, 356, 360
Rigolo de la Vrignaie, 81, 90, 95, 111, 115, 201, 351, 353, 356, 360
Roberts, Evan, 113, 115, 121, 133, 134, 135, 141, 151, 162, 179
Robertson, Gavin, 138
roe deer, 22, 35, 40, 41
Roman, 16, 17, 95
Romano, 97, 98, 99, 105
Romans, 17, 18
Rossi, Rita, 113, 114, 123
rough-coat, 50, 95, 97, 99, 103, 104, 105, 106, 109, 110
rough-coated, 15, 18, 19, 23, 33, 37, 50, 55, 73, 74, 78, 81, 89, 90, 92, 95, 96, 99, 105, 110, 175, 195, 211, 222
rough-coats, 38, 52, 75, 81, 95, 100, 101, 103, 104, 105, 106, 109, 110
rough-haired, 18, 20, 95
Royal Combattant, 33
Ruiten, Nancy, 200
Ryeford Chase, 77, 80, 82, 83

S

saber, 230, 232, 234, 235, 237, 241, 269
sable, 219, 220, 315
Saintonge, 21, 31, 97

Saintongeois, 21, 30
Salaün, Pierre, 6, 70, 91, 92, 94, 137, 150, 161
Salto de Crislaure of Morebess, 82, 114, 128, 129, 131, 132, 133, 134, 135, 136, 137, 138, 149, 151, 152, 153, 160, 161, 162, 186, 187, 188, 191, 350, 355, 356, 357, 358, 359, 360, 362
Sandringham, 75, 100, 105, 106, 107, 108, 109
Sandringham Kennels, 108
Saratoga Kennel Club, 167
SCC, 61, 62, 63, 64, 65, 68, 69, 70
scent, 16, 27, 28, 29, 42, 58, 73, 86, 87, 88, 183, 199, 205, 235, 239, 244, 322, 324, 325, 326, 338
scenthounds, 16, 20, 28, 29, 56, 61, 85, 175, 244, 284, 323, 339, 340
scenting ability, 20, 27, 41, 42, 58, 74, 261
Scharnberg, James "Jim", 6, 92, 93, 94, 343
Schweisswork, 183, 184, 205
scissors, 236, 292, 293
Scotland, 32, 73, 75, 96, 99, 122, 130, 131, 149, 179, 180
Scottish Kennel Club, 180
Search and Rescue, 322, 323
Segusian, 18
Seiffert, Mildred, 80, 95, 111, 115, 135, 179, 201
seizures, 275, 276
Serange, Bernard, 212
Shaw, Vero, 97
sheath, 266, 289
shoulders, 225, 227, 229, 231, 234, 236
showring, 39, 41, 71, 83, 89, 93, 110, 113, 117, 123, 128, 129, 131, 139, 151, 153, 163, 174, 181, 191, 200, 205, 211, 221, 241, 262, 303, 343
Skerritt, Bernie, 114, 115, 127
Skerritt, Linda, 7, 10, 115, 127, 148, 151, 159
skin, 155, 226, 227, 230, 266, 268, 277, 341

skull, 210, 213, 225, 226, 228, 231, 233, 236, 275
Skycastle, 89, 91, 92, 93, 94, 150, 343
Skycastle Duchess, 93
Skycastle Estèle des Ajoncs de l'Aulne, 93
smell, 27, 212, 253, 267, 323, 324, 335, 340
Smith, A. Croxton, 98, 109, 209
Smith, Mary, 103, 104
smooth-coat, 50, 95, 99, 103, 106, 107
smooth-coated, 32, 53, 54, 94, 95, 104, 106
smooth-coats, 37, 96, 103, 104
Snelling, Anne, 125, 145, 147, 156, 157, 162
Société Centrale, 33, 35, 55, 57, 60, 222
Société Centrale's Livre d'Origines Français, 33
Société de Vénerie, 41, 57, 58
Société Zoologique d'Acclimitation, 49
Sport of Kings, 17, 47
St. Hubert, see Hubert, Saint
St. Louis, see Louis IX (Saint Louis)
Steidel, Kitty, 6, 10, 139, 145, 148, 152, 162, 170
stern, 225, 227, 228, 230, 231, 232, 234, 237
sternum, 216, 217, 225, 234, 237, 238, 296, 303
Stock-Keeper journal, 104, 107
Streeter, John and Elizabeth, 89, 90, 91, 92, 113, 147, 150, 151
stud, 33, 34, 36, 38, 52, 53, 77, 82, 91, 100, 101, 103, 113, 120, 121, 127, 129, 135, 136, 150, 151, 154, 157, 163, 178, 181, 188, 189, 199, 282, 285, 286, 287, 290
stud dog, 33, 34, 36, 91, 127, 136, 151, 154, 163, 178, 181, 188, 189, 282, 285, 286, 290
style, 27, 40, 75, 85, 88, 90, 173, 174, 208, 209, 210, 211, 244, 324, 326
subluxation, 272, 273
Suggested Scale of Points, 45

Supermatch, 144, 147, 152
Sweden, 112, 120, 123, 149, 152, 184, 186, 187, 189, 201, 202, 203, 205, 214
Sweetdean, 82, 125

T

T'Annetta, 90, 111, 112, 350, 351, 353, 355, 356, 358, 360, 362
T'Arlette, 111, 112, 201
tail, 38, 69, 71, 90, 151, 211, 235, 237, 238, 239, 241, 266, 267, 288, 303, 311
Talisman, 101, 299, 303
Tambour, 33, 100, 101, 102, 103, 106, 109, 349
Tambourin, 33, 36, 52
tan, 52, 66, 99, 100, 128, 175, 219, 220, 222, 230, 232, 315, 316, 317
Tangaer, 132, 133, 138
tawny, 220
teeth, 116, 233, 236, 266, 269, 298, 301, 302
teething, 251
temperament, 69, 140, 145, 175, 208, 211, 231, 235, 282, 285, 297, 302, 307, 314, 328, 341
testicles, 233, 235
Theory and Practice of Rational Breeding, 209
therapy, 341, 343
therapy dogs, 341
thighs, 225, 227, 229, 232, 234, 237
Thomas, Joseph B., 25, 307
thorax, 296
thyroid, 277, 278, 287
tie, 288, 289, 293
Tixier, René, 6, 40, 41, 65, 70, 83, 114, 128, 164, 174, 196, 197, 198, 316, 317, 318
Tottie, Mabel, 6, 101, 102, 103, 104, 108, 109, 110, 141
toy, 249, 332, 335
toys, 251, 299, 329, 331, 332, 333
track, 240, 322, 323, 325, 326, 329

tracking, 166, 183, 184, 188, 203, 204, 205, 321, 322, 323, 325, 326, 335
Tribert, M. 33
tri-color, 33, 97, 98, 102, 103, 104, 107, 213, 214, 220, 232
Trogens Thyras, 202, 203
Tutankhamun, 16
Twinrivers, 113, 120, 123, 124, 125, 126, 127, 130, 134, 139, 140, 149, 151, 152, 162, 352, 353, 354
Twinrivers Alouette, 120, 123, 125, 352, 353
Twinrivers Danielle, 125, 139
Twinrivers Duchesse, 126, 127, 128, 149, 354

U

U.K., 91, 111, 115, 124, 128, 135, 136, 220, 307, 315, 316, 319
U.S.A., 139, 178, 220, 307, 315, 316, 319, 327, 341
underbites, 270
undercoat, 211, 226, 234, 237, 241, 303, 304, 315
Underhill, Tom, 148, 155
undershot, 69

V

vaccines, 248, 258, 264
van Bylandt, Count Henry, 223
Valentine, Nick, 6, 77, 80, 82, 83, 87, 88, 91, 113, 130
Väntans Enda E-vita, 203, 204
Vårforsens Jum-Jum, 203, 204
variance, 312, 313, 314
Varon, 113, 114, 116, 120, 128, 129, 131, 132, 133, 134, 135, 136, 138, 139, 149, 151, 152, 153, 156, 159, 161, 162, 167, 177, 179, 181, 350, 351, 353, 355, 356, 357, 358, 359, 360, 361, 362
Varon Tamburlaine, 136, 137
Varon Tapette, 137, 139, 161, 179, 180, 181

Varon Ulema, 129, 136, 138, 162, 177
Varon Willful of Pauntley, 162, 167
Varon Zorro, 114, 116, 120, 128, 129, 131, 132, 134, 135, 156, 159, 162, 350, 353, 355, 358, 359, 360, 361, 362
Vendée, 9, 15, 17, 18, 19, 21, 30, 31, 35, 37, 38, 39, 53, 55, 56, 59, 61, 62, 63, 85, 91, 97, 188, 193, 211, 221, 222, 349
Vendric, 122, 124, 125, 129, 130, 147, 149, 156, 157, 159, 161, 162
Vendric Vagabond, 124
venery, 16, 21, 25, 29, 30, 47, 84
veterinarian, 201, 215, 218, 250, 264, 268, 270, 274, 282, 293, 294
Villebois-Mareuil, 35, 37, 55
viruses, 295
vitamins, 253, 254
Vlas, Gerard and Thelma, 121, 195, 196, 198, 201
Vlas, Yolande, 6, 197, 198, 215
vocal commands, 86
voice, 12, 27, 58, 73, 74, 79, 81, 201, 233, 235, 241, 244, 259, 269, 331, 333

W

Wakelyns, 81, 85, 125, 126, 127, 129, 131, 144, 149, 151, 152, 153, 155, 156, 158, 159, 352, 353, 354
Wakelyns Angelique, 85, 144
Wakelyns Noblesse, 149, 155, 156, 159
Walhampton pack, 75
Walker, Joan, 112, 115, 120, 198, 201
Walton-Haddon, John and Adele, 122, 129, 136, 141
Watson, Major John, 6, 78
Weight, 226, 228, 230
Wells-Meacham, Joan, 80, 95, 111, 112, 113, 115, 116, 127, 135, 137, 138, 140, 179, 201
Welsh, 19, 77, 128, 179
Welsh Kennel Club, 179
West Lodge, 9, 78, 79, 80, 81, 110

Westerby, 75, 76, 78, 81, 109, 110

Westminster, 105, 125, 147, 167, 168, 170, 172, 178, 179, 180, 182

Westminster Kennel Club, 125, 172, 179, 182

whelping, 102, 264, 282, 283, 292, 293, 294, 295, 299

whelping box, 292, 293

whiskers, 281, 299

white, 6, 21, 33, 36, 53, 77, 81, 98, 99, 100, 103, 106, 108, 113, 114, 115, 121, 125, 127, 131, 132, 133, 135, 151, 172, 212, 213, 218, 219, 220, 221, 229, 230, 231, 232, 233, 234, 235, 236, 238, 269, 276, 292, 293, 301, 315, 316, 317

Wicklund, Barbara, 145, 148, 165, 167, 187, 323

Williams, Rick, 146

Windsor von Schloss Isabella, 112, 120, 351, 353, 356, 358, 360, 362

wire-coated, 308, 310

wire-haired, 82, 98

Woolner, Lionel, 9, 78, 79

working trials, 44, 58

World War I, 36, 55, 59, 73, 74, 110, 207

World War II, 30, 38, 62, 215

worms, 264

X

Xenophon, 16, 20, 27

Y

Young, Betty, 151

CREEPY RIDDLES

Katy Hall and Lisa Eisenberg

pictures by S. D. Schindler

Dial Books for Young Readers
New York

Dial easy-to-read

Published by Dial Books for Young Readers
A member of Penguin Putnam Inc.
375 Hudson Street
New York, New York 10014

The Dial Easy-to-Read logo is a registered trademark of
Dial Books for Young Readers,
a member of Penguin Putnam Inc.
®TM 1,162,718.
First Edition
5 7 9 10 8 6 4

Library of Congress
Cataloging in Publication Data
Hall, Katy.
Creepy riddles/by Katy Hall and Lisa Eisenberg;
pictures by S. D. Schindler.
p.   cm.
ISBN 0-8037-1684-2 (tr.)—ISBN 0-8037-1685-0 (lib.)
1. Riddles. 2. Supernatural—Juvenile humor.
[1. Riddles. 2. Supernatural—Wit and humor.] I. Eisenberg, Lisa.
II. Schindler, S. D., ill. III. Title.
PN6371.5.H375   1998   818'.5402—DC20
94-37524   CIP   AC   r94

The full-color artwork was prepared using pen-and-ink
and watercolor washes.

Reading Level 2.1

To Lisa Eisenberg
K.H.

To Katy Hall
L.E.

*To Julia—still
a riddle, but not a
creepy one!*
S.D.S.

What do werewolves
say when they meet?

"Howl do you do?"

7

What do you call
a room full of ghosts?

A bunch of boo-boos!

8

How do skeletons send their mail?

By Bony Express.

What do witches like to eat
for dessert?

Ice scream!

Why does Dracula buy the
newspaper every night?

So he can read his horror-scope.

Why do witches
wear green eye shadow?

They like the way
it matches their teeth.

What moves through the air,
casts spells, and has no name?

An unidentified flying sorcerer.

How did
the monster football team
win the game?

They kicked a field ghoul!

What would you get
if you crossed a skeleton
and a jar of peanut butter?

Bones that stick to the
roof of your mouth!

What kind of stories
do little ghosts tell
around the campfire?

People stories.

How did the werewolf
send his valentines?

By hairmail!

Which witches like to play croquet?

Wicket witches!

How does a witch
with a broken broom
get to the second floor?

She takes the scarecase.

19

Why did the little fiends join the protest march?

They thought it was a *demon*stration.

Why didn't the little skeleton
want to go to the party?

Because he had no
body to dance with!

What magic words
does a scary godmother
use to do her laundry?

"Wishy-washy!"

What do ghosts love to eat
for dinner?

Ghoulash.

Why is Frankenstein
so helpful?

He's always willing
to give you a hand!

Why did Granny Monster
knit her grandson three socks?

Because she heard
he'd grown another foot.

Where do demons go at night?

Out with their ghoulfriends!

What do sea monsters
like to eat?

Fish-and-ships!

What did the little ghost
order at the restaurant?

Spookghetti!

What do zombies like to drink?

Croaka-Cola!

Why are witch twins
so confusing?

You can never tell
which witch is which!

Why did the Frankenstein monster get a tummy ache?

He kept *bolting* his food!

What color is a chilly ghost?

Boo!

What trees do zombies
like best?

Ceme-trees!

What do ghouls like to do at the amusement park?

Ride the roller ghoster!

What do vampires eat at baseball games?

Fangfurters!

Why is the mad scientist never lonely?

He's good at *making* new friends!

Why did everyone call
the vampire crazy?

They heard he'd gone batty!

What do ghosts put on their mashed potatoes?

Grave-y!

What did the zombie eat
after he had a tooth taken out?

The dentist!

What fairy tale is scary enough
to tell little witches?

Ghouldilocks and the Three Scares.

Why did Frankenstein
fall in love with the witch?

She *swept* him off his feet!

Why did the little witch get a prize in school?

She was the best *spell*er in her class.

What kind of milk do you get from a ghost cow?

Evaporated milk!

What do ghosts
wear when it's raining?

*Boo*ts.

What game do little zombies play at birthday parties?

Swallow the leader!

What do you get if you cross a giant with a vampire?

A *big* pain in the neck!

What did the little vampire
say to the judges when he won
the Batboy Contest?

"Fangs a lot!"

What did the ghost bride
throw to her bridesmaids?

Her *boo*quet!